ALPHONSE CHAPANIS
Human Factors in Systems Engineering

YACOV Y. HAIMES
Risk Modeling, Assessment, and Management

DENNIS M. BUEDE
The Engineering Design of Systems: Models and Methods

ANDREW P. SAGE and JAMES E. ARMSTRONG, Jr.
Introduction to Systems Engineering

WILLIAM B. ROUSE
Essential Challenges of Strategic Management

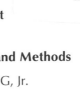

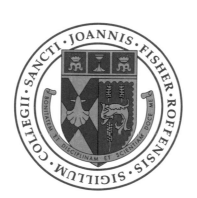

Praise For *Essential Challenges of Strategic Management*

"Bill Rouse brings to this thoughtful work his years of experience as a practitioner, professor, technical management consultant and author. He cuts through the "quick fixes" of the past decade to focus on the critical elements of business success. In this well referenced volume, Bill provides helpful insight to make any business, and in particular any high tech business, perform better."

—DENNIS A. ROBERSON, Senior Vice President &
Chief Technology Officer, Motorola

"Bill Rouse's new book *Essential Challenges of Strategic Management* delivers exactly what it promises: a no-nonsense, to-the-point discussion of the most basic problems confronting senior managers and how to solve them. Based on his experience with thousands of executives, Rouse has boiled down the complex process of strategically managing an enterprise into seven fundamental challenges. Having described and illustrated each challenge, he then provides a useful catalog of best practices for addressing each challenge, as well as specific methods and tools for each practice. I found every page to be rich with useful, practical advice, all based on keen insights about the complex, non-linear functioning of loosely-structured modern organizations. This material is well-researched and supported by specific references. All in all, this book builds on Rouse's excellent past body of work, and weaves it all together in a well-organized, easy-to-understand bible for all strategic managers and leaders."

—DR. STANLEY G. ROSEN, Director of Strategic Planning,
Boeing Satellite Systems

"Bill Rouse captures valuable insights into the challenges that keep managers up at night. A must-read for managers seeking clarity and focus as they lead organizations through chaotic times."

WILLIAM C. KESSLER, Vice President for Enterprise Productivity,
Lockheed Martin Aeronautics Company

"This is a great resource for busy executives and business consultants. Bill Rouse has organized a practical and scholarly discussion of key business challenges and how others have been successful in addressing them. Dr. Rouse's insightful comments and practical advice make this an excellent book to read if you are interested in realizing better business results."

—JOYCE SHIELDS, PH.D., Vice President,
Hay Management Consultants

"Dr. Rouse's essential challenges, with growth at the top of the hierarchy, certainly hit the nail on the head—my experience in leading a large non-profit R&D organization indicates that the stable point between growth and decline is very small and short at best, but probably non-existent. An organization is either growing or declining and, as Dr. Rouse points out, growth is more forgiving. Rouse's observations about the nature of non-profits are right-on."

—EDWARD K. REEDY, Vice President & Director,
Georgia Tech Research Institute

ESSENTIAL CHALLENGES OF STRATEGIC MANAGEMENT

ESSENTIAL CHALLENGES OF STRATEGIC MANAGEMENT

WILLIAM B. ROUSE

A Wiley-Interscience Publication

JOHN WILEY & SONS, INC.

New York • Chichester • Weinheim • Brisbane • Singapore • Toronto

This book is printed on acid-free paper. ∞

Copyright © 2001 by John Wiley & Sons, Inc. All rights reserved.

Published simultaneously in Canada.

For ordering and customer service, call 1-800-CALL-WILEY.

Library of Congress Cataloging in Publication Data:

Rouse, William B.
   Essential challenges of strategic management / William B. Rouse.
      p. cm.—(Wiley series in systems engineering and management)
   "A Wiley-Interscience publication."
   Includes bibliographical references and index.
   ISBN 0-471-38924-2 (cloth : alk. paper)
      1. Strategic planning. 2. Management. 3. Decision making. 4. Strategic planning—Case studies. 5. Management—Case studies. 6. Decision making—Case studies. I. Title. II. Series.

HD30.28 .R6744 2001
658.4'012—dc21   00-043752

Printed in the United States of America.

10 9 8 7 6 5 4 3 2 1

▰▰▰ CONTENTS

These are challenging times for businesses, government agencies, nonprofit organizations, and enterprises in general. Pressures to perform have never been greater, and the business environment has never been faster paced or more complex. Technology changes are also rampant in terms of computer and communications technologies and biotechnology, to name a few.

These pressures to perform are complicated by the fact that most executives and senior managers serve many constituencies. Customers, suppliers, shareholders, employees, and others pull and tug these individuals in numerous directions, trying to assure that the enterprise meets their needs. Usually, it is not possible to make everybody happy.

These well-intentioned and intelligent individuals search for an acceptable, and hopefully profitable, strategy amidst their constituencies and pressures. This search is sometimes muddled, halting, and indecisive—but it is far from aimless or random. The primary difficulty is that formulating a strategy and reaching consensus on pursuing it are laced with challenges.

There are common patterns among these challenges, and most executives and senior managers face quite similar situations. This book focuses on these common challenges. Uncovering and delineating these essential challenges, as well as considering how numerous enterprises address them, results in a compilation of best practices. Advice on how to implement these practices is also included in this book.

PURPOSE AND INTENDED AUDIENCE

The purpose of this book is to clarify and illustrate essential strategic management challenges faced by all enterprises, as well as to explain best practices for addressing these challenges. The goal is also to provide managers options for addressing challenges rather than a single high-powered method or tool. The philosophy is that managers need a portfolio of specialized concepts, principles, methods, and tools—not an overarching panacea.

The audience for this book includes the individuals that I worked with to gain the experiences for this book. These people are executives and senior managers in domains ranging from aerospace to appliances to computers and communications to energy to food services to healthcare and many more. The types of enterprises include for-profit businesses, nonprofit organizations, and government agencies.

This book is intended to provide value to this audience by including discussions on the essential challenges that many executives and senior managers have told me keep them awake at night. Discussions of each challenge begin with an exploration of the nature of the challenge, including consideration of a range of examples. Attention then shifts to why the challenge is difficult—tensions and conflicts, for instance, that tend to make the challenge problematic.

The discussion of each challenge next focuses on best practices gleaned from a wide range of domains. Consideration is given to the bases of the best practices and why they work. Finally, alternative means of supporting best practices are discussed in terms of concepts, principles, methods, and tools for implementing the best practices.

Due to the breadth of alternatives covered in this book, it can be viewed as a mini-handbook for addressing the essential challenges of strategic management. I expect that readers will return to this book again and again as challenges emerge, demand attention, and are addressed and resolved. I also expect, and hope, that users of this book will mail or email me (rouse@mindspring.com) new examples of ways in which the essential challenges are manifested and new insights into how to implement successfully the best practices.

BACKGROUND

I first entered professional life in the late 1960s and early 1970s. The large, electronics company where I worked was awash in posters proclaiming "Zero Defects!" This gave way in the late 1970s and early 1980s to total quality management. The late 1980s and early 1990s were times of business process reengineering. More recently, we have balanced scorecards, open book management, and so forth.

All of these fashions were in part slogans but, more importantly, they usually included substantial methodologies and offered opportunities for tangible improvements. Unfortunately, however, all of the stakeholders—ranging from executives to consultants to academics—conspired to convince each other that a panacea was at hand. The currently fashionable method or tool came to be seen as the solution to *all* problems.

The inevitable result was disappointment and, quite often, finger pointing. People over-promised in part because customers demanded such promises and in part because competitors also overpromised. For a while, in fact, everyone believed the promises. All the stakeholders needed to believe that they had found the key to global competitiveness, lean production, and change management. Consequently, all mutually, but usually unknowingly, conspired to mislead each other.

In the past few years, many executives and senior managers—still smarting from past investments—have been revisiting the fundamentals of management. Puzzling over what really matters, and what doesn't, has led many of these individuals to identify the essential challenges of their jobs. To address these challenges, these executives want sound thinking and a range of best practices, not cure-all prescriptions. This book intends to meet these needs.

OVERVIEW OF CONTENTS

This book includes an introductory chapter, seven subsequent chapters associated with each of the challenges, and a concluding chapter that brings together all of the best practices discussed in earlier chapters. The Introduction discusses the genesis of the essential challenges and the framework within which the challenges are discussed.

The essential challenges that many executives and managers say keep them awake at night include

- Growth: gaining share in saturated/declining markets
- Value: enhancing relationships of processes to benefits and costs
- Focus: pursuing opportunities and avoiding diversions
- Change: competing creatively while maintaining continuity
- Future: investing in inherently unpredictable outcomes
- Knowledge: transforming information to insights to programs
- Time: carefully allocating the organization's scarcest resource

As noted above, a chapter is devoted to each of these challenges.

The concluding chapter summarizes the many best practices introduced in the chapters on each of the challenges. This chapter also integrates the best practices to show how they can be complementary. A cross-cutting discussion of methods and tools is also provided.

ACKNOWLEDGEMENTS

This book is based on extensive experiences with many of the world's top enterprises—including for-profits, nonprofits, and government agencies. The usefulness of the material presented here has been evaluated by numerous presentations and discussions with top management teams of these enterprises. The book is also laced with many observations, concepts, principles, methods, and tools gleaned from relevant professional and academic literature. For these reasons, this mini-handbook for addressing the essential challenges of strategic management is based mostly on the work and insights of others. I greatly appreciate their work and insights, as well as the numerous opportunities to work with many of these individuals as they wrestled with these challenges.

The essential challenges of strategic management transcend any particular methods, tools, or technologies. There are no panaceas for addressing these challenges. There are a range of good practices and some that can reasonably be labeled best practices. Knowledge of these practices, where they apply, and how to apply them are the keys to successfully dealing with the essential challenges. I gratefully acknowledge the many managers, authors, and researchers who have contributed to the body of knowledge compiled in this book.

Atlanta, Georgia   William B. Rouse
June 2000

William B. Rouse is an author, entrepreneur, researcher, and educator. He has founded and led several technology companies and served in leadership positions at several prominent universities. He currently is Chief Executive Officer of Enterprise Support Systems (http://www.ess-advisors.com/). ESS provides software solutions, consulting services, and training in the areas of strategic planning, market/product planning, and organizational change.

Bill has over 30 years of experience in management, marketing, and engineering related to decision-making and problem-solving performance, decision support systems, and information systems. In these areas, he has consulted with over 100 large and small enterprises in the private, public, and nonprofit sectors, where he has worked with several thousand executives and senior managers. His expertise includes individual and organizational decision making and problem solving, as well as design of organizations and information systems.

Bill has written hundreds of journal articles and book chapters and has authored many books, including most recently *Don't Jump to Solutions* (Jossey-Bass, 1998), *Start Where You Are* (Jossey-Bass, 1996), *Best Laid Plans* (Prentice-Hall, 1994), *Catalysts for Change* (Wiley, 1993), *Strategies for Innovation* (Wiley, 1992), and *Design for Success* (Wiley, 1991). He is co-editor of the best-selling *Handbook of Systems Engineering and Management* (Wiley, 1999) and co-editor of the management journal Information • Knowledge • Systems *Management* and its online version IKSM*Online* (http://www.*IKSMOnline*.com/). He edited the eight-volume series *Human/Technology Interaction in Complex Systems* (JAI Press).

Bill is a member of the National Academy of Engineering, a fellow of the Institute of Electrical and Electronics Engineers (IEEE), and a fellow of the Human Factors and Ergonomics Society. He received the Norbert Wiener Award from the IEEE Systems, Man, and Cybernetics Society, a Centennial Medal and Third Millennium Medal from IEEE, and the O. Hugo Schuck Award from the American Automation Control Council. He is listed in *Who's Who in America, Who's Who in Engineering,* and other biographical literature and has been featured in publications such as *Manager's Edge, Vision, Book-Talk, The Futurist, Competitive Edge, Design News*, and *Quality & Excellence.*

Bill has served on a wide range of advisory boards and committees, including Chair of the Committee on Human Factors of the National Research Council and is currently a member of the US Air Force Scientific Advisory Board. He received his B.S. from the University of Rhode Island, and his S.M. and Ph.D. from the Massachusetts Institute of Technology.

CHAPTER ONE

Introduction

My professional life began as an assistant engineer in a large defense electronics company. Hung along the many long halls of the company's offices were colorful posters heralding "Zero Defects" as the overarching goal. In the manufacturing facilities, large blue banners with white letters bore the same Zero Defects message. At the time, I wasn't sure exactly what this slogan meant, but it seemed like a good idea.

Several years later, by then a college professor in engineering, I began to study design decision making and how design processes could be supported. These studies led to frequent encounters with total quality management (TQM). The philosophy and methods of W. Edwards Deming (1986) seemed quite reasonable. Many of the companies with whom I worked appeared to achieve impressive results by adopting this approach.

As my colleagues and I explored the relationships between product design and business strategy, we increasingly encountered executives and senior managers who seemed to expect that TQM could solve all their problems. Deming's 14 points had become a catechism rather than just good management guidelines. These individuals tried to apply TQM to everything, seemingly with faith that following the catechism would yield blessings.

A few years later, the luster of TQM having tarnished, people became enamored with business process reengineering (BPR). The hallmark of BPR was Hammer's exhortation to obliterate rather than automate (Hammer, 1990), as well as Hammer and Champy's (1993) less dramatic advocacy of fundamentally rethinking and radically redesigning business processes. Major corporations embraced these guidelines and pursued massive downsizing almost religiously as processes were redesigned, people eliminated, and costs very significantly reduced.

In recent years, BPR is no longer viewed as the hoped-for panacea and has fallen from favor. Companies have realized that growth of the bottom line (profits) cannot be sustained without growth of the top line (sales). Now, we have profit zones and balanced scorecards, enabled by enterprise resource planning, open book management, knowledge management, and of course, most recently, E-commerce. (These concepts and methods are discussed in later chapters in association with the essential challenge they are intended to

1

address.) There seems to be no limit to top management's willingness to invest large sums in the latest panacea and obviously also no limit to those willing to promote the latest and greatest salvation of business (Micklethwait and Woolridge, 1996; Pinault, 2000).

Despite the hype, the business issues these various concepts and methods were created to address are very real. These business issues need to be addressed, and all managers would like easy-to-understand and easy-to-implement solutions. Furthermore, it is quite natural for managers to want to maximize the leverage of each investment. Thus, it would be great if one solution could solve all problems.

If one concept or method solved all problems, it would quickly be adopted by everyone—certainly, the consulting companies would do their best to ensure this. Eventually, this imagined panacea would redefine the playing field—as the Internet has done recently—and would become a requirement for participation in the game rather than providing a competitive advantage. This possibility, of course, does not limit the attractiveness of promised panaceas.

However, there are no panaceas for addressing all business issues. Despite ardent efforts and persistent longing, TQM, BPR, and so forth are best viewed as addressing particular, important business issues but not all issues (Sage, 1995). Thus, the brief periods during which these approaches achieved panacea status are over, but they remain important elements of management toolkits. There are, fortunately, many good practices—perhaps even best practices—for addressing important business issues.

This book focuses on the essential cross-cutting issues that challenge all businesses and, indeed, all enterprises, including for-profit, nonprofit, and public. This assertion that essential issues cut across a wide range of enterprises immediately raises questions of the nature of these business issues and why they are essential to strategic management. The answers to these questions have emerged from a wide range of executives and senior managers.

For many years, I have been immersed in hundreds of enterprises, working with thousands of executives and senior managers on issues such as overall business strategy, new market offerings, and major organizational changes. In just the past year or two, this has encompassed industries ranging from computers and communication, to aviation, pharmaceutical, retail, R&D/technology organizations, government agencies, and nonprofit organizations.

Throughout these experiences, I have continually discussed with managers the issues that are their greatest concerns—the issues that keep them awake at night. In this process, I have looked for similarities in issues, concerns, and practices articulated by these managers. Two questions framed this exploration.

First, what can be learned from how managers in different types of enterprises address similar issues and concerns? It is clear from pursing this question that enterprises are much more alike than different in terms of essential strategic issues. Although goals, markets, technologies, and so forth may differ substantially, the underlying issues are almost always the same.

This should not be particularly surprising. Political systems, for example, always involve underlying issues of the relative power and interests of stakeholder groups. Economic systems, as another illustration, are always concerned with growth, investment, and productivity. Physical systems all face the underlying issues of speed and stability of response. Thus, the notion that all business systems face the same core set of issues is far from speculative—and also not particularly novel, for example, see Collins and Porras (1994).

Second what good, or possibly best, practices can be gleaned from cross-cutting comparisons of different types of enterprises in a wide range of markets? As this book illustrates, good practices for addressing the essential issues tend to have similar conceptual foundations across enterprises, although the ways in which these practices are implemented can vary substantially for different types of enterprises and markets. The many examples discussed in this book are intended to clarify these similarities and differences.

ESSENTIAL CHALLENGES

The essential challenges of strategic management identified in my explorations with thousands of executives and senior managers are depicted in Figure 1.1. In this section, these challenges are defined, including relationships among challenges. The seven challenges indicated in Figure 1.1 are by no means a somewhat arbitrary set of important business issues. Instead, these challenges are key pieces of the strategy puzzle, which fit together in particular and important ways.

Growth

Growth is the overarching goal and challenge of strategic management. Growth is essential to the well-being of an enterprise. Lack of growth leads, at best, to flat revenues and profits, if any, via cost cutting and eliminating anything not closely linked to sticking to the knitting. This, in turn, tends to limit opportunities for professional and personal growth and, in general, can create a pretty deadly organizational atmosphere.

At worst, lack of growth can lead to slow, or not so slow, declining revenues and profits. Cost cutting tends to become endemic and often severe. A "death spiral" can result in which lack of discretionary resources leads to un-

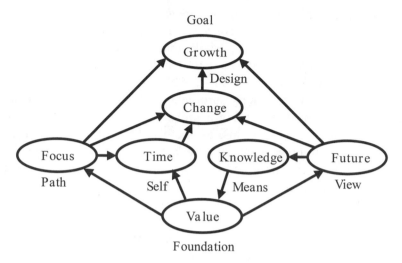

Goal

Figure 1.1. Essential challenges and relationships among challenges

derinvestment in those opportunities needed to just keep heads above water, leading to further decreases in discretionary resources.

As one seasoned CEO put it, "Everyone makes mistakes and everyone encounters things which you cannot control. Growth is more forgiving." Thus, an enterprise must strategically focus on growth to assure—or at least increase the probabilities—that the downside is only lack of growth rather than decline. This challenge is often on the top of a manager's list of critical issues.

Value

Value provides the foundation for growth. The reason an enterprise exists is to provide value to its stakeholders. Many organizations tend to think that the products and services they deliver are synonymous with the value they provide (Rouse, 1998). However, stakeholders usually want the benefits of having these products and services rather than the artifacts or person hours per se. In other words, the products and services are usually means, not ends.

Another common misperception is that what stakeholders valued in the past will continue to be what they value in the future. However, products and services may cease to provide the same benefits as in the past, or these benefits may be inexpensive and widely available. Consequently, relationships with markets change despite enterprises' assumptions to the contrary (Rouse, 1996).

The challenge of value concerns matching stakeholders' needs and desires to the enterprise's competencies in the process of identifying high-value offerings that will justify the investments needed to bring these offerings to market. Ideally, this involves understanding and committing to innovation—creation of change via something new (Rouse, 1992)—in the targeted markets.

Focus

Focus concerns the challenge of deciding the path whereby the enterprise will provide value and grow. Focus involves making decisions to do some things and not do others. It involves deciding to add value in particular ways and not others. Thus, focus involves saying "yes" to a few things and "no" to many.

I have often found that "yes" is much, much easier than "no." Consequently, organizations end up dividing scarce resources among far too many things. Too few resources allocated to too many things leads to false starts and inadequate results. Everyone who won a little in the beginning loses a lot in the end.

The key to avoiding this dilemma is to define and communicate clear decision processes so that all stakeholders know what matters and how decisions are made. This allows decision makers to say "no" in the context of a well-understood framework. People will still be disappointed, but they usually will not perceive the decisions as unjust.

Change

Given a goal (growth), a foundation (value), and a path (focus), the next challenges concerns designing an organization to follow this path, provide this value, and achieve this goal. Rarely is the current organizational design the right one for succeeding with these challenges.

Of course, the old organization is in place and, typically, the only source of sales and profits in the near term. Thus, how do you creatively design and build the new organization you need while also running the organization you've got—all with some degree of consistency and sanity?

This question is further complicated by the fact that the nature of organizations appears to be rapidly changing. Reengineering, downsizing, and rightsizing have changed the terms of the employer-employee social contract. Technology increasingly enables very mobile people and relationships temporally, geographically, and organizationally. Change may be unavoidable, but there should be some strategic advantage gained in the process.

Future

The ways in which you address the challenges of the future strongly affect the most appropriate approaches to the challenges thus far discussed. The future is uncertain, risky, and tends to be a long way off. Consequently, it is usually very difficult to estimate the value of the future. This typically results in heavy discounting of the future.

However, almost all the managers that I discussed this issue with have readily agreed that you have no choice but to invest in the future. You need a view of where you are headed and an investment portfolio aligned with this view. How to make these investment decisions becomes the next question. If we could buy an option on the future, how would we determine what this option is worth?

There are rigorous ways of addressing this question. Some of them borrow from sophisticated financial analysis methods. Others focus on decision-making processes and the multistage execution that should follow decisions. Making the case for the future is certainly a challenge, but this challenge is tractable.

Knowledge

The challenge of knowledge involves at the outset disentangling the term from marketing and sales pitches of all the vendors who stand ready to help you manage knowledge. Before managing knowledge, you need to understand how knowledge influences, or could influence, your enterprise's abilities to provide the value that is your foundation for growth.

More specifically, this challenge concerns understanding how to transform information to value-driven insights to strategic programs of action. This understanding should be gained in the context of critical business issues such as solution pricing or inventory control. In contrast, knowledge in general is seldom of much value—some would argue that it is not even knowledge.

Starting with critical business issues, one can determine what knowledge would make a difference and in what ways. This understanding should determine what information is relevant, how it is processed, and how its use is supported. Although far from a panacea, this form of knowledge management can provide a substantial means to competitive advantage.

Time

Lack of time is almost always the most significant personal issue of executives and senior managers. People say that they spend too much time responding to often meaningless fire drills imposed by superiors, meetings with subordinates to make decisions that the subordinates should have made on their own, meetings in general, and responding to increasingly overwhelming numbers of E-mails. The result, they report, is little time for addressing strategic challenges.

How managers invest their own time reflects their priorities and values, which are, of course, strongly affected by the social and cultural characteristics of an enterprise and the business environment in general. The allocation of time also reflects the leadership style and abilities of managers. Inappropriate allocations of time and ineffective leadership go hand in hand. Covey (1989) and many others have taught this lesson well.

Addressing the challenge of time involves considering first the roles of leaders in strategic management, and next the implications of these roles for how leaders allocate their time. What managers often fail to realize is that their time is one of their organization's scarcest resources. Whereas money, at least in principle, is potentially unlimited, time is not.

Summary

Figure 1.1 also portrays relationships among challenges. Growth is the goal, and value provides the foundation for achieving this goal. Value influences choice of focus (path), investments in the future (view), and allocations of time (self). Focus affects time, and they both, in combination with future, influence change (design). Future also affects knowledge, which provides the means for addressing value. The view (future), path (focus), and design (change) combine to affect the goal (growth).

Clearly, the essential challenges of strategic management are highly interrelated. Dealing effectively with one or two challenges will not compensate for addressing the others poorly. Typically, the challenges presenting the greatest difficulties at the moment receive the most attention. This is understandable and appropriate, as long as managers keep all the challenges in perspective. Balancing how you address the whole set of challenges tends to be a challenge in itself and will be elaborated in the discussion of the challenge of time.

It is useful to note that I have repeatedly tried to identify additional challenges or perhaps replace some of the above challenges with other more compelling or important challenges. I have been aided in this quest by managers at a wide variety of organizations where I have presented the framework underlying this book. Although there have been many suggestions, in-depth discussions of these alternatives have always resulted in retaining the set of challenges just elaborated without change. This does not mean, of course, that eternal truth has been found. Instead, it simply means that a large number of experienced, intelligent, and interested managers have found that this set of challenges works for them.

The next seven chapters are devoted to each of the challenges. Each challenge is considered in terms of its specific nature, numerous examples are given of how the challenge is manifested, and fundamental reasons that underlie the difficulty of the challenge are presented. Recommended practices for addressing each challenge are also discussed and illustrated with numerous examples. These practices cut across for-profit, nonprofit, and government enterprises, as well as domains ranging from aircraft to appliances and from food services to fundraising. Many practices were identified as holistic approaches already in use. Others are natural composites that borrow elements from multiple domains.

Some of the recommended practices are widely used and of sufficient maturity to be designated "best practices." I hasten to note that these practices are, quite simply, good ideas that have worked for others and make sense to consider. This conclusion is, in each instance, backed in part by my experience but mostly via substantial references to the literature. I fervently hope that the phrase "best practices" does *not* become yet another slogan in the pantheon of management panaceas.

ORGANIZATIONAL CONTEXT

It is important at the outset to consider the nature of the roles and activities of executives and senior managers in most enterprises, especially in terms of how these roles and activities affect the ways in which the essential challenges are addressed. Herbert Simon and Henry Mintzberg have developed pioneering insights into these issues. Discussion of these insights provides a foundation on which to frame contemporary thinking on these issues later in this chapter.

Simon's Nobel prize-winning studies of management behaviors provided the basis for many developments in economics as well as much of contemporary cognitive science. The results of his studies of the nature of management rationality are central to understanding people's inclinations and abilities to address the essential challenges of strategic management.

In his book *Models of Man* (Simon, 1957), Simon introduces the concept of *satisficing*. This term is meant to contrast with *optimizing*. Optimizers always make the best decision, carefully balancing all the relevant attributes of a situation. Satisficers make decisions that are "good enough." The likely consequences are satisfactory, even though they may be far from the best achievable.

Satisficing by managers greatly increases the acceptability of *not* effectively addressing the essential challenges. If all you need is a solution or decision that is good enough, then the chances of failing due to inadequate resolution of challenges are substantially decreased. In this way, a large proportion of decisions becomes much easier—in other words, much less challenging.

The acceptability of easier, merely satisfactory decisions does not solely reflect limited abilities of individuals. Simon's later efforts showed how much of human behavior results from conformance to environmental norms and constraints (Simon, 1969). Put simply, satisficing is acceptable because it works in the contexts in which managers act.

For example, top management's lack of a credible "growth story" may be acceptable, despite stated growth goals, because the various stakeholders understand the difficulty of formulating such a story. Furthermore, the results of last year and the last quarter may have been "pretty good. " Why make waves, even if there is a nagging suspicion that problems are likely in the future?

Another important body of work is that of Henry Mintzberg's. He studied how managers spend their time—an issue that is discussed at great length in Chapter 8 on the challenge of time. In a now-classic *Harvard Business Review* article, he debunks various myths about management (Mintzberg, 1975).

Of particular importance to our discussions in this book is his rejection of the idea that managers are reflective, systematic planners. In contrast, managers are very action oriented and spend much of their time reacting to events around them. Their plans are far from elaborate and usually in their heads.

Combining this perspective on management with the notion of satisficing, it becomes very clear why essential challenges are often unresolved. Managers typically have neither the time nor inclinations to do otherwise. Furthermore, making decisions that are *good enough* usually results in the company performing *pretty well*. Although most will agree that they could have done better, the results are nevertheless satisfactory.

As noted earlier, this does not imply that failure to deal with challenges is due solely to limited abilities of executives and managers. Instead, their problem-solving and decision-making behaviors reflect the effects of typical company environments on managers. Their behaviors are necessary adaptations to the ill-structured, ever-changing nature of the marketplace and their companies.

Mintzberg portrays managers as inundated with issues, problems, and decisions, the vast majority of which are relatively minor. They satisfice and respond without reflection because it works. The time horizon for actions and reactions, as well as the changing nature of decision situations, discourage reflective planning and trade-off studies.

My experiences with a wide range and large number of managers have yielded insights that agree with Simon and Mintzberg's characterizations. I have found that few executives and senior managers spend much time on reflective strategizing and planning. Fire fighting gets *much* more attention than fire prevention. Identifying and planting fire-resistant trees gets even less attention than fire prevention.

Business process reengineering has helped to reinforce these tendencies. A total focus on reducing costs, especially operational costs, closes out broader perspectives. Managers who succeed with this focus are promoted to executive positions. As a result, operationally skilled people, who have neither experience with nor orientation to strategic issues, become responsible for these issues.

The Internet economy has also promoted these tendencies. There is no time for strategic thinking. Furthermore, everything is changing every day, so any decisions about how to address essential challenges will inevitably be wrong tomorrow. There is an element of truth to this that is discussed in the next section. Nevertheless, there are fundamentals that do not change, despite the Internet, computers, airplanes, railroads, or steamboats (Rouse, 1996).

As a consequence of the forces elaborated here, many good ideas—in fact, ideas that executives and senior managers have enthusiastically endorsed—are never implemented. Day-to-day business issues demand and get attention. Longer-term views, although intellectually appealing, are preempted by today's problems and contingencies. Best-laid plans do not go awry—they don't go anywhere!

As noted earlier, the problem is not a lack of good intentions or understanding. Instead, as indicated by Simon and Mintzberg, it is the reality of life in most enterprises. There is usually a variety of stakeholders with widely varying values, perceptions, and concerns. There are also numerous economic, social, and cultural forces pulling executives and senior managers in many, often inconsistent, directions. As a consequence, many well-intentioned and intelligent people search for an acceptable, and hopefully profitable, strategy among the various constituencies and pressures.

This search is far from aimless or random. There are common patterns, and most executives and senior managers face similar problems or challenges. This book focuses on these common challenges. At the very least, this book enables managers to see how their challenges are framed and addressed in a wide range of contexts by other managers.

However, in light of Simon and Mintzberg's work, it is clear that simply making managers aware of the ubiquity of the challenges they face is not enough. Most managers—indeed, most people—also need recommended practices for addressing these challenges. Furthermore, these practices should be demonstrably usable and useful. Finally, these practices should be illustrated with concrete, realistic examples. Satisfying these criteria is the challenge faced by this book.

ORGANIZATIONS AS COMPLEX SYSTEMS

The context of managers' roles and activities characterized in the last section reflects the behavioral and social reality of people organizing in pursuit of goals within both local and broader cultures. The phenomena captured by Simon and Mintzberg would doubtlessly apply as well to steamboat ventures in the early 1800s and Internet ventures in the early 2000s. Many aspects of people and organizations are relatively timeless.

However, things do change and these changes affect the ways in which the essential challenges of strategic management are best framed and addressed. Trends in computer and communications technologies are enabling increased globalization and integration of enterprises in domains ranging from retail to publishing to aircraft. The complexity of these global enterprises has greatly changed the ways in which these enterprises are best managed (Rouse, 2000). In particular, highly centralized approaches to management are both less useful and only marginally feasible.

For example, Prahalad (1998) discusses eight "discontinuities" affecting management, including globalization, deregulation and privatization, volatility, convergence, indeterminate industry boundaries, standardization, disintermediation, and ecosensitivity. He suggests five critical management tasks for fostering the competencies necessary for dealing with these discontinuities:

- gaining access to and absorbing new knowledge,
- integrating multiple streams of knowledge,
- sharing across cultures and distance,
- learning to forget, and
- deploying competence across business unit boundaries.

All five of these tasks involve moving beyond traditional approaches to management and moving away from insular, centralized organizational systems.

These trends are also resulting in an increasing number of loosely structured organizations with networks of affiliations and resources that are typically linked solely to specific opportunities rather than to the growth of the overall enterprise per se. Management of such loosely structured enterprises also presents new challenges (Rouse, 1999). For example, managers now must "manage" team members who do not work for them in a traditional sense; thus, they do not control the compensation or advancement of these individuals.

Enhanced communications among all types of organizations—as well as among the stakeholders within these organizations—have further complicated the process of resource allocation in multi-stakeholder, multi-attribute organizational systems. Striking the right balance among interests, across both near and long-term objectives, can be a daunting task (Rouse and Boff, 1999). Well-informed competing interests make the framing of cost/benefit trade-offs particularly important.

This emerging organizational environment is leading to the demise of the "command and control" approach to management. Drucker (1997) notes that, "Increasingly, command and control is being replaced by or intermixed with all kinds of relationships: alliances, joint ventures, minority participations, know-how, and marketing relationships—all relationships in which no one controls and no one commands." In general, "orders" are being replaced by "incentives."

Leadership guru Warren Bennis suggests that replacement of hierarchical organizations by networked organizations requires enhanced trust that involves several types of support (Stewart, 2000). People have to be able to trust in others' competence and work together as communities. Commitment to the same mission is also central, as is truthful communication by leaders. Finally, trust must be seen as good business, not just the mode when things are going well.

Wheatley (1999) argues that failures of complex systems, recently most salient were potential Y2K problems, require new approaches to management, "To function well, or to restore effective functioning, complex systems require collaboration, participation, and openness to information and relationships. These new systems problems force us to dissolve our past practices of hierarchies, boundaries, secrecy, and competition." Many commentators have projected likely increases of such failures.

These trends have caused organizational theorists to reconsider their characterizations of how organizations function and embrace the notion of complex adaptive systems. This trend is driven by a recognition that traditional organizational models are limited in their abilities to represent the fluidity and flexibility of loosely structured organizations. New formalisms are needed.

Complex adaptive systems have several characteristics that, until recently, organizational and management theorists have tended to ignore or assume away (Anderson, 1999; Beinhocker, 1997; Brown and Eisenhardt, 1998; Kelly and Allison, 1999; Wood, 1997).

- They are nonlinear and dynamic and do not inherently reach fixed equilibrium points. The resulting system behaviors may appear to be random or chaotic.

- They are composed of independent agents whose behavior can be described as based on physical, psychological, or social rules, rather than being completely dictated by the dynamics of the system.
- Agents' needs or desires, reflected in their rules, are not homogeneous; therefore, their goals and behaviors are likely to conflict—these conflicts or competitions tend to lead agents to adapt to each other's behaviors.
- Agents are intelligent, learn as they experiment and gain experience, and change behaviors accordingly. Thus, the behavior of the overall system inherently changes over time.
- Adaptation and learning tend to result in self-organizing and patterns of behavior that emerge rather than being designed into the system. The nature of such emergent behaviors may range from valuable innovations or unfortunate accidents.
- There is no single point(s) of control; behaviors of systems are often unpredictable and uncontrollable, and no one is "in charge." Consequently, the behaviors of complex adaptive systems can be influenced more than they can be controlled.

These characteristics differ substantially from the traditional "economic man" view of people and organizations. The monolithic maximization of profit was once viewed as the raison d'être of companies. In contrast, the above characterization reflects the heterogeneous behavioral, social, and cultural nature of organizations.

The complex adaptive systems perspective is much more compatible with the wide range of loosely structured organizational systems that have emerged in recent years. Later in this chapter, the possible nature of overarching strategies for "managing" these types of complex systems is considered.

APPROACHES TO STRATEGY

Thus far, we have considered the nature of the essential challenges, the behavioral and social context within which managers have to address these challenges, and trends toward complex, loosely structured organizations. Our next concern is with how strategy can and should be approached in the process of addressing the challenges.

I hasten to clarify the emphasis of this discussion of approaches to strategy. I make no attempt in this book to outline overall step-by-step procedures for strategy development and implementation such as those presented by, for example, Hunger and Wheelen (1998) and in one of my earlier books (Rouse, 1992). Instead, this book focuses on a small set of critical issues—essential challenges—and provides a range of means for addressing them. This focus enables in-depth treatments of these challenges, which would not be possible if the emphasis was on overall procedures. Given that there are no monolithic best procedures, it is important for managers to have a range of useful and usable concepts, principles, methods, and tools that they can configure and tailor to address their most pressing challenges.

Schools of Thought

There are quite a few alternative ways of thinking about strategy. Mintzberg, Ahlstrand, and Lampel (1998, 1999) have suggested the 10 schools of strategy formation summarized in Table 1.1. This range of alternatives helps to explain quite fundamental differences between, for example, large mature enterprises

TABLE 1.1. Schools of Thought on Strategy Processes

School	Description
Design	Senior management formulates clear, simple, and unique strategies to achieve the essential fit between internal strengths and weaknesses and external threats and opportunities.
Planning	Design school plus formal, decomposable process with distinct steps, delineated by checklists, and supported by techniques which lead to staff replacing senior managers as de facto key players.
Positioning	Reduces strategy to generic positions selected through formal analyses of industry situations.
Entrepreneurial	Centers process on chief executive with process rooted in the mysteries of intuition—emphasizes vision and leader's close control of implementing his or her formulated vision.
Cognitive	Focuses on cognitive biases in strategy making and on cognition as information processing, knowledge structure mapping, and concept attainment.
Learning	Strategies are emergent and can be found throughout the organization, and so-called formulation and implementation intertwine.
Power	Strategy development is a political process that involves bargaining, persuasion, and confrontation among actors who divide power.
Cultural	Strategy development is a social process rooted in culture, involving common interest and integration.
Environmental	Organizations react and adapt to environmental forces and constraints.
Configuration	Organizations are coherent clusters of characteristics and behaviors with states and transformations among states.

(Based on Mintzberg, Ahlstrand, Lampel, 1998, 1999)

and small start-up businesses or, as another example, between for-profit businesses and public agencies. These differences also show why good practices may be best practices in one domain and yet present difficulties in other domains.

For example, I have repeatedly found that best practices from for-profit business do not always transfer successfully to government agencies and nonprofits, despite the sincere desire of many of these types of organizations to be more business like. Compared with businesses, government agencies and nonprofits usually have a much more diverse set of stakeholders with varied and often competing objectives. Consequently, political processes play a much more central role in these organizations.

The breadth of the alternatives in Table 1.1 also helps to keep particular alternatives in perspective. For example, Harvard's Michael Porter, one of the most visible strategy "gurus," recently addressed the basic question, "What is strategy?" (Porter, 1996). He concludes, "Strategy is the creation of a unique and valuable position, involving a different set of activities.". Mintzberg and his colleagues note that this statement fits squarely in the positioning school. However, it has much less significance when interpreted in the frameworks of the other schools.

Thus, the notion of different schools is important to enable keeping good practices in perspective and understanding the conditions under which these practices can be designated "best." Similarly, the many grand ideas articulated by various strategy gurus should be interpreted in the context of the school of thought they represent and adopted with an understanding of the underlying premises of this school.

Five of the schools shown in Table 1.1 are particularly relevant to our discussions—design, planning, positioning, entrepreneurial, and learning. Table 1.2 compares these five schools in terms of the relative attention paid to five issues/criteria: *1*) process leadership, *2*) market opportunities, *3*) customer value, *4*) enterprise capability, and *5*) strategy realization. The merits of each of the five perspectives depend on an organization's preferences for process leadership and the relative priorities of the four other criteria.

To illustrate, it is common for organizations to want a balance of process leadership across the chief executive, senior management, and all employees. Such organizations usually do not want staff dominating the process. It is also typical for organizations to want a rough balance across the four criteria in Table 1.2; often, this desire stems from past experiences in which an imbalance resulted in not meeting expectations.

These preferences argue for a hybrid perspective that blends the design, entrepreneurial, and learning schools of thought. It is also common for organizations to adopt elements of the methodological support and data-driven

TABLE 1.2. Comparison of Five Schools of Thought

	Design	Planning	Positioning	Entre-preneurial	Learning
Process Leadership	Senior Management	Planning Staff	Staff Analysts	Chief Executive	Everyone Participates
Market Opportunity	Driven by SWOT Analysis	Driven by SWOT Analysis	Driven by Market Data	Leader Dependent	External Focus Dependent
Customer Value	Methodology Dependent	Methodology Dependent	Driven by Market Data	Leader Dependent	Culture Dependent
Enterprise Capability	Driven by SWOT Analysis	Driven by SWOT Analysis	Capability Assumed	Leader Dependent	Inherent to Participation
Strategy Realization	Mgt Team Imple-mentation	Programmed Imple-mentation	Implementation Assumed	Leader Controls Imple-mentation	Distributed Imple-mentation

approaches of the planning and positioning schools, respectively, but also carefully avoid the limiting nature of these schools.

Strategy Formation

This hybrid perspective suggests the following requirements for a strategy formation process:

- Strategy formation should be led top down by the chief executive and senior management but fleshed out bottom up throughout the organization by those charged with implementing strategies.
- Strategy formation should involve flowing down the organizational vision, overall goals, and overarching strategies and flowing up detailed goals, strategies, and action plans.
- Strategy formation should be informed, but not solely determined, by data characterizing market opportunities, customer values, and competitive intelligence.
- Strategy formation should include specific consideration of the capabilities needed to implement strategies as well as factors that influence the organization's abilities to sustain successful implementation.

These requirements have important implications for supporting the strategy formation process. Many organizations find strategy formation quite difficult. Studies of the sources of these difficulties have identified three underlying problems (Rouse, 1994):

- People do not know what to do. Strategic thinking is elusive, often preempted by operational matters and hindered by delusions (Rouse, 1998).
- Strategy formation often takes considerable time—sometimes a very long time—as people try to figure out what to do.
- Many strategy formation efforts produce results that people do not value and find useful.

Put simply, people often do not know what to do, their activities consume enormous amounts of time, and these activities do result in anything that they want. Four types of support can substantially remove these difficulties:

First, a clearly defined strategy formation process should be provided. This process should satisfy the above requirements and specify the inputs each participant should expect, the outputs they should produce, and typical schedules and milestones for the overall process. It also should be clear to all participants how strategy formation affects decision making and resource allocation.

Second, each element of the strategy-formation process should be supported with appropriate data, methods, and tools. Data that are of broad value throughout the process should be compiled centrally and distributed to appropriate participants. Methods and tools of broad use should be acquired or created centrally and provided to all relevant participants.

Third, training should be provided to all participants. This training may differ substantially for senior and middle management. However, it is important to avoid the assumption that intelligent, motivated people will figure the process out for themselves. There is tremendous leverage gained when there is a shared mental model about the nature of strategy formation and how it happens in the organization.

Fourth, ongoing coaching should be provided to all participants. Some organizations provide facilitators trained in the strategy formation process to assist teams, at any levels, who encounter difficulties. Coaching can also be provided via a regularly updated web page that addresses frequently asked questions.

Providing these elements of support can create a strategy bureaucracy in itself. To avoid this, most organizations keep the strategy staff quite slim. This can be accomplished, for instance, by having all trained facilitators primarily serve other roles in the organization. Similarly, many elements of training can be delivered by users of the strategy formation process rather than by training specialists.

A strategy formation process that meets the above requirements and provides the needed support is usually viewed by process users as very empowering. They know what to do, are supported in doing it effectively and efficiently, and create strategies and plans that enable achieving the organization's goals. The result should be a shared strategic story of the company's future (Shaw, Brown, and Bromiley, 1998). With such a process in place, organizations are able to leverage their human resources to maximum advantage.

Process Implementation

Success in forming and implementing strategies requires more than just an intellectually coherent process. There are hurdles to jump and barriers to surmount in the process of forming a new strategy for the enterprise. These hurdles and barriers tend to present enormous problems for those attempting to design and implement new directions for an established organization.

Martin (1993) argues that attempts to change are often subverted by organizations' strong tendencies to glorify the past and idealize sunk assets. Sull (1999) observes that organizations are often captured by "active inertia" that inhibits strategy. In general, the practices that helped the enterprise "sail" to its current success often become the "anchors" that retard or stop pursuit of tactics to future success.

Elsewhere (Rouse, 1998), I have focused on the types of delusions that hinder effective strategic thinking. These delusions, or persistent false beliefs, concern an enterprise's perceptions of itself and its markets. The resulting misperceptions cause organizations to entertain poor alternatives, collect inappropriate information, and make wrong decisions. In fact, the alternatives, information, and decisions often would have been quite right if the flawed perceptions had been correct. However, these perceptions were held as truths not as hypotheses to be tested.

Kipp (1999) summarizes several difficulties that must be surmounted to succeed in strategy formation:

- The "right" process is the one that gives you the most direct confrontation with your core challenge; thus, there can be no single "right" process, no panacea.
- Most people would rather talk about operations than strategy; in fact, focusing on today's issues and problems often precludes strategic thinking.

- The absence of appropriate information keeps organizations moving in the same direction, and this direction usually drives what information is compiled.
- Dysfunctional executive teams prevent both breakthrough thinking and follow-through execution—the whole can actually be less than the sum of the parts.
- All organizations are perfectly designed to achieve the results they are getting; hence, they are usually less than perfectly designed for the results they want.
- People have a hard time understanding, much less implementing, a strategy they were not involved in creating, which tends to be true throughout the organization.
- All organizational change begins with personal change—either members of the team need to grow personally, or the members of the team need to change.

These types of difficulties—as well as the aforementioned tendencies and delusions—can cause strategy formation to be a frustrating and unproductive experience. Old debates are revived, people posture regarding sacred cows, and tried and true—but no longer effective—conclusions are reached. Strategic meetings, offsites, and retreats are wrapped up and almost everyone knows that no fundamental progress has been made.

Eisenhardt (1999) argues these natural tendencies can be overcome by viewing strategy formation as a decision-making process. She suggests that the effectiveness of the process can be enhanced by

- building collective intuition that enhances the ability of a top-management team to see threats and opportunities sooner and more accurately,
- stimulating quick conflict to improve quality of strategic thinking without sacrificing significant time,
- maintaining a disciplined pace that drives the decision process to a timely conclusion, and
- defusing political behavior that creates unproductive conflict and wastes time.

These tactics will clearly improve efficiency, but their impact on effectiveness depends totally on complementary tactics for dealing with the fundamental difficulties noted earlier.

This can usually be accomplished, or at least facilitated, by performing an assumption audit (Rouse, 1998). This sometimes painful process involves asking and answering questions such as, "What hard evidence do we have that our products are as good as we like to think they are?" Another example is, "How do we know that the members of the top-management team are as good as we like to think they are?" This process often leads to the conclusion that, unlike Lake Wobegon, everyone and everything are not above average. The painful part is both the recognition of this reality and, just as important, doing something to change this reality.

Beyond dealing with the above hurdles and barriers, there are several other issues that relate to the success of the strategy-formation process. One concerns the linking of strategy to projects (Englund and Graham, 1999). The enterprise's strategy should drive project selection criteria, including the metrics chosen and the relative weights assigned to criteria. In this way, all projects that are undertaken will explicitly support the enterprise's strategy.

As obvious as this advice sounds, projects frequently are unrelated to strategy. I recall asking the CEO of an appliance manufacturing company if the goals and plans of the executives reporting to him were aligned with the company's overall strategic goals. In other words, if all the goals of the executives were achieved, would the company achieve its overall goals? His answer, which is typical, was that he had no idea if this were true.

Having reviewed all of these goals and plans, I knew that people had proposed quite reasonable things that would, without doubt, benefit the company. However, considering the fact that these goals and plans were developed without knowledge of subsequently determined overall goals, it would be very unlikely for the particular sets of contributing goals chosen to be the best set relative to the overall goals. In cases like this, the overall goals become more like long-term wishes rather than driving forces throughout the organization.

Some of this lack of linkage stems from a lack of tools for decomposing overall goals into component goals, as well as rolling up component goals into overall implications. There are many tools available—many of which are discussed in later chapters. However, beyond the ubiquitous spreadsheet, adoption of such tools is not widespread.

In part, this makes much sense. Organizations need to define their own processes for addressing strategic issues, rather than adopting off-the-shelf approaches (Campbell, 1999). Defining these processes can require significant effort. Furthermore, there is often a sense of wanting to get on with strategy rather than getting bogged down in strategy processes.

Extensive experience with this issue using a wide range of strategic planning methods and tools (ESS, 2000) has led to the following conclusion. It is usually very helpful to begin using off-the-shelf processes, in part to make some real progress but also as a means of discovering how you would really like your processes to work. Then, you need to modify the methods and tools you are using, switch to other methods and tools that are modifiable, or develop your own.

This implies a very flexible and adaptive management team and, to an extent, organizational culture. In fact, this flexibility and adaptability, when combined with an openness to external information, knowledge, and skills, are keys to addressing most of the difficulties outlined in this section. Questioning assumptions, seeking new approaches, and adapting to new realities are key behaviors.

Strategy and Complexity

Beyond the difficulties just discussed, we must also address the implications for strategy-formation processes of organizational complexity as elaborated earlier. Consideration of the possible nature of overarching strategies for "managing" complexity leads to a fundamental question. How can one best influence a system in which there are conflicting and competing concerns, values, and perceptions among stakeholders, no one is in charge, and almost all paths lead to failure? Although some of the players, and society in general, will succeed, how can one assure a share in this success?

Beinhocker (1997) argues that "The central challenge in a complex adaptive system is...excelling at conflicting goals simultaneously: having strategies that are both focused and robust; seeking competitive advantage by adapting continuously; operating conservatively and innovating radically; maintaining diversity while establishing standards and routines; and optimizing both scale and flexibility." One way to accomplish this is to provide considerable independence to operating units within the overall enterprise. Kelly and Allison (1999) focus on the value of empowering business units to self-organize and propose four strategic rules for successful self-organizing—trust, learn together, commit deeply, and embrace change—that are compatible with Beinhocker's guidance.

Wood (1997) suggests possible elements of such an overarching strategy. First, the process of strategy formation should be framed as a strategic conversation among stakeholders that results in strategy being driven by environmental forces. Next, a "future navigating process" should be created for learning from uncertainty and dealing with the unexpected, which enables adaptation to environmental changes. Amidst this flow of changing forces, one should adopt an approach to business design that enables finding and protecting profit zones—the high-margin portions of business often surrounded by low-margin portions. Finally, one needs to ensure an ongoing coherence between the business design and capabilities to deliver, together with the capacity for self-renewal.

Brown and Eisenhardt (1998) propose 10 rules of strategy that reflect a similar philosophy and guidance:

- Advantage is temporary and requires continuous change.
- Strategy is diverse, emergent, and complicated.
- Invent new ways to create value.
- Live in the present, as this is the most important time frame.
- Take advantage of past experiences but avoid outdated models.
- Look to the future but avoid extensive plans for the unpredictable.
- Pace change to enable a smooth transition from present to future.
- Grow the strategy in an evolutionary manner.
- Drive strategy from the business level, rather than just top down.
- Readjust the organization to align with emergent opportunities.

Anderson's theory (1999) begins from a similar premise, namely, that the aim of an organization's strategy should become one of evolving temporary advantage more rapidly than competitors. Consequently, managers should establish and modify the direction and the boundaries within which effective, improvised, self-organized solutions can evolve. This should involve small, cheap experiments that recombine the elements of the portfolio of modular business units, ensuring that novelty is deliberately generated without destroying the best elements of past experience. This requires altering the "fitness landscape" for agents and reconfiguring the organizational architecture within which agents adapt. This shapes the context within which strategy emerges. Recommended alterations include changing the domain or niche, changing the incentive and reward systems, countering tendencies to exploit short-term opportunities, and changing the demographics of the organization.

It is difficult to summarize these prescriptions without feeling that the overall guidance is simply be very flexible, do the right things, and design the organization accordingly. Few managers would disagree with this conclusion. However, the key difference emerges when one considers this conclusion at the next level of depth.

Somewhat simplistically, all of the above guidance and advice can be summarized by characterizing management's tasks as the following.

- Defining rules such as goals of the enterprise and boundaries within which these goals should be achieved.

- Allocating resources to proposals for succeeding within these rules, monitoring ongoing success of these efforts, and reallocating resources as needed.

The rules are necessary to ensure that people focus on strategic organizational goals and behave consistently with organizational values—in other words, pursuing the right things in the right ways. Otherwise, component organizations tend to "suboptimize" and focus solely on what's good for them. As straightforward as this sounds, many managers find it quite difficult to specify goals and boundaries rather than behaviors.

Malone and Laubacher (1998) reach similar conclusions regarding managers' roles in defining rules: "One of the primary roles for the large companies that remain in the future may be to establish the rules, standards, and cultures for network organizations operating partly within and partly outside their own boundaries." Thus, as difficult as this task may be, managers are likely to increasingly face these demands as they oversee loosely structured organizations in which they cannot manage, or perhaps even observe, behaviors (Rouse, 1999).

Resource allocation has long been a central management task when resources are scarce and not all proposals can be supported. This task becomes even more important when the behaviors enabled by resources cannot be directly managed. The quality of proposals become crucial and tends to improve when goals and criteria are clear and well communicated, which, of course, reinforces the importance of defining the rules. Proposals are also better executed when continued allocations of resources depend on performance.

Above all, resources—including money, people, facilities, and management attention—serve as strong incentives for behaviors that can no longer be commanded in loosely structured organizations. More specifically, resources are allocated so as to result in desired outcomes via behaviors that conform with organizational values and priorities, that is, the rules. And, in keeping with the adaptive nature of complex systems, the rules tend to evolve with experience and opportunities.

BEST PRACTICES

The purpose of this book is not only to characterize the essential challenges of strategic management but also to recommend how these challenges are "best" addressed. To this end, later chapters discuss a wide range of frameworks, methods, and tools for assessing the nature and extent of challenges, developing creative and effective approaches for dealing with challenges, and implementing and monitoring the success of these approaches.

It is important to underscore what is meant by "best" practices. In some cases, a practice has been rigorously and empirically evaluated relative to competing approaches and shown to provide the greatest benefit, for example, highest probability of profitability. In other cases, a practice has become a de facto standard approach among widely admired companies, although there has been no rigorous evaluation to assess the merits of this practice.

In many cases, a practice has yet to be widely employed but makes considerable sense, and all results to date are supportive of its likely merits. In some of these cases, there are published works explaining and arguing the benefits of a practice. In a few cases, there is only experiential support for a practice. In all cases, readers have to decide the relevance of a practice to their enterprises and the sufficiency of the support for the merits of the practice.

The nature and extent of support for each practice are discussed when the practice is introduced. Also considered are methods and tools for implementing best practices. The final chapter discusses the ways in which the range of best practice, methods, and tools presented in this book can be integrated and viewed more holistically.

BRIEF OVERVIEW

The next seven chapters address the essential challenges in the order discussed earlier: goal (growth), foundation (value), path (focus), design (change), view (future), means (knowledge), and self (time). These challenges are discussed in terms of the following characteristics:

- nature of challenge,
- examples,
- difficulty of challenge,
- best practices, and
- methods and tools

Several issues that cut across all of the challenges are also discussed. One such issue is risk. This concerns the kinds of things that can go wrong, how to assess whether these things are happening, and, potentially, how to mitigate the consequences of such occurrences.

Another cross-cutting issue is resources. Needs and implications for human and financial resources are pervasive for all of the essential challenges. Organizational design is an important related issue. Each chapter considers the ways in which these issues interact with approaches to the challenge being addressed.

The nature of the markets or constituencies served by an enterprise strongly affects the relevance of best practices and how they should be implemented and managed. Discussions in each chapter explicitly distinguish the implications for different types of enterprises, including for-profits in different markets, nonprofits, and government agencies.

The final chapter summarizes the best practices, methods, and tools identified throughout this book. A procedure is described for assessing the extent to which the challenges are being successfully addressed in your organization. Finally, an integrated view of all practices, methods, and tools is presented.

REFERENCES

Anderson, P. (1999). Complexity theory and organizational science. *Organizational Science* 10(3): 216–232.

Beinhocker, E. D. (1997). Strategy at the edge of chaos. *The McKinsey Quarterly* Winter: 24–40.

Brown, S. L., and Eisenhardt, K. M. (1998). *Competing on the Edge: Strategy as Structured Chaos*. Boston, MA: Harvard Business School.

Campbell, A. (1999). Tailored, not benchmarked: a fresh look at corporate planning. *Harvard Business Review* March–April: 41–50.

Collins, J. C., and Porras, J. I. (1994). *Built to Last: Successful Habits of Visionary Companies*. New York: Harper Business.

Covey, S. R. (1989). *The Seven Habits of Highly Effective People*. New York: Simon & Schuster.

Deming, W. E. (1986). *Out of Crisis*. Cambridge, MA: MIT Press.

Drucker, P. F. (1997).Toward the new organization. *Leader to Leader 3*: 6–8.

Eisenhardt, K. M. (1999). Strategy as strategic decision making. *Sloan Management Review* Spring: 65–72.

Englund, R. L., and Graham, R. J. (1999). Linking projects to strategy. *Journal of Product Innovation Management* 16(1): 52–64.

ESS. (2000). http://www.ess-advisors.com/software.htm. Atlanta, GA: Enterprise Support Systems.

Hammer, M. (1990). Reengineering work: don't automate, obliterate. *Harvard Business Review* 68(4): 104–112.

Hammer, M., and Champy, J. (1993). *Reengineering the Corporation: A Manifesto for Business Revolution*. New York: Harper Business.

Hunger, J. D., and Wheelen, T. L. (1998). *Strategic Management* (6th ed.). Reading, MA: Addision-Wesley.

Kelly, S., and Allison, M. A. (1999). *The Complexity Advantage: How the Science of Complexity Can Help Your Business Achieve Peak Performance*. New York: McGraw-Hill.

Kipp, M. F. (1999). The challenges of strategy: seven lessons. *Strategy & Leadership* 27(1): 32–33.

Malone, T. W., and Laubacher, R. J., (1998). The dawn of the e-lance economy. *Harvard Business Review* September–October: 145–152.

Martin, R. (1993). Changing the mind of the corporation. *Harvard Business Review* November–December: 5–12.

Micklethwait, J., and Woolridge, A. (1996). *Witch Doctors: Making Sense of the Management Gurus*. New York: Times Business.

Mintzberg, H. (1975). The manager's job: folklore and fact. *Harvard Business Review* July–August: 49–61.

Mintzberg, H., Ahlstrand, B., and Lampel, J. (1998). *Strategy Safari: A Guided Tour Through the Wilds of Strategic Management*. New York: Free Press.

Mintzberg, H., and Lampel, J. (1999). Reflecting on the strategy process. *Sloan Management Review* Spring: 21–30.

Pinault, L. (2000). *Consulting Demons: Inside the Unscrupulous World of Global Corporate Consulting*. New York: Harper Business.

Porter, M. E. (1996). What is strategy? *Harvard Business Review* 74(6): 61–78.

Prahalad, C. K. (1998). Managing discontinuities: the emerging challenges. *Research Technology Management* 41(3): 14–22.

Rouse, W. B. (1992). *Strategies for Innovations: Creating Successful Products, Systems, and Organizations*. New York: Wiley.

Rouse, W. B. (1994). *Best Laid Plans*. Englewood Cliffs, NJ: Prentice-Hall.

Rouse, W. B. (1996). *Start Where You Are: Matching Your Strategy to Your Marketplace*. San Francisco, CA: Jossey-Bass.

Rouse, W. B. (1998). *Don't Jump to Solutions: Thirteen Delusions That Undermine Strategic Thinking*. San Francisco, CA: Jossey-Bass.

Rouse, W. B. (1999). Connectivity, creativity, and chaos: challenges of loosely-structured organizations. *Information • Knowledge • Systems Management* 1(2): 117–131.

Rouse, W. B. (2000). Managing complexity: disease control as a complex adaptive system. *Information • Knowledge • Systems Management* 2.

Rouse, W. B., and Boff, K. R. (1999). Making the case for investments in human effectiveness. *Information • Knowledge • Systems Management* 1(3): 225–247.

Sage, A. P. (1995). *Systems Management for Information Technology and Software Engineering*. New York: Wiley.

Shaw, G., Brown, R., and Bromiley, P.(1998). Strategic stories: how 3M is rewriting business planning. *Harvard Business Review* May-June: 41–50.

Simon, H. A. (1957). *Models of Man: Social and Rational*. New York: Wiley.

Simon, H. A. (1969). *The Sciences of the Artificial*. Cambridge, MA: MIT Press.

Stewart, T. A. (2000). Whom can you trust? It's not so easy to tell. *Fortune* June 12: 331–334.

Sull, D. N. (1999). Why good companies go bad. *Harvard Business Review* July-August: 42–52.

Wheatley, M. J. (1999). When complex systems fail: new roles for leaders. *Leader to Leader* Winter: 11.

Wood, R. (1997). The future of strategy: the role of the new sciences. In: *Proceedings of International Conference on Complex Systems*. Boston, MA: New England Complex Systems Institute.

CHAPTER TWO

Growth

Growth is a primary objective of almost all of the many enterprises with whom I have worked. Indeed, many of these efforts were initiated because of a lack of growth. Failure to sustain growth had hurt the company's share price, executive's incentive compensation, employee bonuses, and company morale. As one executive said, "This is not a fun situation."

Occasionally, an enterprise has questioned the need to grow. Why not focus on providing continually increasing value with stable revenues and profits? This seems reasonable, at least philosophically. To many, this seems like the ideal corporate citizen. However, this approach to growth presents a range of practical difficulties.

First and foremost, the flow of customers and revenues is rarely, if ever, constant and uninterrupted. Avoiding growth means turning away customers in good times and decline in bad times. More specifically, customers turned away can be sorely missed when the "sure thing," sales, unexpectedly disappear, perhaps due to uncontrollable external forces.

Another problem with lack of growth, intentional or otherwise, is the impact on the organizational culture. One senior manager of a company mired in a lack of growth commented, "We are all just watching each other get older." Such situations tend to limit opportunities for personal growth, especially for younger, less-senior personnel. The spirit and energy level of such organizations tend to drift downward.

Lack of growth can also lead to what a senior manager in another enterprise termed "an income replacement model." Everyone works to ensure continuity of the revenue streams on which their livelihoods depend. Once they have met these "quotas," they revert to just doing their jobs. In such situations, the purpose of the enterprise slowly but surely becomes solely continued employment for current employees.

All in all, perhaps after reflecting on the above issues, most enterprises want to grow. At the very least, this is due to a strong desire to avoid decline. Most managers usually come to the realization that a stable organization that neither grows nor declines is very difficult to achieve. Simply staying in place almost always requires that you try to move forward.

There is more to growth, however, then simply decline avoidance. Growth usually results in increased impact and greater resources—profits in some cases and discretionary monies in other cases. This enables rewarding those responsible for growth, as well as investing in continued growth of both the enterprise and employees. Overall, it's a lot more fun to be part of a growing organization.

NATURE OF GROWTH

In contrast to the microeconomic view of growth just elaborated, there are broader perspectives that consider companies as wholes and even broader macroeconomic views that look at industries or the economy as the unit of analysis. It is particularly useful in this book to discuss company-level points of view.

Theories of Growth

There are many theories of business growth, for example, those detailed in the *Economist* (1999). A traditional theory is that companies' pursuits of economies of scale lead to mergers and acquisitions, as well as organic growth. Such growth is eventually limited, at least in principle by diminishing returns for further consolidation and in practice by mechanisms such as anti-trust regulations. The finite size of all markets is, of course, the ultimate limit. For examples, once everyone eats your burgers and drinks your colas, it is very difficult to sustain growth rates, unless you do something different.

Another traditional theory emphasizes the cyclical nature of markets, technologies, and companies (Rouse, 1996). According to this view, companies inevitably move through (typically five) stages of initiation, growth, maturity, consolidation, and decline. Varian's (2000) version of this theory also includes five stages: experimentation, capitalization, management, hypercompetition, and consolidation. He uses this framework to discuss past growth markets (e.g., telephones) and contemporary growth markets such as cellular phones and E-commerce, indicating the current stages of a range of high-tech markets. Pfeiffer (2000) discusses the inevitable and impending consolidation of Internet sites, noting that there are 10,000 Internet companies too many.

Of course, it is difficult to argue with the idea that companies are formed, grow for a period, and inevitably decline. The crucial issue is the length of stages and how transitions between stages occur. Collins and Porras (1994) convincingly show how numerous companies have reinvented themselves, moving from maturity back to growth. A very good example is Motorola, which has moved from batteries to radios to pagers to cell phones over several decades. Thus, the existence of cycles and transitions does not tell us much, except perhaps when it may be prudent to fold our bets.

A more recent theory of growth focuses on the notion that core competencies drive growth. Skills in technology, marketing, and so forth provide competitive advantages that yield increased sales and possibly market shares. Further growth may be obtained by transferring these skills to adjacent markets, for example, retailing skills and infrastructure transferred by Circuit City to Car Max. In contrast, companies with inferior skills in key areas lose out to their competitors. The not surprising "bottom line" of this view is that companies that are better at what they do tend to perform better than companies that are not as good at what they do. Furthermore, companies that venture outside their competencies seeking growth are unlikely to succeed.

The above theories would seem to imply straightforward transitions among phases and exploitation of competencies leading to smooth growth—or decline. However, as recently shown by Paul Geroski, smooth growth or decline seldom appears in real growth data (Economist, 1999). Instead, growth data portray "random walks" with no apparent underlying smooth transitions. Geroski hypothesizes that this is due to erratic innovation by companies. Rather than regularly introducing innovations, most companies innovate in response to competition and crises, leading to on-again, off-again growth—or decline.

Companies' difficulties with innovation do not stem solely from a lack of impetus. As Christensen (1997) compellingly shows, large enterprises often have great difficulty taking advantage of potential innovations in which they have invested. An underlying problem is that innovations seldom yield large revenues and profits in the near term. However, near-term growth is usually a dominating objective for large companies. Consequently, potential innovations get limited attention and resources in such firms. Innovation is discussed at length in the next chapter on the challenge of value.

Competing theories of growth are increasingly being evaluated using computer simulations. For example, Ballot and Taymaz (1999) have developed a computer model of the Swedish economy that enables study of behaviors of firms. Casti (1997) discusses the overall approach of using "would-be worlds" for studies of behaviors in domains ranging from the stock market to the insurance industry to grocery stores. Thus, it is possible to simulate the implementation of a growth strategy before deciding to actually implement this strategy.

Many of these simulations are based on complex systems representations as discussed in Chapter 1. In particular, organizational systems are represented in terms of "intelligent agents" that act on the basis of the rules of the game, learn from their individual actions, and subsequently modify the rules.

The agents may be individual consumers or employees, whole companies, or perhaps industries. The choice depends on the questions driving the development of such models. Complex systems are considered in more depth in Chapter 5, which addresses the challenge of change.

Situation Assessment

A central issue in developing successful growth strategies is understanding your current and emerging relationships with your markets. In *Start Where You Are* (Rouse, 1996), I discuss and illustrate an approach to performing this type of situation assessment. The overall premise is that knowing where you are is an essential first step to getting where you want to be.

The situation assessment methodology, and a tool which is discussed later in this chapter, is based on an extensive study of three industries: transportation, computers, and defense. This study involved fascinating examinations of steamboats, railroads, automobiles, aircraft, calculators, typewriters, cash registers, tabulators, computers, and so on. Similar patterns emerged in all of these industries. A new technology matured to the point of practical application. Fairly quickly, hundreds and often thousands of businesses were formed to exploit this opportunity; eventually, consolidation resulted in a handful of remaining competitors.

I recall, in particular, reading about competition in the steamboat industry in the early and mid-1800s. Steamers with a new hull design or a new engine design might enable cutting 1 hour off the trip from New York to Boston. Passengers would flock to this new type of boat. However, the originators of this innovation might within a year bemoan the fact that yet a newer hull or engine had cut further time off the trip and captured all the passengers. Last year's innovation was relegated to carrying low-margin freight.

Commentaries from this period wonder at the pace of technological change. Similar stories are quite common from other periods in the 200-year span studied. This year's innovations displace last year's innovations, and, much less often, last year's dominant competitors are displaced by new players. At the very least, however, the originators of the latest innovations are making much higher profit margins than those providing last year's offerings.

On the surface, this pattern fits quite well the classical cyclical theory of business growth. However, this description is not sufficiently rich to enable the insights needed to make strategic management decisions. We need a level of description that portrays the experiences and possibilities for a particular company in a broader industry context. In other words, we need to describe patterns of growth at a level that is compatible with the strategic alternatives typically available to managers.

Table 2.1 summarizes the 10 common business situations identified in this study. The overarching situation assessment question is, "Where am I now and where am I headed?" To support addressing this question, a set 41 current and leading indicators—thus, 82 in all—were gleaned from the business histories studied. Situation assessment involves estimating the levels of each of these indicators for your enterprise. The *Situation Assessment Advisor*, described later in this chapter, then provides a knowledge-based assessment of your current situation and your most likely transitions to future situations. Numerous historical examples are provided of how other companies dealt with the situations that one may currently face or likely face in the future. More general advice for dealing with your assessed situations is also provided.

It should not be surprising that there are several dominant patterns of transitions among the 10 common situations in Table 2.1. As shown in Figure 2.1, transitions from steady growth to consolidation are fairly common, whereas transitions from vision quest to consolidation are quite rare. The predominant transition paths among the 10 business situations can provide important insights. Anticipating, recognizing, and responding to these transitions are important elements of strategic thinking and should strongly influence strategic planning.

The pattern of transitions experienced by a specific company constitutes the story of this business. There are five common stories that I call classic life cycle, false start, death spiral, reinventing the company, and branching and pruning. These stories illustrate patterns that are both desirable and undesirable.

Classic Life Cycle

This is the classic story reflected in the more traditional theories of growth discussed earlier. Typically, this story involves steps with names such as birth, growth, maturation, and decline. With the use of the 10 common situations, this pattern can be described as follows:

Vision Quest – Evolution – Crossover – Crossing the Chasm – Steady Growth – Consolidation – Silent War – Paradigm Lost – Commodity Trap – Process

This story can be interpreted in terms of broad relationships with markets. The vision quest, evolution, crossover, and crossing the chasm situations are elements of being ahead of the market. Crossing the chasm, steady growth, and consolidation situations relate to the market catching up. Finally, the silent war, paradigm lost situations, and potentially the commodity trap and process situations can reflect the market passing by.

TABLE 2.1. Ten Common Business Situations

Situation	Definition
Vision Quest	A situation where you are trying to create a relationship with the marketplace, usually for products and services that are ahead of the markets expressed needs and wants.
Evolution	A situation where development of your relationship with the marketplace takes substantial time as your technologies, processes, and overall market proposition mature.
Crossover	A situation where either your success depends on importing key technologies and processes from other domains, or your success depends on exporting your technologies or processes to other markets.
Crossing the Chasm	A situation where you must transition from selling to innovators and early adopters to a more pragmatic relationship with the early majority in the broader marketplace—originated by Geoffrey Moore in his book *Crossing the Chasm* (1991).
Steady Growth	A situation where sales and profits repeatedly increase as your relationship with the market becomes strongly established; quite often, market share increases in an overall market that is also increasing.
Consolidation	A situation where the number of competitors and the fierceness of the competition increase to the point that price cutting and increased costs result in many mergers, acquisitions, and business failures.
Silent War	A situation where you do not recognize competing companies or technologies, or perhaps recognize and discount them; they thereby become strong competitors while you offer little if any resistance—originated by Ira Magaziner and Mark Patinkin in their book *The Silent War* (1989).
Paradigm Lost	A situation where your technologies, processes, market propositions, and so forth become obsolete, often suddenly, due to new approaches and competitors, which results in damage to your relationship with the marketplace; phrase was originated by John Casti in his book *Paradigms Lost* (1989).
Commodity Trap	A situation where most or all competitors are selling the same products or services due to de facto or actual standards, with the result that you must focus on quality, service, and price as the dominant competitive attributes.
Process	A situation where improvements of processes, rather than new product innovations, are the central competitive issue; substantial investments are usually required if you are to beat your competitors' quality, service, and prices.

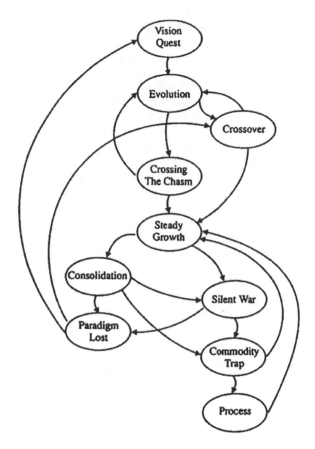

Figure 2.1. Typical transitions among business situations

The business life cycle reflected in this story is often considered to be inevitable. However, this is far from true. The comprehensive and compelling analysis provided by Collins and Porras in *Built to Last* (1994) makes this very clear. They show how companies such as Hewlett-Packard and Motorola have continued to renew themselves.

False Start
This story is quite common among new ventures. It also is common for new product lines within existing companies. There are two versions of this story:

Vision Quest – Evolution – Crossover – Evolution

or

Vision Quest – Evolution – Crossing the Chasm – Evolution

This story is one of continually trying to gain momentum and then losing it.

I have encountered this story frequently among university spin offs. Small, new ventures are formed on the basis of a specific technical idea. In the United States, they may seed this company by winning a Small Business Innovation and Research (SBIR) contract with the federal government. In principle, this seed money, and perhaps a second round of such funding, should result in commercialization of the founding technical idea.

What frequently happens, however, is that these new ventures repeatedly apply for SBIR contracts. I have known a couple of companies who have won over 100 of these contracts without ever getting a product to market. People who manage small business incubators, which are prevalent at US universities, have told me of many instances of companies who settle in and solely focus on SBIR contracts. I have seen the same behaviors in small companies supported by similar mechanisms in other countries.

I have also experienced this story in much larger companies who attempt to launch new product lines that are rather different from their existing product lines. A good recent example in the United States is the many companies who have entertained pursuing the health care market. I have worked with four defense electronics companies who considered applying their technologies and skills to either medical electronics or health information systems.

In one company, they actually made a large sale, but the customer went bankrupt. Two other companies have transitioned from evolution to crossover to evolution at least once. The fourth company quickly developed a business plan, evaluated its chances of success relative to other opportunities, and decided to terminate this effort. This last case is the only success story among the four.

You may wonder why I label such a decision a success. This company quickly developed and evaluated an alternative and then stopped all further investments in this alternative once they determined that it was not their best choice. This is good planning. Successfully considering an alternative does not mean that you have to decide to pursue this alternative. In fact, if you are only willing to consider alternatives that you are sure will subsequently be pursued, you are being much too conservative. A key to being able to avoid undesirable situations is the ability, and willingness, to quickly consider and evaluate a variety of ways of proceeding.

Death Spiral

You want to avoid false starts or, hopefully, exit them quickly. You also want to avoid death spirals or, again, find your way out quickly. This story is probably quite familiar:

Steady Growth – Consolidation – Commodity Trap – Consolidation

Note that I have not indicated how steady growth was achieved as this is not central to this story.

We saw this story repeatedly in the aforementioned analysis of companies in the transportation, computer, and defense industries since 1800. In 1850, there where 2,500 railroad companies; in 1900, there were 30. We identified comparable ratios for steamboats, automobiles, aircraft, calculators, cash registers, typewriters, and tabulators.

A good relatively recent example is the defense industry. In the 1990s

- Lockheed acquired General Dynamics' aircraft division,
- Martin Marietta acquired General Electric's military electronics division,
- Northrop acquired Grumman,
- Raytheon acquired E-Systems,
- Lockheed and Martin merged,
- Raytheon acquired Hughes' military electronics business, and
- Boeing acquired McDonnell-Douglas.

In addition, numerous small defense contractors have merged or left the market. Many companies, or business units within companies, are caught in death spirals.

In this story, you either want to be one of the surviving companies or you want to be acquired with attractive terms. Simply closing your doors and selling your hard assets are not desirable results, although many companies, especially lower-tiered subcontractors, have little choice.

For would-be acquirers—with discretionary resources available—prevalent death spiral stories can be wonderful. I have been involved with companies who have acquired other companies for no cash and the assumption of the acquired company's debt, which the acquirer promptly renegotiated with the financial institutions involved. In one case, the acquirer made back their investment in 6 months.

If you do not have the resources—or energy—to acquire other players, you should make yourself as attractive as possible. This means maximizing short-term sales and profits, avoiding investments, and making your financial statements look as rosy as possible. Alternatively, you can try to break out of the death spiral by redeploying your resources in other markets where their are fewer players or less capable players. The following two stories illustrate how this might be accomplished.

Reinventing the Company

One approach to avoiding classic life cycles and death spirals is to reinvent your company or, in effect, create a new company. There are two common stories in this pattern:

Steady Growth – Consolidation – Paradigm Lost – Crossover – Steady Growth

or

Steady Growth – Consolidation – Paradigm Lost – Vision Quest – Evolution – Crossing the Chasm – Steady Growth

As with the death spiral, I have not indicated how steady growth was initially achieved.

These two versions of this story involve either encountering a paradigm lost situation or precipitating this situation. In the former case, you have little choice but react. In the latter, you may be choosing to act much earlier than necessary but while you have the resources to act.

In the first pattern, you transition to a crossover situation by either acquiring technology and people or moving your technology and people to new markets. In the second pattern, you create the technology and grow the people needed for competitive advantage. If you are skilled at accomplishing these transitions, you may be able to keep your company continually growing by harvesting resources from declining stories and investing these resources in potential growth stories.

A good example of a company that is highly skilled in this manner is Motorola. I have had the good fortune to work with several Motorola business units and a couple hundred managers and executives. As noted earlier, they started in batteries, moved to radios and televisions, and then moved again to semiconductors, pagers, cellular phones, and other products. This process continues, with the latest quest being biochips.

A particularly important aspect of how Motorola and other companies reinvent themselves involves entertaining and investing in multiple stories. Some of these stories turn out to be false starts, and investments are stopped. Some become modest successes and may or may not be continued. A few— and only a few are needed—become significant successes. These receive substantial investments until paradigm lost situations emerge or are precipitated.

Branching and Pruning

Branching and pruning provide another way to avoid classic life cycle and death spiral stories. Three common versions of this story are as follows:

Steady Growth – Consolidation – Paradigm Lost – Commodity Trap – Process – Steady Growth

or

Steady Growth – Consolidation – Paradigm Lost – Crossover – Steady Growth

or

Steady Growth – Consolidation – Paradigm Lost – Vision Quest – Evolution – Crossing the Chasm – Steady Growth

As in the earlier examples, how steady growth is initially achieved is not central to this story.

This story is similar to reinventing the company, with a few important exceptions. First, you do not necessarily transition away from mature markets. Second, you actively encourage the pursuit of a large number of versions of these stories—in other words, much branching. Third, you communicate very clear criteria for continued investment in a story—thus, decisive pruning.

Built to Last (Collins and Porras, 1994), from which I borrowed the name of this story, provides a detailed discussion of an exemplary player of branching and pruning stories, namely 3M (Minnesota Mining and Manufacturing Company). 3M is well known for its many divisions and hundreds of product lines. The company is constantly branching and pruning.

In my interactions with 3M, I have been impressed with the autonomy of its divisions. All clearly understand the branching and pruning process, which they usually have replicated locally. The continued success of 3M provides substantial evidence of the power of understanding your relationships with your markets, their likely changes, and how to quickly respond and remain innovative in these markets.

The five typical business stories portray predominant patterns among the 10 common situations or relationships with markets. These stories illustrate how particular patterns of situations portend specific consequences for companies who play out these stories. Growth, lack of growth, or decline underlies all of these stories:

- Classic life cycle—Growth is achieved, but slips away into decline.
- False start—Growth never emerges.
- Death spiral—Growth transitions to steep decline.
- Reinventing the company—Old growth is replaced with new growth.
- Branching and pruning—Many growth paths are tried; a few flourish.

Thus, the challenge of growth is pervasive and must be addressed, one way or another, by all enterprises.

CHALLENGE OF GROWTH

The need to grow affects different types of enterprises in varying ways. In rapidly growing markets, it is usually relatively easy to find opportunities for growth. It takes skills and resources to pursue these opportunities successfully. However, it seldom requires fundamental rethinking of the nature of the enterprise or the marketplace.

Enterprises in mature markets find growth much more challenging. Growth requires gaining shares in saturated markets. Worse yet, such enterprises may need to find profits in declining markets. This happens in many large markets that are dominated by a few competitors that can only grow by taking market shares from each other. The other choice is doing something significantly different, which mature companies find quite difficult to do.

It is very easy to identify examples of this challenge. Major companies in markets ranging from airplanes, to appliances, automobiles, beverages, burgers, and computers face this challenge. How can you achieve strong, sustained growth in markets where you already have the dominant share? Wresting market share from competitors is clearly a possible answer, but this approaching is eventually self-limiting. Once you sell all the airplanes or all the burgers, what do you do next?

This challenge is particularly difficult because there is a very strong tendency to continue making your largest investments in the competitive approaches that helped you achieve your past levels of success (Martin, 1993). Thus, for example, the very limited possibilities for future sales of aircraft only slightly deters companies and government from making substantial investments in aeronautics and related areas.

When confronted with the assertion that airplanes 50 years from now will look pretty much like they look now, managers in these enterprises will readily admit this possibility. On the other hand, they find it very difficult to align their instincts and emotions with the idea that the halcyon days of this technology have past. They maintain persistent false beliefs—delusions—despite enormous amounts of contradictory data.

Delusions like this are completely understandable (Rouse, 1996). There are enormous economic, social, and psychological costs of recognizing and accepting the true state of affairs. Many thousands of people's jobs and several billion dollars of sales may be impacted. Consequently, managers usually cling to old markets and paradigms, often investing enormous sums in hopes that they can keep going until "normalcy" returns.

Of course, not all situations seem so dire. Some companies attribute weak growth to the cyclical nature of markets for lumber, paper, steel, and so forth. They argue for investing in the down cycle and harvesting during the up cycle. This argument holds best for commodity markets where everyone is selling basically the same products, and price, quality, and service are all that matter—the commodity trap and process situations discussed earlier.

Growing in maturing and/or cyclical markets is admittedly difficult. However, trying to succeed in the same old ways exacerbates these difficulties. How can companies possibly sustain or regain strong growth by relying solely on strategies linked to past situations and opportunities? As obvious as the answer to this question may seem, dead horses get regularly beaten and wheels are constantly reinvented.

MARKETS AND TECHNOLOGIES

It is important to break out of delusions and move beyond outmoded strategies. Figure 2.2 provides a framework for accomplishing this.

This framework focuses on two critical questions that underlie formulation of growth strategies. First, what do you sell and to whom? Second, how do you enable competitive offerings? More succinctly, what markets do you address and what technologies do you employ? I hasten to emphasize that technology is defined here quite broadly as the means whereby products, processes, and organizations function.

There is a very strong tendency to focus solely on current products in current markets and invest in technologies that will provide near-term enhancements of the performance of these products. Peters and Waterman, in their 1982 classic, *In Search of Excellence*, concluded that sticking to the knitting was a hallmark of success. The value of this prescription strongly depends on the knitting being in a growth market.

The total quality management movement in the late 1970s and early 1980s emphasized quality and cost issues and prompted process investments for the purpose of improving enterprise performance, only a portion of which in-

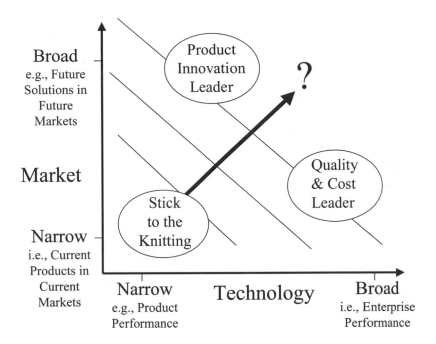

Figure 2.2. Market/technology strategies

volves product performance. The obsession with business process reengineering in the late 1980s and early 1990s did much to reinforce this notion. The focus was very much on improving the bottom lines of financial statements.

However, cost cutting is inherently limited. Eventually, sustained growth requires steady increases of top lines—revenues or sales. This need dictates consideration of market/technology strategies that go beyond sticking to the knitting or quality and cost leadership. This involves entertaining future solutions in future markets. It also involves considering possibilities for becoming a product innovation leader in these broader markets.

Of course, you should keep in mind that you do not have to choose just one position among the three delimited in Figure 2.2. It is more important to consider your current balance among these positions and the balance most appropriate to achieving your growth goals. Then, you need to determine how to move the current balance to the desired balance.

The issues discussed in the section raise fundamental questions of the underlying value of current market offerings and how value will be defined and perceived in the future. Chapter 3, which focuses on value, discusses this idea in great detail. First, however, we need to consider alternative ways to conceptualize growth strategies.

STRATEGIES FOR GROWTH

It is important to reinforce the ideas introduced earlier concerning the extent to which business practices are undergoing fundamental changes. The prognostications range from Peter Drucker reporting the demise of command and control management (Drucker, 1997), to Lester Thurow's advising to look for growth opportunities via social and developmental disequilibriums, rather than just technological change (Thurow, 1999). Numerous commentators and business publications have heralded a new order of things and the need to formulate strategies with these profound changes in mind.

However, as this section illustrates, many if not most of the alternative strategies for growth are far from novel. The relative attractiveness of these strategies are no doubt affected by ongoing changes in business practices. Furthermore, the ways in which these strategies are best implemented are strongly influenced by contemporary thinking regarding management and leadership. Nevertheless, the possible ways to grow a business have been with us for a long time.

Acquisitions and Mergers

A very common growth strategy involves acquisitions and mergers. Rather than attempting to create organic growth, this strategy focuses on "buying" revenues and profits by acquisitions or mergers that will immediately swell both top and bottom lines. Although this strategy often leads to bad choices, it does, if implemented well, produce the desired results.

Considering the common business situations in Table 2.1, this strategy is frequently a mainstay of attempts to stay in a steady growth situation. Acquisitions and mergers are also often evident for businesses in consolidation, commodity trap, and process situations. Companies plagued by paradigm lost or silent war situations may also be acquired but often at a steep discount to acquire underlying assets.

Newell in the retail industry has used acquisitions and mergers as the centerpiece of its growth strategy, although its relatively recent acquisition of Rubbermaid has not gone smoothly. As discussed earlier, this strategy has been dominant of late in the defense industry. Lockheed Martin and Raytheon, however, have consequently seen their market values severely eroded by their inabilities to deliver promised efficiencies.

In general, acquisitions and mergers can be attractive when they increase profits and earnings per share, as well as increase orders booked and likely future sales. Also important is strategic fit, which includes impacts on depth and breadth of offerings and capabilities, as well as overall technology fit. The impact on image is a further concern, especially growth image but also technology image.

All of these positive attributes have to come at an acceptable cost in terms of cash, share dilution, debt, assumed liabilities, and so forth. Almost all acquisitions and mergers increase the top line. The bottom line, however, often suffers immediately due to costs of closing the deal and ongoing debt service, and much longer if the combination of synergy in the marketplace and increased efficiency are not realized.

Enhancing Productivity

Another strategy for growth involves enhancing productivity through improved processes and information technology (Womack and Jones, 1996; Kessler, 1999). The result, hopefully, is higher-quality, lower-cost market offerings, leading to greater market share and profits. Referring to Table 2.1, this strategy is dominant for companies in process situations. In fact, it is often the hallmark of the transition from commodity trap to process situations.

Not surprisingly, these situations are most often encountered by companies in mature industries. It often takes such companies a long time to reach the conclusion that a transition from commodity trap to process is needed. Typically, this is due to an inability to recognize and accept the commodity nature of their market offerings. Most people have great difficulty accepting that what they once viewed as "leading edge" has become a commodity.

The aviation industry is a good example of a mature industry. As noted earlier, all airplanes look pretty much alike and will continue so. Aircraft performance improvements have only marginal, if any, impacts on airlines' profits. On the other hand, process improvements that decrease costs are very appealing to airlines. In the context of Figure 2.2, aircraft manufacturers' investments should be shifted from product performance to enterprise performance. In fact, Boeing and Lockheed Martin have been shifting investments in this way.

As important as increasing productivity can be to growth, this strategy may provide only fleeting advantage. Almost all major players in most mature markets are playing some version of this game—this is readily apparent among automobile manufacturers. Thus, you either have to be very good at constantly improving productivity or have additional, complementary growth strategies.

Wal-Mart, Home Depot, and Southwest Airlines are very good at constantly improving productivity. Consequently, they can provide very attractive prices for their commodity products and services. They have also developed an image as the best place to buy these products and services. This makes it difficult to compete with these companies solely on the basis of productivity.

Organic Growth Strategies

Beyond buying growth via acquisitions and mergers, and trying to grow existing product and service lines, there is a broad class of growth strategies that involve doing new things, or at least old things in significantly new ways. Most of the strategies in this class involve investing in innovative new products and services, including brand extensions.

This class of growth strategies is potentially more profitable but also more risky. If successful, this can yield substantial competitive advantages and profit margins. It also can lead to sizable losses. Because it is very difficult to attain a high batting average for new offerings, it is important to bat often and bat well. Batting often enables accepting the many strikeouts and pop flies. Batting well includes working quickly and knowing when to stop investing in a particular opportunity.

Hewlett Packard and 3M are, historically at least, very good at this. A high percentage of their sales comes from products and services introduced in the last 3–5 years. In Chapters 3 and 4, which consider the challenges of value and focus, respectively, we consider how to understand opportunities for innovation and how to decide among alterative new offerings, respectively.

Growing via new product and service offerings may involve finding new "market space" to provide opportunities for targeting innovations. Kim and Mauborgne (1999) suggest several ways to create the needed opportunities:

- Look to create substitutes for traditional solutions; for example, Home Depot replaced contractors for home repair and remodeling and eventually also came to be a primary provider to small contractors.
- Look across strategic groups within an industry; for example, Toyota's Lexus redefined the group once dominated by Cadillac and Lincoln and, due to superior products, severely undercut their leadership.
- Redefine the buyer group of the industry; for example, Bloomberg focused on traders as buyers of their computer-supported financial services rather than IT managers, and defined the nature of these offerings by traders' needs.
- Look across complementary product and service offerings that go beyond the traditional bounds of the industry; for example, Borders and Barnes & Noble redefined book buying, enhancing this experience with coffee, music, and so forth.
- Rethink the functional-emotional orientation of product or service functionality; for example, Swiss watch maker SMH transformed watches to fashion statements, typically resulting in people owning several watches to match clothing styles.

- Participate in shaping external trends over time; for example, Cisco anticipated growing demand for high-speed data exchange and became a key player in standards-setting processes for networking.

As these guidelines illustrate, new product innovation is not just a matter of creating interesting new gizmos. The market segments to be targeted (or created) and the positioning of new products in these segments require careful strategic thinking.

Kim and Mauborgne's (1999) suggestions can be used to review your current market offerings and consider strategic moves to create more market space for these offerings. None of the example companies noted above involved these companies leaping to totally new markets with totally new products. Instead, they involved broadening or shifting the definitions of customers or expanding market offerings to satisfy a broader range of customers' needs.

Hax and Wilde (1999) suggest three distinct strategic alternatives that are particularly relevant when pursing such growth strategies. One strategy is to focus on competing in terms of *product economics*. The emphasis might be low cost, for example, Nucor and Southwest Airlines, or product differentiation, for example, Lexus or Ritz-Carlton. The customers targeted and the approach to marketing and sales are, obviously, quite different with these two emphases.

Another alternative strategy focuses on *customer economics* in terms of reducing their costs and/or increasing their profits. Information technology service providers such as EDS and communications service providers such as MCI Worldcom emphasize these benefits of their offerings. This strategy mostly applies to business-to-business selling. However, there are business-to-consumer examples; for example, Home Depot has changed the customer economics of home repair and remodeling more than they have lowered the costs of materials and tools.

The third alternative involves competing on the basis of *systems economics*. This includes notions such as complementor lock-in, competitor lock-out, and proprietary standards. The best examples of this are Intel and Microsoft, which have locked in many millions of users to Intel microprocessors and Microsoft operating systems. More recently, Amazon has locked in customers by providing very responsive online services, tailored to past purchases and preferences. In both cases, customers view the costs of switching to other providers as too high to entertain alternatives.

As you look for ways to expand your market space, you also need to consider the economics (i.e., product, customer, or system) that will drive competitiveness in these broadened markets. You also need to consider alternatives that go beyond the smooth transitions to adjacent markets and offerings depicted thus far. This involves the possibility of discontinuous innovation.

Kaplan (1999) focuses on discontinuous innovation. He notes that, whereas traditional strategy formulation focuses on reducing uncertainty, discontinuous innovation requires viewing uncertainty as opportunity. In Chapter 6, which addresses the future as a challenge, we discuss methods for determining the value of options with uncertain outcomes. Succinctly, the value of an option to act in the future can be much more attractive than having to invest substantial amounts now in highly uncertain future outcomes.

Kaplan proposes four strategies for fostering discontinuous innovation. One strategy is radical cannibalism, whereby you exit ongoing businesses and use the proceeds to invest in newer growth opportunities. A good recent illustration of this strategy is provided by Hughes Electronics Corporation, which is owned by General Motors. In the past few years, Hughes sold off its aerospace, defense, and automobile electronics businesses and invested in growing its consumer direct-broadcast satellite business, in the process transforming itself from an arms maker to a satellite broadcasting giant (Harris, 2000).

Another strategy Kaplan terms competitive displacement involves broadening the boundaries of the business charter, including perhaps exploring tangential industries. Disney's success in selling total vacation offerings (i.e., rather than just theme park tickets) and Boeing's move into total solutions (i.e., airplane, training, spares, maintenance, etc.) are good examples of companies broadening their strategies to include all the economic activity associated with, in these cases, their theme parks or airplanes.

Another strategy for discontinuous innovation involves creating markets. Markets for cable television, cellular phones, and personal computers did not exist until relatively recently. Most consumers did not expect to pay for television viewing, did not see needs for mobile communication, and could not imagine owning computers. Now, we are coming to see these products and services as necessities.

A broader version of this strategy concerns creating industries, not just markets. Medical electronics is a good example, especially implantable electronics, for example, pacemakers. This multibillion dollar industry is likely to see continued strong growth with advances in genomics and nanotechnology that will enable, respectively, knowing what to sense and control and being small enough to provide this functionality.

The strategies for growth discussed in this section may all seem quite risky. This tends to be true and warrants a systematic approach to evaluating alternatives. O'Brien and Fadem (1999) discuss how DuPont decided where to grow. They began by reviewing macro trends in society and the economy and determined the likely market issues implied by these trends. They also considered major technology trends and how these trends might combine with market issues to create potentially attractive markets.

They compared and prioritized trends, issues, and opportunities using 25 criteria embodied in scoring scales. Use of this approach for evaluating new business initiatives creates a pipeline of 50–60 potential growth businesses, the more mature of which are managed by the corporate new business development division. Systematic processes such as these are discussed in more detail in Chapter 4, which addresses the challenge of focus. At this point, it is perhaps sufficient to indicate that such systematic processes are invaluable for identifying and managing risks.

An issue that often emerges concerns the speed at which growth strategies are formulated and implemented. There is a tendency, especially in recent years, to think that time to market is critical and being first to market is almost essential to reaping big rewards. Consequently, people want to formulate growth strategies quickly and get on with succeeding.

Lambert and Slater (1999) address the popular wisdom that the keys to market success are *1*) first to market, *2*) fast product development cycle, and *3*) on-time schedule performance. Based on a thorough review of the literature and a conceptual model of market-driven project management, they suggest that more firmly based principles are *1*) effective market introduction timing, *2*) first to mind share, and *3*) managed responsiveness. Succinctly, they argued for well-planned and responsively controlled—rather than ballistic—new product development and introduction. We return to this issue in Chapter 3.

The foregoing may lead you to believe that growth strategies can be derived from one or more of the frameworks discussed in this section. Although this is a possibility, it is very much a rarity. Strategic thinking surrounding growth almost always starts with ideas and intuitions about where growth is possible and desirable. These ideas and intuitions should be viewed as hypotheses to be evaluated using the frameworks outlined here. At the very least, these frameworks should be used as "sanity checks" to ensure that appealing ideas and intuitions make sense in terms of markets, technologies, finances, and so forth.

GROWING ELECTRONICALLY

It is impossible to think about growth without paying some attention to the Internet and its potential impact on your enterprise, either as it currently exists or as you envision it. As noted earlier, Peter Drucker (1999) likened the probable impact of the Internet to the impacts of the railroads in the second half of the 19th century. The ability to transfer goods efficiently over long distances changed many business models and provided many opportunities for growth. The Internet is doing the same thing.

It is useful to think about this trend in two different ways. A primary impact of the Internet is the ability to substantially improve things that you were already doing. Order taking and tracking, as well as product support, are among the most compelling examples. Companies like Cisco and Marshall Industries have employed the Internet to dramatically cut the costs of these processes while significantly improving customer services. Seybold (1998) provides numerous examples of these types of E-commerce successes.

It is important to distinguish between two types of E-commerce: business to consumer (B to C) and business to business (B to B). Amazon has been one of the most visible B to C companies, with immense stock market capitalization despite having yet to earn any profits. There are thousands of other "E-tailers" in the B to C side of E-commerce, and the growth *rate* of this side has started to decrease. Some have argued that consolidation is not far away (Varian, 2000).

In contrast, the B to B side of E-commerce is experiencing explosive growth. With Y2K apparently safely behind us, the consulting companies who were once Y2K specialists have transformed themselves into E-commerce specialists. Companies in industries ranging from aircraft manufacturers to building materials distributors are investing heavily in trying to gain the efficiencies experienced by companies like Cisco and Marshall. This approach to growth fits squarely in category of enhancing productivity discussed earlier.

Another impact of the Internet is the ability to sell information products and services that were heretofore prohibitively expensive. Evans and Wurster (1997) discuss the resulting new economics of information. They use the example of the cheap, adequate *Encarta*, which took away much of the market for the expensive, high-quality *Britannica* to support three assertions. First, they argue that every business is an information business. Second, the value of market channels and hierarchy will decline due to the "hyperarchy" of networking. Finally, the economics of printing will result in decreased nonelectronic publishing.

Subsequently, Evans and Wurster (1999) focus on the importance of the emergence of separate businesses that provide "navigation" to other businesses' products and services—and a key factor in the decline of the value of traditional channels. They discuss the dimensions of E-strategy for such businesses in terms of

- Reach—access and connection to alternatives,
- Affiliation—whose interests the business represents, and
- Richness—depth and detail of information.

They use this framework to suggest alternative strategies for four different types of players: pure navigators (e.g., Yahoo), electronic retailers (e.g., Amazon), incumbent product manufacturers (e.g., Proctor & Gamble), and incumbent category killer retailers (e.g., Wal-Mart).

Shapiro and Varian (1998) argue, quite convincingly, that fundamental principles of economics still apply in the realm of networks and information. They start with the simple principle that the selling price of any product or service tends to the marginal cost of production and distribution. In competitive markets, the players will continually push marginal costs down—thus, prices tend to go down. For information products distributed over the Internet, the marginal costs are zero! Consequently, companies will tend to give their information products away—and customers will expect information products to be free.

This principle explains why so many Internet businesses are trying to make money on advertising. They trade free content for your willingness to put up with banners and blinkers proclaiming the wonders of everything from security software to simulated sex. As irritating as this can be, we have long demonstrated our willingness to be manipulated by such messages via television.

Shapiro and Varian suggest that differentiation can help you to escape the fate of having to give away your products. They suggest you do this by selling customers personalized products at personalized prices. This requires in-depth understanding of customers' needs and values so that you know what to put in the package and which things can command higher prices. For example, some customers value time much more than others.

Put simply, the idea is to sell roughly the same things to different people for different prices. Sounds great, but the network economy enables everyone to know the lowest price for anything. Shapiro and Varian suggest that you avoid this with versioning. With a modular design, based on a common platform, you can create different versions of your products tailored to the desires of different market segments. Although you want to avoid blunders, like putting Cadillac badges on Chevrolets, this principle can help provide the differentiation you need at costs you can endure.

Another economic principle is lock-in. The essence of lock-in is that customers' future options are constrained by the choices they make now. Once a customer commits to your information products, invests in gaining competence in using these products, and becomes dependent on the tailored information you provide, it will be expensive for them to change providers. The switching costs are likely to be too high. Such customers are locked in. An installed base of locked-in customers can be a company's most valuable asset.

Yet another principle concerns network externalities and positive feedback. The value of some information products, for instance telephones, is much greater if many people use these products. The more people in the network, the better. In this way, larger networks get larger—this is called positive feedback. For obvious reasons, therefore, you are likely to want to grow the network of users of your information products.

Glazer (1999) discusses growing in rapidly changing markets, such as those associated with the Internet, in which there is frequent turnover in the general stock of knowledge or information embodied in products and possessed by competitors and consumers. He suggests that the customer information file (CIF) is central to this competition. A CIF is composed of the following for each customer: characteristics of customer, responses to company decisions, purchase history, and potential profit. Mining the CIF becomes key to adapting quickly to rapid market changes. These data can also be invaluable to situation assessment as discussed earlier and illustrated later in this chapter.

Building on Drucker's characterization of the Internet being like the railroads, we have moved into an era of E-commerce where, for most companies, the primary concern is how to take advantage of railroads, not start new railroad companies. The Internet can be a very important way to enable growth strategies, but the Internet, in itself, is unlikely to be a growth strategy. For example, the Internet can enable dramatic improvements in customer relationship management (Amazon is a great example), but the essence of these relationships depends on the value companies provide, the challenge we address in the next chapter.

SUPPORTING GROWTH STRATEGIES

Success with the strategies for growth discussed in this chapter is highly related to abilities to formulate and execute the strategies well. Information technology is often a key element of executing well. However, clear formulation, articulation, and communication of these strategies are more important. Inconsistent and incoherent strategies executed poorly are the hallmark of *former* growth companies.

This section discusses two primary elements of supporting formulation and implementation of growth strategies. One element concerns information needed for these processes, much of which often relates to external trends and events. The other element involves methods and tools for supporting these processes.

Competitive Intelligence

Identifying, evaluating, and choosing among alternative growth strategies can require extensive information. (In Chapter 7, which addresses the challenge of knowledge, we distinguish among data, information, and knowledge, but these subtleties are not central at this point.) Of course, this need does not deter people from making major investments in the absence of information. I have been repeatedly amazed when managers avoid spending $100,000 to collect evidence to ensure that investments they are entertaining make sense and, instead, commit immediately to the $100,000,000 required to pursue an intuitively appealing but unfounded strategy.

Most people would rather make well-founded strategic decisions. There are a variety of types of information of potential use. Internal information concerning sales, profits, and market share of the enterprise's products and services in various market segments is invaluable and often surprisingly difficult to obtain, especially for past years. Similar information for competitors is also of great interest and, equally surprising, often relatively easy to obtain. This type of information is important to determining where you are, that is, situation assessment.

The information needed to entertain alternative futures is much broader and usually oriented toward external economic, social, and technological trends and events. Competitive intelligence is a phrase often used for the activities associated with researching and compiling this broader information. Competitive intelligence is discussed in detail in Chapter 7; the brief overview here is needed to show its relationship to formulation and execution of growth strategies.

Herring (1999) discusses a process for identifying key competitive intelligence topics that is driven by interviews of key decision makers focused on

- strategic decisions and issues,
- early warning topics, and
- key players in the marketplace.

When one reviews the examples of questions that he suggests to ask decisions makers, it is clear that identifying key topics involves more of a dialogue than a step-by-step methodology. This dialogue enables subsequently focusing on information that will likely make a difference rather than the immense amount of information that would be interesting but not key to decision making.

John Pepper, former CEO of Proctor & Gamble, provides a good illustration of this type of focus in his discussion of the role of competitive intelligence at Proctor & Gamble (Pepper, 1999). He characterizes the company as focused on stretch, innovation, and speed. Competitive intelligence efforts at Proctor & Gamble emphasize benchmarking and addressing three questions:

- How do we generate greater innovation to reach our stretch goals?
- How do we recognize our people, their knowledge, and their ideas and convert these into action?
- How do we capitalize as fully as we can on emerging technologies in communications, both internally and externally, to make the best use of that knowledge?

There is a fairly natural tendency to view competitive intelligence as synonymous with market research. Sharp (2000) argues that this view undermines the effectiveness of competitive intelligence. She also discusses the impacts of management perceptions that information is either free or too expensive, is too time consuming to compile, and seldom impacts eventual decisions. All in all, there are strong pragmatic forces that tend to limit or undermine effective compilation of information needed to support strategic decision making.

Settecase (1999) provides a straightforward, albeit qualitative, approach to performing competitiveness assessments. This approach focuses on eight elements of competitiveness:

1. Organizational structure
2. Global presence
3. Products and methodologies
4. Operations
5. Research and development
6. Market image
7. Growth strategy
8. Management

These elements and the finer-grained characteristics of these elements provide a good means for self-assessment of an enterprise's abilities to competitively pursue alternative growth strategies. Quite often, I find that companies devise strategies that would be excellent if they were capable of competitively implementing these strategies. In general, it is much easier to come up with good ideas—in other words, be inventive—than it is to transform these ideas to innovations in the marketplace. This distinction is pursued in some detail in Chapter 3.

Shaker and Gembicki (1999) discuss major trends that are impacting the role and nature of competitive intelligence. Heightened competitiveness combined with increasingly prevalent loosely structured organizations are making fast and flexible intelligence essential. Similarly, more traditional slow and inflexible information-gathering processes are likely to lose their value.

There is, obviously, much more to competitive intelligence than introduced here. The later chapter on knowledge elaborates on this field in the context of knowledge management. The key point here is that formulation and implementation of growth strategies are enhanced when based on well-founded competitiveness assumptions. Competitive intelligence provides the means to identifying such assumptions.

Situation Assessment Advisor

The process of transforming concepts and principles of strategic growth to creation of strategies and plans can be greatly enhanced by useful and usable methods and tools. It certainly is possible, and quite often the practice, to just "wing it." However, most managers would rather have well-founded strategies and plans. At the same time, most of these people are not at all patient with abstract, time-consuming processes that provide only general, rather than specific, value added to the process of strategic thinking and planning.

In each chapter that addresses one of the essential challenges of strategic management, one or more methods and tools are discussed. Most of these methods and tools are computer based. However, the concern here is more with the conceptual basis and value of the methods and tools rather than how to interact with the associated computer software. Internet references are provided to online descriptions of these methods and tools.

Figure 2.3 shows an example situation assessment from the *Situation Assessment Advisor* (ESS, 2000) or the "light" version of this tool available in *Strategic Thinking* (Rouse, 1999). These tools embody the situation assessment methodology discussed earlier in this chapter. They also include a hypertext version of *Start Where Your Are* (Rouse, 1996) and extensive online advice.

The screen in Figure 2.3 shows the results of having estimated the aforementioned 82 current and leading indicators of the relationships of a hypothetical software company to its markets. The knowledge base of the advisor has enabled translation of these estimates to assessments of both current and likely future situations. Note that this company is now in steady growth, but close to consolidation, and consolidation is looming strongly in the future.

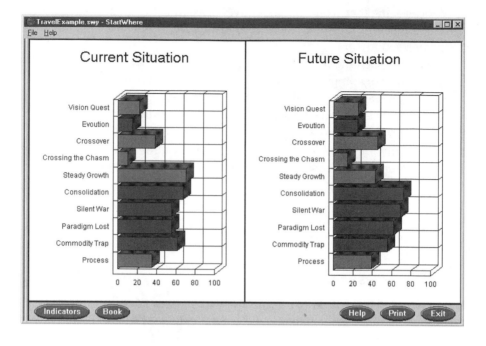

Figure 2.3. Example from the *Situation Assessment Advisor*

This tool is typically used by management teams, working as a group, to address and resolve several issues:

- What do the current and leading indicators mean in the context of our enterprise and what are our estimates of these indicators?
- To what extent do we agree with the tool's assessment of our current and future situations, or how do we differ?
- Considering component and sensitivity analyses, do we need to reconsider our estimates of any of the indicators?
- Do any of the examples of how other companies have addressed our current and future situations provide relevant guidance to us?
- In light of all of the above, what assessment do we agree on, and what are the strategic implications of this assessment?

The types of dialogues listed above often lead to unexpected conclusions. For instance, we used this tool to support the top management team of a large-contract food services company. After debating the current and leading indicators extensively, especially relative to their interpretation for a contract services company, the team reached agreement that the current and future situations were not very attractive. Consolidation and commodity trap were the dominant alternatives.

One executive commented that it would nice to be in another business. Someone else asked whether anyone in the food business made good margins. Another person said that higher-end restaurants did pretty well. Then, the CEO said, "Let's just assume that we are in the food business, not the contract food services business. We can redo the assessment and, if we like it, then we can decide how to actually be in the food business."

The team restarted the process, changed the interpretations of many of the indicators, and concluded that steady, profitable growth was achievable if the assumption of being in the food business could be justified. This lead to considerable discussion about how this assumption could be made true. Ideas raised included substantially upgrading food offerings and services, with commensurate price increases. Everyone agreed that consumers are quite willing to pay more if they perceive good value.

This example illustrates a very important aspect of using computer-based methods and tools to support strategic thinking. To a great extent, the overriding purpose of such tools is to get the right people to have the right discussions on the right topics at the right time and support this process with information, computation, and advice. The real creativity and all the decisions come from the users of such tools, not from the tools themselves.

CONCLUSIONS

This chapter began with a discussion of the importance of growth, including the various implications of not growing. Alternative theories of growth were discussed, as well as a method for determining where you are in the growth process. Growth strategies were first explored using a market/technology framework, in which technology is interpreted quite broadly in terms of the means to create and deliver market offerings. Specific types of growth strategies were then considered, including mergers and acquisitions, productivity improvements, and organic growth possibilities, the latter two of which might be supported by E-commerce technologies. Finally, we discussed how information, methods, and tools can support the formulation and pursuit of growth strategies.

All of the growth strategies discussed have associated risks, including

- mergers and acquisitions may not meet expectations, with promised synergies and efficiencies not emerging,

- productivity improvements may result in being able to do very efficiently what you should no longer be doing at all,
- organic growth strategies may draw away vital resources from current lines of business but not yield needed returns.

How can you minimize or at least manage these risks? First of all, use of information, methods, and tools as discussed earlier can ensure that you are making good bets. Nevertheless, they are still bets.

In general, you can hedge bets by diversifying your portfolio. At an extreme, you might try pursuing all of the above three types of strategies in parallel. More reasonably, you could pursue multiple opportunities for organic growth, perhaps nurturing several possible new market offerings and winnowing this set as you learn more.

Diversification can also increase another risk, namely, financial and human resources being spread too thinly to be effective. Consequently, the success of all strategies may depend on the same resources—especially human resources. In this case, diversification may increase rather than decrease risks because the likelihood of success of each opportunity is no longer independent of the probability of success of the other opportunities.

There are also risks of your current organization not being compatible with new strategies. For example, functional "stovepipes" may hinder the collaboration needed for new strategies to succeed. Another frequent problem is a mismatch between current incentive and reward systems and future directions. Overall, there are many ways in which "what is" can be a tremendous hindrance to "want might be."

Later chapters revisit the cross-cutting issues of risks, resources, organization, and so on. In general, these issues are intrinsic to business. You can not eliminate them. However, your abilities to manage and balance them are often critical determinants of success.

KEY QUESTIONS

Successfully addressing the challenge of growth involves answering several key questions, hopefully supported by the concepts, principles, methods, and tools discussed in this chapter:

- What are your growth goals, what will achieving these goals enable, and what consequences will result if you fail to achieve these goals?

- What are your current and emerging relationships with your markets, and what key indicators would have to change to improve your situation?
- Where can you create the market space you need to grow, and how capable are you of making this happen?
- What is your overall growth strategy, what plans have been formulated, who is responsible for these plans, and how will you measure progress?
- What methods and tools are you using to support your growth strategy?

REFERENCES

Ballot, G., and Taymaz, E. (1999). Technological change, learning and macro-economic coordination: an evolutionary model. *Journal of Artificial Societies and Social Simulation* 2(2).

Casti, J. (1989). *Paradigms Lost: Images of Man in the Mirror of Science.* New York: Morrow.

Casti, J. L. (1997). *Would-Be Worlds: How Simulation Is Changing the Frontiers of Science.* New York: Wiley.

Christensen, C. M. (1997). *The Innovator's Dilemma: When New Technologies Cause Great Firms to Fail.* Boston, MA: Harvard Business School.

Collins, J. C., and Porras, J. I. (1994). *Built to Last: Successful Habits of Visionary Companies.* New York: Harper Business.

Drucker, P. F. (1997).Toward the new organization. *Leader to Leader* 3: 6–8.

Drucker, P. F. (1999). Beyond the information revolution. *Atlantic Monthly* October: 47–47.

Economist. (1999). The corporate-growth paradox. *The Economist* July 17: 70.

ESS. (2000). *Situation Assessment Advisor.* http://www.ess-advisors.com/software.htm. Atlanta, GA: Enterprise Support Systems.

Evans, P. B., and Wurster, T. S. (1997). Strategy and the new economics of information. *Harvard Business Review* September–October: 71–82.

Evans, P., and Wurster, T. S. (1999). Getting real about virtual commerce. *Harvard Business Review* 77(6): 85–94.

Glazer, R. (1999). Winning in smart markets. *Sloan Management Review* 40(4): 59–69.

Harris, R. (2000). Direct hit: how Hughes transformed itself from arms maker to satellite broadcasting giant. *CFO* March: 41–50.

Hax, A. C., and Wilde, D. L. II (1999). The Delta model: adaptive management for a changing world. *Sloan Management Review* 40(2): 11–28.

Herring, J. P. (1999). Key intelligence topics: a process to identify and define intelligence needs. *Competitive Intelligence Review* 10(2): 4–14.

Kaplan, S. M. (1999). Discontinuous innovation and the growth paradox. *Strategy and Leadership* 29(2): 16–21.

Kessler, W. C. (1999). Implementing lean thinking. *Information • Knowledge • Systems Management* 1(2, Summer) 99-103.

Kim, W. C., and Mauborgne, R, (1999). Creating new market space. *Harvard Business Review* January–February: 83–93.

Lambert, D., and Slater, S. F. (1999). First, fast, and on time: the path to success. Or is it? *Journal of Product Innovation Management* 16(5): 427–438.

Magaziner, I., and Patinkin, M. (1989). *The Silent War*. New York: Random House.

Malone, T. W., and Laubacher, R. J. (1998). The dawn of the e-lance economy. *Harvard Business Review* September–October: 145–152.

Martin, R. (1993). Changing the mind of the corporation. *Harvard Business Review* November–December: 5–12.

Mintzberg, H., and Lampel, J. (1999). Reflecting on the strategy process. *Sloan Management Review*: Spring: 21–30.

Moore, G. A. (1991). *Crossing the Chasm: Marketing and Selling Technology Products to Mainstream Customers*. New York: Harper Business.

O'Brien, T. C., and Fadem, T. J. (1999). Identifying new business opportunities. *Research Technology Management* 42(5): 15–19.

Pepper, J. E. (1999). Competitive intelligence at Proctor & Gamble. *Competitive Intelligence Review* 10(4): 4–9.

Peters, T. J., and Waterman, R. H. Jr. (1982). *In Search of Excellence: Lessons From America's Best-Run Companies*. New York: Harper & Row.

Pfeiffer, E. W. (2000). Where are we in the revolution? *Forbes ASAP* February 21: 68–70.

Porter, M. E. (1996). What is strategy? *Harvard Business Review* 74(6): 61–78.

Rouse, W. B. (1996). *Start Where You Are: Matching Your Strategy to Your Marketplace*. San Francisco, CA: Jossey-Bass.

Rouse, W. B. (1999). *Strategic Thinking*. Atlanta, GA: Enterprise Support Systems.

Settecase, M. (1999). The competitiveness assessment model: a thought-structuring approach to analysis. *Competitive Intelligence Review* 10(3): 43–50.

Seybold, P. B. (1998). *Customers.com: How to Create a Profitable Business Strategy for the Internet and Beyond*. New York: Times Business.

Shaker, S. M., and Gembicki, M. P. (1999). Competitive intelligence: a futurist's perspective. *Competitive Intelligence Magazine* January–March: 24–27.

Shapiro, C., and Varian, H. R. (1998). *Information Rules: A Strategic Guide to the Network Economy*. Boston, MA: Harvard Business School.

Sharp, S. (2000). Ten myths that cripple competitive intelligence. *Competitive Intelligence Magazine* January–March: 37–40.

Thurow, L. C. (1999). Building wealth. *Atlantic Monthly* June: 57–69.

Varian, H. (2000). Habits of highly effective revolutions. *Forbes ASAP* February 21: 73–76.

Womack, J. P., and Jones, D. T. (1996). *Lean Thinking: Banish Waste and Create Wealth in Your Corporation*. New York: Simon & Schuster.

CHAPTER THREE

Value

It is rare to encounter an enterprise that does not claim to be focused on providing value to customers or, more broadly, providing value to stakeholders or constituencies. Yet, in many cases, this assertion is more a slogan than an operating principle. This slogan permeates brochures and proposals but is not readily apparent in day-to-day business practices.

Value means different things to different stakeholders. For customers, value relates to the benefits of products and services relative to their costs. For employees, value is concerned with the nature of their jobs, the work environment, compensation, benefits, and so forth. Stockholders usually focus on share price in particular and overall market valuation in general.

Finding the "sweet spot" among all these expectations of an enterprise is a continual challenge. Customers like low prices, employees like high wages, and stockholders like high profits. Furthermore, competitors will do their best to move the sweet spot by providing, for example, new benefits without price increases or comparable benefits for lower prices.

It is very difficult to maintain, and especially enhance, your market position without continually adding to the value provided. Customers expect new and better products and services, particularly if you would like to be able to raise prices. Employees expect raises and improved benefits. Stockholders expect continual growth of revenues and profits; public companies that fail to meet these expectations quickly see share prices swoon.

A sure way to avoid these dilemmas is through innovation. When companies continually provide new benefits and/or current benefits in new ways, customers do not object to higher prices—or at least do not expect price decreases. Sales of new products and services with strong profit margins will enable good salaries and benefits to be provided, thereby ensuring retention of the best employees. Strong margins will also keep share prices growing.

Unfortunately, as noted by *The Economist* (1999), "Unlike cutting jobs or making an acquisition, innovation does not happen just because the chief executive wills it." This appears to be particularly difficult for large companies whose methods for achieving past successes continue to dominate people's attention and investment resources. A further problem, which is later discussed in depth, is that innovations often provide only modest near-term returns in which many large companies are not interested.

This chapter focuses first on the broad challenge of continually enhancing value and then on strategies for addressing this challenge by continually providing market innovations. The types of innovations considered range from new products and services to new business models for providing existing products and services. As noted in Chapter 1, the challenge of value is the foundation challenge of strategic management. Understanding the ways in which your enterprise provides value to its stakeholders and then continually enhancing—and occasionally reinventing—how value is provided should be a driving strategic priority.

NATURE OF VALUE

Specific definitions of value for customers depends on the particular market domain. For example, whereas clock speed, memory capacity, and screen size are typically important attributes of computers, you never hear these same attributes discussed for burgers or colas. Later in this chapter, methods for characterizing the value attached to attributes of products and services are discussed.

Similarly, the specific definitions of value for employees depend on the particular work domain. Although everyone is concerned about compensation, the broader set of attributes that affect perceived value varies substantially from production workers to executives to college professors to performing artists. Later discussion also addresses characterizing these differences.

Defining value is more straightforward for stockholders. The value of a share of stock is highly related to a company's earnings, particularly the anticipated growth rate of its earnings. Growth of revenue and margins are good predictors of earnings growth. Faltering revenue growth and declining margins—perhaps due to increased competition or market saturation—are good predictors of earnings decline. Share prices usually reflect perceptions of such growth or decline.

To a great extent, the stock market valuation of a company is a good overall, albeit surrogate, measure of the company's current and anticipated ability to provide value to customers and, less directly, to employees. This measure also has the very desirable characteristic of applying to all public companies. This enables comparisons across industries and time.

Slywotsky (1996) presents an insightful analysis of how value waxes and wanes or, in his terms, migrates. He defines value migration as a pattern of increasing obsolescence of traditional business designs toward others that are better designed to maximize utility for customers and profit for companies. He argues that market value—defined as shares outstanding times stock price plus long-term debt—is a measure of the power of a business design to create and capture value.

Using the ratio of market value to annual revenue of a company, Slywotsky compares industries and companies within industries to illustrate three stages of value migration: value inflow, value stability, and value outflow. The central questions, therefore, become how to anticipate value stability and in particular value outflow and then how to avert these transitions. He suggests several possible patterns of value migration:

- multidirectional migration, for example, large integrated steel manufacturers lose substantial market share to specialty materials companies,
- migration to a nonprofit industry, for example, hyper-competitive price cutting by the airlines creates an industry with no cumulative profit since its inception,
- blockbuster migration, for example, value growth in the pharmaceutical industry driven by science-driven discovery yields high-margin breakthroughs,
- multicategory migration, for example, coffee, a commodity, is transformed to multiple category offerings, including high-end offerings such as Starbucks,
- from integration to specialization, for example, integrated providers such as IBM and Digital lose substantial markets share to Intel, Microsoft, Dell, and so forth,
- from conventional selling to low-cost distribution, for example, high-volume, low-cost providers such as Wal-Mart and Costco capture commodity retail markets, and
- from conventional selling to high-end solutions, for example, Hewlett-Packard shifts from selling hardware to selling business solutions with seamless global support.

Slywotsky suggests detecting and anticipating value migration by focusing on three overarching issues:

- nature of your customers' economics and needs, particularly the implications for future priorities,
- relative performance—economics and customer satisfaction—of alternative business designs in your industry, and

- patterns of value migration that underlie your current market position, as well as trends in your industry and adjacent industries.

Understanding changing customer priorities, relative performance of business designs, and emerging patterns of value migration provides the basis for reconsidering the value you provide and the business design whereby you provide this value.

Rethinking value and business designs should include more detailed consideration of value as perceived by customers, employees, and other stakeholders. Market value, as an overall metric, enables diagnosis of needs for change. However, market value can only be improved by specific changes, usually at customer or employee levels, rather than at market levels.

Rucci, Kirn, and Quinn (1998) provide a good example of changes at these levels in their report on improving the value/profit chain at Sears. Their underlying premise is that a compelling place to work is more likely to be a compelling place to shop, which will, in turn, be a compelling place to invest. This premise offers the promise of being able to increase market value by improving processes within stores.

They present a statistical model that relates employee attitude to customer impressions to revenue growth. This model was used to design a program to improve employee satisfaction and attitudes. Measured results indicate a 4% increase in employee satisfaction, 4% increase in customer satisfaction, $200 million increase in revenue, and $0.25 billion increase in market value. Thus, the logic of the model appears to reflect the reality of actual results.

Developing useful value chain models such as this requires understanding how an organization truly functions. Mintzberg and Van der Heyden (1999) suggest creation of "organigraphs" to depict how organizations really function—what an organization is, why it exists, and what it does. Not surprisingly, they conclude that typical organization charts provide few insights into how problems are addressed, decisions are made, and value is really provided.

This conclusion relates to Argyris and Schon' s (1978) characterizations of organizations. In particular, there are usually substantial differences between the theory in principle and theory in practice of how an organization functions. Furthermore, organizations are often captured by single-loop learning whereby they attempt to continually refine and optimize their current ways of functioning. Double-loop learning, in contrast, questions current ways and entertains whole new ways of functioning. This can be crucial if new ways of providing value are needed.

The notion of mental models is particularly relevant. Mental models are the cognitive constructs that enable understanding how something functions, forming expectations of how it will behave, and attempting to influence control over these behaviors (Rouse and Morris, 1986). Senge (1990) popularized this idea in the context of organizational learning, including possible explanations of learning disabilities.

It has been shown that incompatible mental models among team members relate to poor team performance (Rouse, Cannon-Bowers, and Salas, 1992). In particular, teams with incompatible models tend to overcommunicate—for example, trying to clarify meanings and expectations—only to achieve unsatisfactory results. Organizations attempting to change the ways in which they provide value can encounter such problems, typified by endless, unproductive meetings. We return to the topics in the last few paragraphs in Chapter 5, which is devoted to the challenge of change.

The nature of value and how value changes are key elements to understanding companies' relationships with markets and how these relationships change (Rouse, 1996). Yesterday's innovation becomes tomorrow's commodity. Becoming better and better at providing this commodity is very unlikely to yield the margins enjoyed when it was an innovation.

Understanding the multi-stakeholder, multi-attribute nature of value can be critical to devising new ways of delivering value (Rouse, 1991, 1994). Typically, the various players in the value chain have differing concerns, preferences, and perceptions, all of which have to be addressed successfully to ensure that the chain works. Later in this chapter, methods and tools for representing and evaluating such value chains are discussed.

INNOVATION

Innovation is the introduction of change via something new (Rouse, 1992). Many innovations take advantage of one or more inventions—new devices or processes—but these inventions are not the innovations. The vast majority of inventions and good ideas in general do not result in change. They do not become part of products or services in people's hands, being used to be productive, make life easier or safer, or bring enjoyment.

The distinction between innovation and invention is very important. Many of the enterprises with whom I have worked consider themselves to be innovative, despite flat sales and sagging profits. Usually, I find that they are reasonably inventive but not as innovative as they perceive themselves to be. Presented with this observation, they often say, "But, our employees are full of good ideas and have created lots of neat things."

This assertion is almost always correct. Their perceptions that their employees are inventive are usually well founded. However, at the same time, this plethora of inventions has seldom resulted in change in these companies' markets. Value provided to the marketplace has not increased. Their inventions did not result in innovations.

I hasten to note that the position I am advocating is somewhat risky. Most people like to consider themselves and their colleagues innovative. They want to view their inventions as evidence of being innovative. Convincing them that these inventions are potential innovations rather than inherently innovations can become a bit confrontational.

Fortunately, once you come to expect these negative reactions, you can move smoothly beyond them. Furthermore, it can be critical to get your management team—or your customer's management team—to realize that the inability to transform inventions to innovations is a plausible explanation of the company's value shortfalls in the marketplace. The inevitable next question, of course, is what to do about it.

Difficulty of Innovation

Innovation appears to be ubiquitous in the "new economy." Many executives and senior managers with whom I interact attribute much of the this innovation to small, often start-up companies. In contrast, large enterprise seem to have difficulty innovating, despite having many more human and financial resources.

The Economist (1999) discusses the worries of large firms about needs for and difficulties of innovation, perhaps stemming from feelings of inadequacy about the market valuations of newly minted Internet-based companies. This perceived need may be justified, considering that the top 20% of firms in *Fortune*'s annual innovation survey have achieved double the shareholder returns of their peers. They conclude that the two particular strengths needed to innovate are difficult to create by dictate: *1)* a culture that looks for new ideas and *2)* leaders who know which ones to back.

Christensen (1997), in his best-selling *The Innovator's Dilemma*, provides a deeper explanation for this state of affairs. Large organizations usually achieved their size and success by innovating in some way. Subsequently, the whole enterprise becomes devoted to refining and extending this innovation. The culture creates and reinforces belief in the innovativeness of what they are doing. Thus, they have difficulty entertaining new ways of providing value.

This difficulty is exacerbated by their needs to sustain the growth rates that earned them their current success. Because innovations almost always initially provide modest returns, pursuit of new innovations will not contribute substantially to sustaining growth in the near term. Hence, many large companies pursue mergers and acquisitions to gain innovative offerings well beyond the incubation stage.

Christensen and Overdorf (2000) extend this analysis, discussing the factors that affect an organization's capacity to change, including resources, processes, and values. They indicate two particular values that affect companies' abilities to innovate:

- how they judge acceptable gross margins and
- how big an opportunity has to be before it can be interesting.

As companies become large, their overhead structures and growth needs result in an inability to enter small, emerging markets because of these values. Early stages of innovation cannot satisfy the hurdle rates for margins and revenue. They suggest three ways to overcome these limitations:

- create new capabilities internally, for example, by forming "heavyweight teams" focused on pursuing potential innovations,
- create capabilities through spinout organizations, with strong CEO support, each of which is solely focused on a particular innovation,
- create capabilities through acquisitions of organizations who have already succeeded in innovating in the desired direction(s).

Sharma (1999) argues that several additional, and more specific, difficulties underlie a large firms' inabilities to innovate:

- Stage-gate and other screening processes tend to discourage many more ideas that they encourage;
- Raw initiative alone cannot compensate for lack of relevant experience—hence, new directions can be much more difficult than might be expected;
- Strong forces favor internal staffing of projects, thus reinforcing current beliefs and priorities, as well as limiting the experience base;
- Although there are many advantages to collaboration, it can be difficult to do well, especially when changes are driven by crises;
- Large launches are risky, and hence discouraged, but also tend to provide greater advantages and rewards.

He suggests several management approaches for dealing with these difficulties. These include broadening the strategic envelope by, for example, paying careful attention to knowledge and skills gained from current projects that have implications beyond these projects. He also argues for strategic pacing that recognizes the irrevocable nature of choices when innovating—you cannot realistically keep all your options open. Finally, he suggests strategic partnerships to leverage internal and external resources, both financial and human.

Praether and Gundry (1996) provide yet another level of analysis that identifies several pitfalls that hinder innovation:

- Identifying the wrong problem—this obvious pitfall emerges surprisingly often; for example, when Coke perceived that Pepsi might surpass their cola market share, Coke tried to fix the problem by creating a sweeter Coca-Cola.
- Judging ideas too quickly—people are taught to make a decision quickly and move on and are promoted for abilities to see the flaws in any idea. Therefore, they tend to rule out ideas as soon as they see a defect rather than refining them to find the possibilities.
- Stopping with the first good idea—because problems create a tension calling for relief, people often jump at the first idea that relieves the stress. The first good idea is almost never the best one; it is often just the one most easy to recall.
- Failing to "get the bandits on the train"—great ideas often don't get implemented because they threaten somebody else's territory. Avoiding this requires thinking about whose support is necessary to implement the idea and then finding a way to get them involved.
- Obeying rules that don't exist—a Gary Larsen cartoon shows two cowboys crouched behind a covered wagon as flaming arrows shoot over their heads. One says to the other, "Hey, they're lighting the arrows! Can they do that?" Assumptions about the rules of the game need to be questioned.

Rouse and Boff (1994) identify further hindrances to innovation. They interviewed senior science and technology (S&T) managers in the Department of Defense (DOD) regarding how S&T investments lead to returns for DOD. They asked each manager to identify a success story and a failure story and then answer detailed questions about how the success or failure emerged. The predominant finding of this study related to the central roles that particular individuals play in successful transitions of S&T investments to fielded innovations.

For all the success stories identified, the champions have to go around the organizational system to achieve success. Furthermore, the commitments of champions often are substantially beyond what government incentive and reward systems could repay. A number of managers commented that successful transitions in DOD, and perhaps elsewhere, often depend on what are, in effect, commitments by champions that are irrational from an organizational perspective.

Thus, there are a wide variety of organizational impediments to innovation, most of which are exacerbated by growth, size, and previous success. Small, start-up enterprises do not have cultures and organizational systems in the way. Furthermore, they inherently have to focus on the idea that prompted the formation of the enterprise. However, what often goes unreported is the simple fact that the vast majority of start-ups do not succeed in innovating. Although they may succeed at inventing, this technical success is seldom translated to market success.

James Burke, the well-known commentator on BBC' s production *Connections*, has compiled a fascinating history of innovation, tracing roughly 300 technologies from the Renaissance to modern times. His book, *The Pinball Effect* (1996), shows how the eventual payoffs from inventions are almost always greater for unanticipated applications than for the originally envisioned applications. Furthermore, the originators of inventions are seldom the ones who reap the greatest rewards. Innovations often emerge from tortured paths of unmet expectations and overlooked serendipity, until finally we end up with penicillin or Post-It notes.

Given all these difficulties, it is natural to ask about the overall status of innovation. Buderi (1999) reviews various attempts to quantify innovation. He discusses the Porter-Stern National Innovation Index, which is based on eight variables, including international patents filed, research and development (R&D) spending, share of gross domestic product (GDP) spent on higher education and so forth. This index suggests that the United States will lose the lead in innovation, mostly due to less spent on R&D and higher education. Critics argue that this index does not account for unpatentable innovations relating to integration of technologies and the lack of patenting in rapidly moving areas like the Internet.

Buderi also discusses Francis Narin's three factors used in ranking of high-tech firms:

- citation intensity—how often a patent is cited in other patents,
- science link—number of scientific papers cited in a patent, and
- technology cycle time—median age of patents cited in recent patents.

Market-to-book value ratios are higher for companies that score well on these three factors. Another approach to quantification is Baruch Lev's measure of knowledge capital (Mintz, 1998), which indicates a huge market premium for companies whose earnings far surpass what would be expected based solely on their financial and physical assets. Lev's knowledge capital metrics are discussed in detail in Chapter 7, which addresses the challenge of knowledge.

Concerns about innovation and the difficulties underlying success have also resulted in public policy debates, which have outcomes that may interact with how individual enterprises choose to address this challenge. Ceruzzi (1998) discusses the unexpected nature of innovations and their dependence on fundamental research. He also notes that this dependence is usually only apparent after the fact. Furthermore, in the United States at least, a large portion of government-sponsored fundamental research was originally justified for military purposes and hence sponsored by the DOD. This investment has dramatically decreased in the past 10 years, causing concerns that the seeds of nonmilitary innovations are no longer being planted.

Rycroft and Kash (1999, 2000) focus on large-scale innovations, for example, the Internet, which are unlikely to emerge from efforts of single inventors/entrepreneurs. They argue that such innovations require public policies that foster development of network resources across stakeholder organizations, create experimentation/learning opportunities for stakeholders, and both seed and enhance market opportunities. This obviously implies a strong, facilitating role for government; however, lately, government has been less willing to play.

The concerns of Ceruzzi, Rycroft, and Kash raise the fundamental question of the extent to which private sector innovation depends on government investments in fundamental research. In other words, to what extent are private sector innovations the result of harvesting knowledge and skills that would not exist without government investments in discovery and risk reduction?

From an individual company's point of view, this suggests that leveraging the returns from government investments should be an element of the company's innovation strategy. Of course, it also raises the possibility that this source may be less dependable in the future. This risk is high for domains like aeronautics but less a problem for domains like medicine.

Product Innovation

Despite all the difficulties and issues just discussed, innovations do certainly occur. This is particularly evident for new product innovations. Fortunately, a wealth of studies have delved into the factors that affect successful product innovations. In this section, these factors are discussed. Consideration of specific methods—for example, stage-gate processes and portfolio management methods—is delayed until Chapter 4, in which the challenge of focus is addressed.

It is useful to begin by outlining the scope of product innovation. Stevens and Burley (1997), in an article that is emerging as a classic, compile and integrate a wide range of studies of product innovation success. They conclude that it takes 3,000 raw ideas to produce one commercial success. These 3,000 ideas translate into roughly 300 actual proposed efforts. I am aware of a few companies who have tracked proposals vs. successful products and the 300-to-1 ratio is quite consistent with their statistics.

Similarly, Nichols (1994) notes that drug companies must investigate roughly 10,000 compounds for one drug to reach the market. Although these are scientific investigations rather than the product ideas considered by Steven and Burley, the ratio of thousands to one is in the same ballpark for both domains. The implication is that a tremendous winnowing process among ideation, invention, and innovation must occur. Furthermore, all along the way, good bets may be screened out and bad bets retained.

Success in new product development has been found to relate to factors concerning processes, time, people, and technology. Process factors relate to understanding markets, competitors, and technologies. Smith, Herbein, and Morris (1999) discuss front-end innovation at AlliedSignal and Alcoa. They suggest critical success factors for the fuzzy front end of innovation:

- identification of transitions in key markets and technologies,
- knowledge of relevant external scientific breakthroughs,
- competitors' patent activities and long-term business strategies,
- new business intelligence for evolving market gaps,
- technology/business core strengths and weaknesses, and
- understanding of cross-business opportunities.

Guiltman (1999) presents a framework that suggests the strategic and tactical challenges to be addressed depending on the specific market behavior to be influenced. Behaviors include *1*) trial and repurchase, *2*) customer migration and, and *3*) innovation adoption and diffusion. Major decisions to be made include strategic decisions, such as market targeted, leadership (first in or follow), and relative innovativeness; and tactical decisions, such as promotion activities, sales and distribution support, pricing, nature of product, and timing. On the basis of an extensive review of the literature, Guiltman proposes a framework that includes two dimensions: relative advantage (i.e., perceived uniqueness, importance, and relevance of benefits provided) and degree of compatibility (i.e., ease of adoption). The four quadrants in this framework suggest very different choices among the decision alternatives just noted.

Lynn, Mazzuca, Morone, and Paulson (1998) argue that learning is the critical success factor in developing truly new products. To learn more, they suggest that teams should not expect to get processes right the first time. Consequently, they need to be receptive to external information, embrace it, and build on it. Overall, structuring the team to learn can overcome difficulties of less than desirable initial processes.

Davidson, Clamen, and Karol (1999), after reviewing many sources and studies, suggest guiding principles for new product development. The overall process needs clarity, providing a clear path to action. The process should be owned by everyone but include strong leadership from the top. The new product planning process also should be integrated with all other business processes and, finally, provide flexibility in its execution.

Also important is support of the process with appropriate methods and tools. For example, Cooper, Edgett, and Kleinschmidt (1998, 1999, 2000) report that companies who employ portfolio management methods experience significantly greater success from their investments, especially if the size of the portfolio matches the resources available and companies do not place excessive reliance on purely financial metrics. Portfolio methods are discussed in more detail in Chapter 4.

Beyond probability of success, time is an overarching variable in new product development. Indeed, excessive time is often correlated with decreased probability of success. Melsa (1999) discusses the problem of reducing time to market. He indicates the need to develop a time-based mindset and rethink the product realization process to support incremental innovation, reuse of existing product technology, and use of external sources of product technology. He also argues for cross-functional training, colocation of product realization teams, and concurrent development of products and processes. Finally, he advocates process measurement and the use of real-time market data to drive change.

Gupta and Souder (1998) discuss key drivers of reduced cycle time, based on survey results of almost 40 companies. They conclude that cycle time is reduced by extensive user involvement, effective management of teams, extensive supplier involvement, an effective design philosophy and practices, and effective organizational learning processes. Clearly, inefficient gathering of information and inefficient functioning of teams increases cycle time.

As noted in Chapter 2, Lambert and Slater (1999) challenge the popular wisdom that the keys to new product success are first to market, a fast product development cycle, and on-time schedule performance. Instead, they argue for effective market introduction timing, first to mindshare, and managed responsiveness, thus implying well-planned and responsive new product development and introduction.

People issues also affect the likely success of new product development. Of particular importance are the roles of managers, champions, and teams. Of course, people problems in general can also be significant contributors to new product failures. These people problems can often be attributed to failures to deal appropriately with the aforementioned process factors.

Englund and Graham (1999) review actions that upper managers can take to create an environment for more successful projects in their organization. Successful upper managers assure selection of projects with strategic emphases and provide explicit links between projects and strategies. They create management teams to make these selections, using consistent criteria to prioritize projects while also assuring that numbers of projects and resources are compatible. They also develop means to manage resources appropriately.

Markham and Griffin (1998) report on an insightful empirical study of the impacts of product champions, based on survey responses from almost 400 firms. Overall, champions slightly improve project and program performance but do not directly produce any discernible overall effects on new product development performance at the firm level. The impact of champion support for projects appears to be indirect through program success, innovation strategy, process implementation, and program success.

Lester (1998) discusses critical success factors for new product development, with emphasis on use of cross-functional teams. He advocates shared understanding across team members of the process for new product development, as well as providing teams with help, support, and guidance. He suggests team formation events to help members learn to work together. He also argues for timely update and redirection of project plans to keep team members aligned.

Production innovation success is also affected by the nature of technologies adopted and how they are employed. Robertson and Ulrich (1998) advocate the use of common product platforms to enable reuse of product technologies and to decrease time to market, costs, and risks. Thomke and Reinertsen (1998) provide similar advice in the context of managing development flexibility in uncertain product development environments. They see three ways of raising flexibility: adopting flexible technologies, adopting rigorous management processes, and employing modular architectures with minimal coupling between modules.

Tatikonda and Rosenthal (2000) review the impacts of technology novelty and project complexity on product development project execution success, based on a survey of 120 new product development projects from almost 60 firms for assembled goods. They find that technology novelty is strongly associated with poor unit cost and time to market results, whereas project complexity is strongly associated with poor unit cost outcomes. They also conclude that process technology novelty is more problematic than product technology novelty. The ideas of product platforms and modular architectures can substantially reduce both product and process novelty.

Robert Cooper (1999), a long-time and substantial contributor to our understanding of new product development, discusses the invisible success factors in product innovation. His common denominators of success include

- do up-front homework;
- build in the voice of the customer;
- seek differentiated, superior products;
- demand sharp, stable, and early product definition;
- plan and resource the market launch—early in the game;
- build tough go/kill decision points into your process—a funnel, not a tunnel;
- organize around true cross-functional project teams; and
- build an international orientation into your new product process.

He also suggests blockers of success; these include

- ignorance ("we don't know what should be done");
- lack of skills ("we don't know how to do it and/or we underestimate what's involved");
- a failed or misapplied new product process;
- too much confidence ("we already know the answers")
- lack of discipline and no leadership;
- being in just too big a hurry; and
- too many projects and not enough resources (a lack of money and people to do the job).

This brief review of the factors that affect new product innovations serves to support an overall observation. There are a variety of interacting things that you have to do well to achieve superior product innovation results. If you ignore these things, your chances of success are, at best, no better than the odds identified by Stevens and Burley. On the other hand, if you pay careful attention to these factors, you can substantially increase your chances of being a market innovator.

CHALLENGE OF VALUE

Value inherently migrates—the high-value products and services of today are unlikely to be the high-value products and services of tomorrow. For example, the high-margin automobiles and personal computers of the past are now low-margin commodities or near commodities. Airplanes are quickly evolving toward similar market relationships.

To escape such commodity traps, companies have to provide value in new ways, either changing the value proposition for existing products and services or developing new product and service offerings. Both paths involve innovation in the sense of introducing change via something new. Unfortunately, for the reasons outlined earlier, the major existing players in the market often have great difficulty innovating.

The value challenge poses the fundamental question of the extent to which your business processes provide benefits and costs as perceived by the marketplace. This question can be painful to address because many business processes are often focused on supporting the status quo, which may or may not directly provide compelling value to key stakeholders. In fact, the emergence and growth of many processes were never driven by stakeholder benefits.

The nature and roles of staff functions in many large organizations provide a good example. The chartering of these functions, as well as the resources they require, often reflect attempts to support executives and senior managers rather than provide value to customers. As another illustration, efforts to improve strategic thinking and planning also often become ends in themselves rather than investments explicitly linked to enhancements of business value added.

The difficulty is that many processes have emerged and grown for reasons that may no longer be evident and are not necessarily benefit or cost oriented. Processes acquire constituencies of their own, involving services, resources, and jobs that can be very difficult to reconsider when one attempts to make adding value a driver rather than an afterthought. Consequently, success in innovating is often blocked (Cooper, 1999).

Addressing this fundamental question of the value provided by existing processes provides the basis for developing a deep understanding of the value provided by products and services. This exploration of value also enables natural consideration of ways to enhance the value provided, as well as identification of new ways to provide value and new types of value to provide. The key is to transform analyses of "what is" into explorations of "what might be."

STRATEGIES FOR VALUE

This section discusses a range of strategies for enhancing value. Central to all of the guidance provided is the notion of a value proposition. Although there are a variety of definitions of this concept, I have found the following most useful:

> Benefits provided to stakeholders (i.e., customers, users, and so forth), expressed in terms of what they value, relative to costs born by stakeholders, again in terms of costs they experience, to gain these benefits.

Note that the providers' activities and the extent to which providers value these activities are not relevant. In other words, value is almost always an ends issue rather than a means issue. As obvious as this definition may be, a wide range of enterprises are managed as if their activities are the primary value they provide.

Starbucks is an excellent example of a company that understands its value proposition (Schultz, 1997). This company has successfully transformed an everyday product into an emotional experience of warmth, community, and quality. More than many other enterprises, Starbucks clearly knows what value it intends to provide. There are clearly many activities that go on in the background to enable the value that customers perceive, but they serve rather than lead the process of providing value.

As discussed briefly in Chapter 2, Kaplan (1999) outlines alternative strategies for discontinuous innovation and enhancing value. Four broad strategies are suggested, each with a couple of guiding questions:

- Radical cannibalism
  - *What forces could lead to the demise of your business?*
  - *What emerging technologies could displace the current value you provide to the market?*
- Competitive displacement
  - *What is the root end-user need that your business satisfies?*
  - *How does the fundamental value you provide get satisfied within industries outside of your own?*
- Market invention
  - *If the entire world represented your customer base, how would you segment your markets and what needs could you satisfy within each segment?*
  - *What larger systems do your products operate within, and how might you incorporate a larger value set into your offering?*
- Industry genesis
  - *What value would your technology provide if it were 10–20 times smaller than it is today?*

- *What unique combinations of technology or functionality might provide a new form of value?*

Note that these four broad strategies and eight questions do not constitute a menu of innovation strategies in themselves. Instead, this guidance is intended to prompt exploration of your enterprise's fundamental value proposition, the likely future if it remains unchanged, and alternative futures based on new value propositions.

Hamel (2000), drawing on experiences of companies like Enron, General Electric, Charles Schwab, and Virgin, discusses 10 rules for designing an organizational culture that inspires innovation:

- set unreasonable expectations—no one outperforms their aspirations,
- stretch your business definition—elastic definitions help curb conservative instincts,
- create a cause, not a business—success is often a side effect of personal dedication,
- listen to new voices—industries get reinvented by outsiders free from prejudices,
- design an open market for ideas—radical ideas are the only way to create wealth,
- offer an open market for capital—investments that avoid any downside also tend to limit the upside,
- open up the market for talent—good people vote with their feet,
- lower the risks of experimentation—resolve uncertainty via low-cost experimentation,
- make like a cell, divide and divide—spin-offs create space for new thinking and business models, and
- pay your innovators well, really well—create wealth by sharing it.

These ten rules for innovation provide good overall guidance, with implications for other challenges discussed in later chapters, e.g., change and the future. Of course, beyond overall guidance, you need to consider specific ways of innovating and providing value.

Slywotsky and Morrison (1997) discuss value strategy in terms of profit zones. They discuss 22 basic profit models. These models differ by your role in the overall value chain (e.g., in control), your standing in the product life cycle (e.g., innovator), your relative costs (e.g., cost leader), your standing in market share or installed base (e.g., leader), and your market image (e.g., standard or brand leader). These models are useful for characterizing both where you are and where you want to be.

Differences between where you are and where you aspire to be should drive reconsideration of your business design. Slywotsky and Morrison discuss business design using four dimensions:

- customer selection—what customers do I want to serve?
- value capture—how do I make a profit?
- differentiation/strategic control—how do I protect my profit stream?
- scope—what activities do I perform?

They suggest the following questions to guide reconsideration of your business design, with the goal of moving your company into one of the profit zones:

- Who are my customers?
- How are their priorities changing?
- Who should be my customer?
- How can I add value to the customer?
- How can I become the customer's first choice?
- What is my profit model?
- What is my current business design?
- Who are my real competitors?
- What is my toughest competitor's business design?
- What is my next business design?
- What is my strategic control point?
- What is my company worth?

To take full advantage of the broad guidance provided by Kaplan, Slywotsky, and Morrison, it is necessary to understand your current processes and the extent to which they do or do not provide value. Such an assessment can be surprisingly difficult to do.

A primary source of this difficulty is the inability to attribute costs appropriately. Financial reports often aggregate across value streams and disaggregation becomes impossible. Activity-based cost accounting, which is later discussed, provides a clear path to linking activities to value added. This assumes, of course, that value streams can be agreed on.

The obvious logic of this approach is often obscured by many organizations' difficulties dealing with internally valued activities with strong constituencies but minimal external value added. In such situations, moving away from the status quo can be quite difficult. I have sometimes found this difficulty to be nearly insurmountable in government agencies and nonprofits where political constituencies block reallocations of resources.

A related issue concerns developing market-driven processes focused on benefits to key stakeholders. With this orientation, the status quo has very little status—the market rules. A primary difficulty is the typical shortsightedness of the marketplace. Today's unique value added may be tomorrow's commodity. This works well for the consumer but not very well for the provider.

A variation of this issue involves focusing on the value provided to stakeholders rather than just cost recovery. The central concern here involves understanding the value provided rather than solely focusing on the cost of providing it. In this situation, activity-based accounting is not of much help, other than as a baseline. Instead, the key issue is understanding value propositions.

The importance of focusing on value provided to marketplace stakeholders seems obvious. However, this is often not a natural act, especially for large, established enterprises, especially when prosperity has come to be viewed as an entitlement. It may take crises to precipitate shifting the focus to value provided. Furthermore, it may take years before these crises are recognized and accepted.

This pattern of insularity, lack of recognition, and slowly emerging acceptance has played out repeatedly in recent years in industries ranging from automobiles to aircraft to consumer goods. New chief executives and substantial layoffs suddenly occur. However, some companies understand this pattern, know how to anticipate, and know how to strategically manage such inevitable transitions (Collins and Porras, 1994).

SUPPORTING VALUE STRATEGIES

Essential support for all of the strategies that address the challenges discussed in this book includes information on market opportunities, competitive threats, technology trends, organizational weaknesses, and so forth. Approaches to pursuing such information were briefly discussed in Chapter 2, which addressed the challenge of growth. This topic is pursued in more detail in Chapter 7, which addresses the challenge of knowledge.

Human-Centered Design

One aspect of these information needs deserves particular attention. This concerns the question of what stakeholder-related information to collect, how to collect it, and when it is needed. These questions can be systematically considered and answered using a methodology called human-centered design (Rouse, 1991, 1994).

This methodology focuses on identifying all the stakeholders in the value chain associated with the success of a product or service. Central to this approach is gaining an understanding of stakeholders' concerns, values, and perceptions. This understanding enables assessing stakeholders' perceptions of the benefits and costs of current products and services, as well as projecting their likely perceptions of future products and services.

This type of information can enable creation of models of customer and market purchasing behaviors. Such models can be qualitative or quantitative and provide a means for predicting the relative value of alternative offerings, including competitors' offerings. Gensch and colleagues (1990) discuss development of such models and present data that show the financial returns from making decisions with the support of such models.

Compilation and interpretation of this type of information can be accomplished via a four-phase process that begins by using the information collection methods of naturalists, moves on to the methods of market researchers, and subsequently employs more formal methods of product test and evaluation. Each phase of this process is specified in terms of both the questions to be asked and the most appropriate methods and tools for addressing these questions (Rouse, 1991). The ways in which this information is used are described below in the discussion of the *Product Planning Advisor.*

Multi-Attribute Utility Models

Multiattribute utility theory provides a broadly applicable way to represent how people perceive value (Keeney and Raiffa, 1993; Hammond, Keeney, and Raiffa, 1998). Of particular importance, multi-attribute utility models provide a means for dealing with situations involving mixtures of economic and noneconomic attributes. To illustrate, consider how to represent stakeholders' perceptions of costs and benefits.

Let cost attribute i at time j be denoted by c_{ij}, where $i = 1, 2,...L$ and $j = 0, 1,...N$, and let benefit attribute i and time j be denoted by b_{ij}, where $i = 1, 2,...M$ and $j = 0, 1,...N$. The values of these costs and benefits are transformed to common utility scales using $u(c_{ij})$ and $u(b_{ij})$. These utility functions serve as inputs to the overall utility calculation at time j as shown below

$$U(\underline{c}_j, \underline{b}_j) = U[u(c_{1j}), u(c_{2j}),...u(c_{Lj}), u(b_{1j}), u(b_{2j}),...u(b_{Mj})]$$

which provides the basis for an overall calculation across time using

$$U(\underline{C}, \underline{B}) = U[U(\underline{c}_1, \underline{b}_1), U(\underline{c}_2, \underline{b}_2),...U(\underline{c}_N, \underline{b}_N)]$$

Note that the time value of costs and benefits, discussed in Chapter 6, which addresses the challenge of the future, can be included in these equations by dealing with the time value of costs and benefits explicitly and separately from uncertainty. An alternative approach involves assessing utility functions for discounted costs and benefits. With this approach, streams of costs and benefits are collapsed across time, for example, in terms of net present value, before the values are transformed to utility scales. The validity of this simpler approach depends on the extent to which people's preferences for discounted costs and benefits reflect their true preferences.

The mappings from c_{ij} and b_{ij} to $u(c_{ij})$ and $u(b_{ij})$, respectively, enable dealing with the subjectivity of preferences for noneconomic returns. In other words, utility theory enables one to quantify and compare things that are often perceived as difficult to objectify. Unfortunately, models based on utility theory do not always reflect the ways in which human decision making actually works.

Subjective expected utility (SEU) theory reflects these human tendencies. Thus, to the extent that one accepts that perceptions are reality, one needs to consider the SEU point of view when one makes expected utility calculations. In fact, one should consider making these calculations using both objective and subjective probabilities to gain an understanding of the sensitivity of the results to perceptual differences.

Once one admits the subjective, one needs to address the issue of whose perceptions are considered. Most decisions involve multiple stakeholders. It is, therefore, common for multiple stakeholders to influence a decision. Consequently, the cost/benefit models need to take into account multiple sets of preferences. The result is a group utility model such as

$$U = U[U_1(\underline{C},\underline{B}), U_2(\underline{C},\underline{B}), ... U_K(\underline{C},\underline{B})]$$

where K is the number of stakeholders.

Formulation of such a model requires that two important issues be resolved. First, mappings from attributes to utilities must enable comparisons across stakeholders. In other words, one has to assume that $u = 0.8$, for example, implies the same value gained or lost for all stakeholders, although the mapping from attribute to utility may vary for each stakeholder. Thus, all stakeholders may, for instance, have different needs or desires for safety and, hence, different utility functions. They also may have different time horizons within which they expect benefits. However, once the mapping from attributes to utility is performed and utility metrics are determined, one has to assume that these metrics can be compared quantitatively.

The second important issue concerns the relative importance of stakeholders. The above equation implies that the overall utility attached to each stakeholder's utility can differ. For example, it is often the case that primary stakeholders' preferences receive more weight than the preferences of secondary stakeholders. The difficulty of this issue is obvious. Who decides? Is there a super stakeholder, for instance? In many cases, shareholders can be viewed as these super stakeholders. However, for organizations with diverse constituencies such as government agencies and nonprofits, the lack of a super stakeholder can present difficulties.

Beyond these two more theoretical issues, there are substantial practical issues associated with determining the functional forms of $u(c_{ij})$ and $u(b_{ij})$ and the parameters within these functional relationships. This also is true for the higher level forms represented by the above equations. As the number of stakeholders (K), cost attributes (L), benefit attributes (M), and time periods (N) increases, these practical assessment problems can be quite daunting. Nevertheless, the overall multi-attribute approach provides a powerful framework for representing stakeholders' perceptions of value.

Quality Function Deployment

Beyond representing value, one needs to represent how to affect value. Quality function deployment (QFD), originally developed by Mitsubishi, provides a means for representing relationships between desires of stakeholders and the means open to variation for achieving these desires (Hauser and Clausing, 1988). QFD involves a series of matrices. The rows of each matrix denote things to be affected, whereas the columns denote things that can be manipulated to cause the desired effects.

For example, the rows on the initial matrix may be stakeholders' desires and the columns may be possible product functionality. For the next matrix, the rows would be product functionality and the columns might be alternative technologies. For the third matrix, the rows would become technologies and the columns might be alternative manufacturing processes. The series of matrices usually continues until one has depicted the full causal chain from market desires to the variables that one intends to manipulate to satisfy desires.

Above each matrix is also included a representation of the interactions of columns, for example, interactions of functions. These interactions are depicted in a triangular matrix, rotated to provide a "roof" to the matrix below. The visual appearance resulting is why QFD is often termed the "house of quality." As might be imagined, compiling the information necessary to complete the entries in a full series of such houses can be overwhelming. Nevertheless, the kernel of the QFD concept can be quite useful without having to construct whole villages of houses.

Product Planning Advisor

The *Product Planning Advisor* (ESS, 2000) combines multi-stakeholder value chains, multi-attribute utility theory, and QFD, as well as the human-centered design methods from *Design for Success* (Rouse, 1991). This tool supports formulation and manipulation of integrated market/product models as summarized in Figure 3.1.

Use of this planning and analysis tool involves several steps:

- identify goals,
- identify stakeholders,
- define measures,
- define functionality,
- define solutions, and
- assess solutions

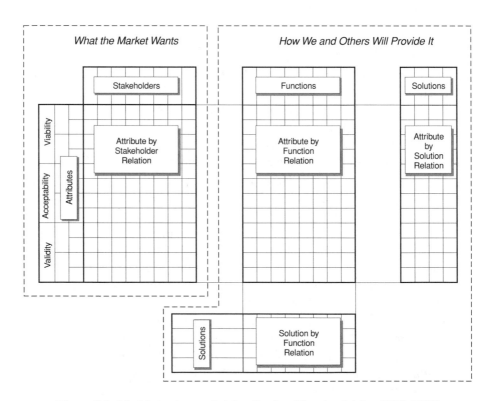

Figure 3.1. Model structure underlying *Product Planning Advisor* (ESS, 2000)

The initial step focuses on identifying the goals of the product planning effort. These goals typically involve competing in particular markets, gaining specific competitive advantages, and securing certain results. For example, goals might be to introduce a $25 processor in low-end markets and achieve a 30% market share within 3 years.

The next step involves defining stakeholders in successful pursuit of goals. Stakeholders usually include customers, users, distributors, and so forth in the marketplace. Also important are internal stakeholders such as marketing, sales, engineering, manufacturing, and so forth in the enterprise creating the product. There are also usually stakeholders who provide the financial resources and are designated with labels such as corporate or shareholders or investors.

Defining measures involves specifying the attributes of importance to each stakeholder and formulating multi-attribute utility models for each stakeholder. There is often substantial uncertainty associated with defining such attributes and relationships. Sensitivity analysis is typically used, in the assess solutions step, to determine when uncertainties might affect the merits of potential product planning decisions.

Defining functionality concerns determining the functions and features of the product that will influence attainment of attribute levels. This involves a simplified version of QFD, in which the positive or negative impacts of functions/features on attributes are specified. For example, enhanced built-in diagnostics may enhance mean time to repair for a product, while also negatively impacting the applicability of current maintenance training.

As indicated in Figure 3.1, defining solutions involves specifying sets of functions/features and the attribute levels expected to be achieved by each set. Solutions usually include the salient alternative offerings, by both you and your competitors. We have found that one particularly strong competitor is often ignored—the status quo. This alternative has several inherent competitive advantages in terms of costs, difficulty of learning, and so forth.

Assessing solutions concerns using the underlying object-oriented market/product models created in the earlier steps to determine relative competitive advantages, as well as perform sensitivity and "what if?" analyses. The *Product Planning Advisor* also uses the underlying models to provide recommendations of where to focus product enhancements—that is, which attributes and which functions—to most improve the competitiveness of offerings.

In hundreds of product-planning workshops, this tool has been found to be most effective when used by cross-functional teams to formulate and manipulate market/product models in an interactive manner. This enables teams to determine impacts of assumptions and explore alternative offerings. A particularly valuable use of this tool involves determining likely strategies and responses of competitors. In Chapter 9, which discusses best practices in general, we consider in depth the roles of methods and tools.

Activity-Based Cost Accounting

The above methods and tools focus on defining value and determining ways of providing value in terms of functions, features, and attribute levels that will provide competitive offerings. Another aspect of value concerns the activities or processes associated with providing value. As indicated earlier, a central concern in the challenge of value is assuring that processes are aligned and tuned to support the enterprise's value streams.

One way of addressing this issue is to focus on where resources are being spent and determine how these expenditures relate to the value provided. This can be a somewhat surprisingly difficult question to answer. The difficulty is primarily due to how costs are traditionally captured. The "culprit" is almost always overhead accounts.

It is not unusual, for example, for the ratio of total costs to direct labor costs to be three or even much greater. Roughly speaking, this means that one-third, or less, of total costs can be attributed to hands-on providing of value. The other two-thirds, or more, relate to management, infrastructure, and functions such as accounting, finance, human resources, and so forth.

Increased focus on value fairly quickly leads to the question of how to attribute this lion's share of resources to value streams such as products and services. This attribution process can be quite controversial, as product-line managers try to avoid having costs attributed to them and support-function managers try to justify their existence. Support-function managers do not want to be trapped in the undifferentiated overhead pool; however, product-line managers want to minimize their "taxes" for support functions.

A key to moving away from large, undifferentiated overhead cost accounts can be adoption of activity-based cost (ABC) accounting that directly links activities to value (Cooper and Kaplan, 1988). Adoption of this approach usually leads to painful questions of why certain activities are performed because there appears to be little if any linkage to value. In some cases, activities are regulatory requirements. However, in many cases incumbency ("we've always done this") is the only justification of the activities. Discussion of ABC accounting is beyond the scope of this chapter. Nevertheless, it is important to realize that the things you count and the ways you count them often limit your ability to understand and improve value.

CONCLUSIONS

This chapter began with discussions of the meaning of value, how value changes or migrates, and the role of innovation in continually enhancing the value of your market offerings. Considerable attention was devoted to the nature of innovation and the underlying difficulties, with particular emphasis on new product innovations. Approaches to developing value strategies were discussed, as well as methods and tools for supporting development and execution of these strategies.

Pursuing new value strategies forces consideration of several risks and resource issues. Of particular importance, how can you adopt and invest in new value strategies while, at the same time, continuing execution of the old strategies that are providing most of the resources? This is a fundamental change management question which is considered in Chapter 6, which addresses the challenge of change.

However, it is useful to consider the overall trade-off this poses. What should be your relative investment in a low-risk, low-margin strategy vs. a high-risk, high-margin strategy? What if the low-risk alternative is clearly a "sunset" business, whereas the high-risk alternative may be a "sunrise" business? How can you be sure that the sun, if it rises, will shine on you?

These basic questions of risks and rewards are addressed in detail in the next chapter. Nevertheless, it is important to recognize in this chapter that significant changes in the ways you provide value involve risks and resource requirements that go beyond "business as usual." You cannot change the fundamental nature of your enterprise and its relationships with stakeholders without accepting risks and investing resources.

Of course, there is a low-risk alternative. If you simply maintain your current offerings, processes, and so forth, you will, without doubt, eventually decline into oblivion. The uncertainty associated with this strategy is very low—it is almost guaranteed. The consequences are quite negative, but there is little uncertainty that you will experience these consequences. Most people are willing to take some risks to avoid these "sure-thing" results. The next chapter discusses how to place such bets prudently.

KEY QUESTIONS

To successfully address the challenge of value, you should consider the following key questions and explore answers based on the concepts, principles, methods, and tools discussed in this chapter:

- Who are the stakeholders in the value provided by your enterprise?

- What is the value provided to these stakeholders by your products and services?
- How has this value changed in recent years and likely to change in the future?
- How well does your organization transform inventions into innovations?
- What are success and failure stories and what factors impacted these results?
- Which of the common barriers to innovation are prevalent in your enterprise?
- What is your value/innovation strategy and how is it supported?

REFERENCES

Argyris, C., and Schon, D. A. (1978). *Organizational Learning: A Theory of Action Perspective*. Reading, MA: Addison-Wesley.

Buderi, R. (1999). In search of innovation. *Technology Review* November–December: 42–51.

Burke, J. (1996). *The Pinball Effect: How Renaissance Water Gardens Made the Carburetor Possible and Other Journeys Through Knowledge*. Boston, MA: Little, Brown.

Ceruzzi, P. (1998). Non-standard models of innovation. *Knowledge, Technology and Policy* 11(3): 40–49.

Christensen, C. M. (1997). *The Innovator's Dilemma: When New Technologies Cause Great Firms to Fail*. Boston, MA: Harvard Business School.

Christensen, C. M., and Overdorf, M. (2000). Meeting the challenge of disruptive change. *Harvard Business Review* March–April: 66–76.

Collins, J. C., and Porras, J. I. (1994). *Built to Last: Successful Habits of Visionary Companies*. New York: Harper Business.

Cooper, R. G. (1999). The invisible success factors in product innovation. *Journal of Product Innovation Management* 16(2): 115–133.

Cooper, R. G., Edgett, S. J., and Kleinschmidt, E. J. (1998). *Portfolio Management for New Products*. Reading, MA: Addison-Wesley.

Cooper, R. G., Edgett, S. J., and Kleinschmidt, E. J. (1999). New product portfolio management: Practices and performance. *Journal of Product Innovation Management* 16(4): 333–351.

Cooper, R. G., Edgett, S. J., and Kleinschmidt, E. J. (2000). New problems, new solutions: Making portfolio management more effective. *Research Technology Management* 43(2): 18–33.

Cooper, R., and Kaplan, R. S. (1988). Measure costs right: making the right decisions. *Harvard Business Review* September–October: 96–103.

Davidson, J. M., Clamen, A., and Karol, R. A. (1999). Learning from the best new product developers. *Research Technology Management* 42(4): 12–18.

Economist. (1999). Fear of the unknown. *The Economist* December 4: 61-62.

Englund, R. L., and Graham, R. J. (1999). Linking projects to strategy. *Journal of Product Innovation Management* 16(1): 52–64.

ESS. (2000). *Product Planning Advisor*. http://www.ess-advisors.com/software.htm. Atlanta, GA: Enterprise Support Systems.

Gensch, D. H., Aversa, N., and Moore, S. P. (1990). A choice-modeling market information system that enabled ABB Electric to expand its market share. *Interfaces* 20: 6–25.

Guiltman, J. P. (1999). Launch strategy, launch tactics, and demand outcomes. *Journal of Product Innovation Management* 16(6): 509–529.

Gupta, A. K., and Souder, W. E. (1998). Key drivers of reduced cycle time. *Research Technology Management* 41(4): 38–43.

Hamel, G. (2000). Reinvent your company. *Fortune* June 12: 99–118.

Hammond, J. S., Keeney, R. L., and Raiffa, H. (1998). *Smart Choices: A Practical Guide to Making Better Decisions*. Boston, MA: Harvard Business School.

Hauser, J. R., and Clausing, D. (1988). The house of quality. *Harvard Business Review* May–June: 63–73.

Kaplan, S. M. (1999). Discontinuous innovation and the growth paradox. *Strategy and Leadership* 29(2): 16–21.

Keeney, R. L., and Raiffa, H. (1993). *Decisions With Multiple Objectives: Preferences and Value Tradeoffs*. Cambridge, UK: Cambridge University Press.

Lambert, D., and Slater, S. F. (1999). First, fast, an on time: the path to success. Or is it? *Journal of Product Innovation Management* 16(5): 427–438.

Lester, D. H. (1998). Critical success factors for new product development. *Research Technology Management* 41(1): 36–43.

Lynn, G. S., Mazzuca, M., Morone, J. G., and Paulson, A. S. (1998). Learning is the critical success factor in developing truly new products. *Research Technology Management* 41(3): 45–51.

Markham, S. K., and Griffin, A. (1998). The breakfast of champions: associations between champions and product development environments, practices, and performance. *Journal of Product Innovation Management* 15(5): 436–454.

Melsa, J. L. (1999). Reducing the time-to-market interval. *Information • Knowledge • Systems Management* 1(1): 15–31.

Mintz, S. L. (1998). A better approach to estimating knowledge capital. *CFO* February: 29–37.

Mintzberg, H., and Van der Heyden, L. (1999). Organigraphs: drawing how companies really work. *Harvard Business Review* September–October: 87–94.

Nichols, N. A. (1994). Scientific management at Merck: an interview with CFO Judy Lewent. *Harvard Business Review* January–February: 88–99.

Praether, C. W., and Gundry, L. K. (1996). *Blueprints for Innovation*. New York: AMACOM.

Robertson, D., and Ulrich, K. (1998). Planning for product platforms. *Sloan Management Review* Summer: 19–31.

Rouse, W. B. (1991). *Design for Success: A Human-Centered Approach to Designing Successful Products and Systems*. New York: Wiley.

Rouse, W. B. (1992). *Strategies for Innovation: Creating Successful Products, Systems, and Organizations*. New York: Wiley.

Rouse, W. B. (1994). *Best Laid Plans*. New York: Prentice-Hall.

Rouse, W. B. (1996). *Start Where You Are: Matching Your Strategy to Your Marketplace*. San Francisco, CA: Jossey-Bass.

Rouse, W. B., and Boff, K. R. (1994). *Technology Transfer From R&D to Applications*. Wright-Patterson AFB: Armstrong Research Laboratory.

Rouse, W. B., Cannon-Bowers, J. A., and Salas, E. (1992). The role of mental models in team performance in complex systems. *IEEE Transactions on Systems, Man, and Cybernetics* 22(6): 1296–1307.

Rouse, W. B., and Morris, N. M. (1986). On looking into the black box: Prospects and limits in the search for mental models. *Psychological Bulletin* 100(3): 349–363.

Rucci, A. J., Kirn, S. P., and Quinn, R. T. (1998). The employee-customer-profit chain at Sears. *Harvard Business Review* January–February: 83–97.

Rycroft, R. W., and Kash, D. E. (1999). Innovation policy for complex technologies. *Issues in Science and Technology* 16(1).

Rycroft, R. W., and Kash, D. E. (2000). Steering complex innovation. *Research Technology Management* 43(3): 18–23.

Schultz, H. (1997). *Pour Your Heart Into It: How Starbucks Built a Company One Cup at a Time*. New York: Hyperion.

Senge, P. M. (1990). *The Fifth Discipline: The Art and Practice of the Learning Organization*. New York: Doubleday/Currency.

Sharma, A. (1999). Central dilemmas in managing innovation is large firms. *California Management Review,* 41(3, Spring): 146-164.

Slywotsky, A. J. (1996). *Value Migration: How to Think Several Moves Ahead of the Competition*. Boston, MA: Harvard Business School.

Slywotsky, A. J., and Morrison, D. J. (1997). *The Profit Zone: How Strategic Business Design Will Lead You to Tomorrow's Profits*. New York: Times Books.

Smith, G. R., Herbein, W. C., and Morris, R. C. (1999). Front-end innovation at AlliedSignal and Alcoa. *Research Technology Management* 42(6): 15–24.

Stevens, G. A. and Burley, J. (1997). 3000 raw ideas = 1 commercial success! *Research Technology Management* 40(3): 16–27.

Tatikonda, M., and Rosenthal, S. R. (2000). Technology novelty, project complexity, and product development project execution success: a deeper look at task uncertainty in product innovation. *IEEE Transactions on Engineering Management* 47(1): 74–87.

Thomke, S., and Reinertsen, D. (1998). Agile product development: managing development flexibility in uncertain environments. *California Management Review* 41(1): 8–30.

CHAPTER FOUR

Focus

Most enterprises operate in environments that are rich in possibilities—opportunity seems to always be knocking. In particular, dramatic increases in the power and ubiquity of computer and communication networks seem to offer endless possibilities for enhancing revenues, decreasing costs, and increasing profits. On the other hand, resources are almost always limited. Only a few possibilities can be pursued well. If available resources are spread too thinly, all investments suffer.

Thus, most organizations, some sooner and many later, eventually reach the conclusion that they need to focus their human and financial resources on a few high-leverage possibilities. They also eventually come to realize that much of the apparent wealth of possibilities represents diversions not opportunities. The question then becomes one of identifying and committing to the opportunities, while also avoiding the diversions.

This is a decision-making question. The primary concerns include framing, evaluating, and making decisions. This chapter addresses these concerns and presents concepts, principles, methods, and tools for decision making in general and strategic focusing in particular. The overarching theme is that good decision-making processes greatly enhance organizations' abilities to focus successfully.

CHALLENGE OF FOCUS

Focus as a challenge involves, as just noted, pursuing opportunities and avoiding diversions. Organizations tend to seriously entertain many more alternatives than are reasonable, relative to the organization's goals, strategies, plans, and resources. Much of the time of senior management tends to be consumed considering these alternatives; this is addressed in detail in Chapter 8, which addresses the challenge of time.

A good example of this phenomenon is the many "what ifs" posed by customers, suppliers, employees, and so forth. Ideas usually abound; however, most of these ideas, although reasonable, are not good ideas. For instance, the CEO of a mid-sized appliance company told me that almost all ideas for new appliances are diversions and only occasionally is there a real opportunity. As another illustration quite close to home, most of the latest leading-edge technologies and management methods and tools will not, in retrospect at least, have been worthy investments.

The difficulty of this challenge is that some alternatives really are opportunities. Although the vast majority are undoubtedly diversions, how can you determine which are which? What is needed are methods and tools for rapid pruning of option trees. At the same time, however, you do not want methods and tools that discourage generation of option trees!

A significant portion of this difficulty is due to a range of decision-making disabilities often exhibited by organizations. Common disabilities include

- assumptions that are not explicit and consequently not questioned,
- a lack of information vital to understanding the implications of alternatives,
- prolonged waiting for consensus to emerge, resulting in de facto decisions,
- lack of decision-making mechanisms, creating decision "vacuums,"
- key stakeholders are not involved (and commitment to decisions suffers), and
- decisions are made but, for various reasons, never implemented.

Later in this chapter, we explore the underlying psychological sources of these types of disabilities. Many of the methods and tools later discussed provide means to counteract these natural tendencies.

Magasin and Gehlen (1999) provide an insightful study of a company that exhibited several of these disabilities in the process of addressing issues surrounding violations of environmental regulations. The resulting decisions were sufficiently flawed to lead to criminal charges against the officers of the company and the demise of the business. The consequences of poor decision making are not usually this obvious and dramatic. Instead, poor decision making slowly eats away at the resources and value of the enterprise.

These types of problems are pervasive. I have many times worked with senior management teams who patiently try to coax consensus into emerging. Typically, the leader of the team is organizationally empowered to make the decision in question. However, he or she feels more comfortable slowly building consensus and assuring that everyone "buys in" to the decision.

It is important to ensure that team members feel their points of view have received due consideration. A point can be reached, however, where total agreement is not possible and a decision should be made. Indeed, a good definition of consensus is agreement to act despite possible disagreements about elements of the course of action. All too often, managers wait for "signals" that everyone agrees with and will commit to a course of action—and such managers will not announce a decision until this agreement and commitment are obvious.

I have been involved in many decision-making situations in which all available information supported a particular course of action. Furthermore, sensitivity analyses had shown that no foreseeable outcomes for uncertain attributes would change the relative attractiveness of this alternative. However, the senior managers continued to hesitate.

In several cases, I asked the team, "In light of all our discussions and analyses, are there any imaginable circumstances where the currently most attractive alternative would become other than the best choice?" After everyone agreed that there were no such circumstances, the senior person on the team said something like, "Given this agreement, we should be able to reach a conclusion on this choice within the next month or so."

I then said, "Why don't you decide right now? You all agree that there are no imaginable circumstances where any other choice would be better." In all cases, this comment lead to the team leader saying., "Right now?" My response was, "Yes, unless I am missing something." In one case, the leader slowly looked around the table, not speaking, just looking. Other key people were nodding their heads yes. He looked back at me and said, "Okay, let's decide and move ahead."

In all of these situations, various team members have later approached me indicating their support for having the decision made. Even people who disagreed with the decision were supportive. The process had worked; the data had been compiled and analyzed in various ways, everyone got to speak their piece and argue with assumptions and interpretations, a decision was made, and the team was moving on to implement this decision.

These teams reached a consensus to move forward. Those who disagreed with the decision were nevertheless committed to help pursue success. If success failed to result or emerged too slowly, these people would undoubtedly revive past arguments against the chosen course of action. The team would expect and support this. However, until results began to emerge, the team was unanimous in moving forward.

Another pervasive problem is lack of processes for making decisions. In many efforts with nonprofits and government agencies, in particular, I have encountered an absence of methods for making decisions, especially big decisions. In these types of organizations, there are often very diverse constituencies, typically with a wide range of interests and concerns. Not infrequently, these interests and concerns are in conflict.

For example, a military service may decide to close an under-used facility and shift resources to higher-priority areas. Congressional members in the district involved will likely block this reallocation if it affects jobs in their districts. At lower levels, resources targeted for high-priority investments may be redirected to lower-priority areas because of personal whims of new senior stakeholders. There are often no ways to make binding decisions that cannot be reversed by other stakeholders or political processes in general.

As another example, nonprofits usually serve a wide range of stakeholders who have interests related to issues, diseases, locations, and so forth. One group of stakeholders, for instance, may be committed to funding for research on childhood cancer at universities in a particular state. In contrast, another group may be advocates of funding for breast cancer patient support groups in poor, urban areas. Trade-offs across such disparate interests are quite difficult.

One way to address such difficult trade-offs is to first agree on decision-making processes, for example, majority-rule voting, and then debate the alternatives. Obviously, this is the way that the public and their representatives become involved in government decision making. However, for trade-offs such as just illustrated, it often makes sense to look more deeply at costs and benefits (e.g., lives saved or improved) in the process of reaching a decision.

A primary hurdle in attempting to reach agreement on decision-making processes for addressing these types of trade-offs is the strong tendency of advocacy groups to derail processes if they do not feel their causes will fare well in terms of the issues emphasized by the processes. I have had numerous senior managers in these types of organizations tell that they did not care about the process employed, the premises assumed, or the philosophy adopted as long as their cause won its share of the resources.

In the types of situations just discussed with interminable consensus building and lack of decision processes, one usually finds that power, influence, and control of resources become paramount. Control of the agenda is often central. If one can control what gets discussed and, in some situations, what issues get considered for possible voting, one can cause de facto decisions. This approach is particularly effective for preserving the status quo.

The organizational phenomena just discussed are important to this chapter in that they can completely undermine efforts to focus. Although these phenomena are far more prevalent in organizations like nonprofits and government agencies, they can emerge in for-profit organizations, particularly large, established enterprises with strong cultures that support the status quo. Before considering how to deal with such forces, it is important to consider the underlying nature of decision making.

NATURE OF DECISION MAKING

To understand human decision making—and enhance decision making via methods and tools—it is necessary to understand the typical context of decision making. As discussed in Chapter 1, decision making rarely involves reflective strategic thinking, data collection and analysis, and in-depth debate (Mintzberg, 1975). In part, this is due to the press of events in typically time-pressured organizational environments. It is also due to managers' tendencies to satisfice in the sense of seeking solutions that are "good enough" rather than optimal (Simon, 1957).

Beyond the time pressure and willingness to accept satisfactory solutions, there is the simple fact that, in most situations, managers make very good decisions without formal analyses and extensive debates. As extensive studies by Gary Klein and others have shown (Klein et al., 1993; Klein, 1998), highly experienced decision makers in natural environments—rather than artificial environments constructed to assess their abilities—are usually able to employ readily-available cues to recognize high-quality courses of action. They do not need to study data and generate alternatives; they know what to do.

Thus, most of the time, experienced decision makers perform very well and need little assistance. Difficulties arise when unfamiliar and infrequent circumstances arise for which past experience is insufficient for knowing what to do. This is particularly problematic when decision makers continue to think that their instincts and intuitions provide a sufficient basis for decision making.

Possible biases and other limitations of human decision making have been researched for several decades, led by people such as Daniel Kahneman, Paul Slovic, and Amos Tversky (1982). Many early findings were criticized for being based on artificial laboratory tasks rather than the context-rich realities of actual decision making. Over time, however, evidence has accumulated supporting the notion that the strengths of human decision making, such as identified by Klein and his colleagues, can become weaknesses in some situations.

Hammond, Keeney, and Raiffa (1999) provide a recent summary of these limitations in terms of a set of decision-making traps. They present everyday examples of the types of biases, heuristics, and other limitations explored by Kahneman et al. The decision-making traps of Hammond et al., augmented by a few others from further sources, include

- anchoring and adjustment—initial estimates of magnitudes and probabilities strongly influence further adjustment of these estimates, providing ample opportunity for biases due to the ways questions are posed;

- status quo—there are strong tendencies to defend current situations and avoid breaking away from them, often despite strong evidence that current situations are far from attractive;
- sunk-cost—managers are inclined to making current and future decisions that justify past decisions, seeking to be consistent despite the fact that new information is available;
- confirming evidence—people tend to seek information that supports intuitions and preferences, what they already want to do, rather than confirming and disconfirming evidence relative to all alternatives;
- framing—the ways in which problems are stated, for example, in terms of gains vs. losses, strongly affect people's preferences regarding outcomes, despite the fact that alternative problem statements are equivalent;
- estimating and forecasting—people exhibit poor abilities to estimate quantities with which they have little experience, for example, probabilities, and when little feedback of the accuracy of past estimates is received;
- overconfidence—there are tendencies to perceive that estimates and predictions are much better than experience indicates, for example, ignoring possibilities of failure, perhaps due to the ease with which success can be envisioned;
- prudence—managers are sometimes overcautious relative to extreme cases, for example, stockpiling inventories in case demand follows the best-case scenario or over-hedging against the worst-case scenario;
- availability—estimates are related to the ease with which relevant instances come to mind; hence, past strong experiences, for example, highly publicized disasters, overly influence estimates of probabilities;
- representativeness—estimates are related to the extent to which data seem representative of hypotheses;- for example, people can be uncomfortable with the statistically expected value when this particular value is atypical; and
- causality and attribution—people tend to misattribute causes, for example, attributing their own successes to skills and hard work and their failures to unavoidable external forces, while doing the opposite for others' successes and failures.

Interestingly, these biases and limitations are very useful for much of life, providing convenient shortcuts and enabling avoidance of time-consuming analyses of most decisions. Later, we discuss ways to avoid the consequences of these limitations in situations in which these consequences are likely to be unattractive.

Beyond these well-circumscribed limitations, there are several broader phenomena that affect organizational abilities to focus. When focus is likely to require significant organizational change, there are a range of delusions that can hinder decision making (Rouse, 1998a). These delusions are influenced, in part, by perceptions that are governed by underlying needs and beliefs (Rouse, 1993). For example, the need to feel that certain competencies are central to an organization tends to result in beliefs that such is undeniable, and this strongly affects perceptions of changes that require different competencies. The notion of organizational delusions, as well as relationships among needs, beliefs, and perceptions, are discussed at length in Chapter 5.

Abilities to focus are also affected by the nature and roles of champions. As discussed in the context of value and innovation in Chapter 3, champions play important and sometimes subtle roles (Rouse and Boff, 1994; Markham and Griffin, 1998). They are often key to the success of new directions, especially when these new directions can only be pursued by working around existing organizational practices. On the other hand, old directions often also have champions who strongly advocate the status quo and may creatively find ways to work around decision processes that potentially favor new directions. Of particular importance, these champions often have many fans among those toiling to preserve the status quo.

As Mintzberg and Van der Heyden (1999) emphasize, it is important to understand how an organization really works when trying to achieve focus, especially if the focus sought represents a new direction. Such changes can be very difficult in the presence of significant organizational learning disabilities (Senge, 1990) or when the organization is trapped in single-loop learning (Argyris and Schon, 1978). We explore these issues in depth in Chapter 5.

The foregoing paints a picture of rather seriously flawed human decision-making abilities. These limitations are very real and need to be addressed. However, they should be kept in perspective in the sense that much of managers' decision making is unaffected by these limitations. Experienced managers' instincts and intuitions are usually pretty good. The main area of concern is those situations in which unfamiliar and infrequent issues predominate. For most managers, achieving a new organizational focus is one of these types of situations.

STRATEGIES FOR FOCUS

If one looks across the many references cited in this chapter, seeking a single best practice that all the pundits agree on, the result will be quite clear. Everyone agrees that good decision-making processes produce good decisions. By good decisions, I mean decisions that are well-founded in terms of explicit assumptions and use of information; decisions that consider an appropriate number of alternatives and uncertainties associated with them; and decisions that are understood by key stakeholders and have their commitment.

Good decision processes satisfy these criteria and also make explicit the nature of outcomes sought and behaviors necessary for achieving these outcomes (Rouse, 1992, 1994). This may involve creating "scorecards" that clearly delineate what matters and how it is to be measured. Some processes include explicit linkages to the behaviors needed to score highly, for example, in terms of innovation as discussed in Chapter 3. In general, however, such behavioral linkages can be difficult to specify.

Adoption of a decision process also involves depicting and making choices in terms of the relationships of alternatives to clearly articulated and communicated goals, strategies, and plans. In other words, in adopting a decision process, management also adopts the discipline and consistency to frame decisions in the context of the goal-plan hierarchy of the organization. This hierarchy is central to achieving focus in that it provides a direct basis for pruning alternatives.

This practice implies top-down clarification of goals and plans. However, this "sense making" role for top management does not imply that all the elements of this hierarchy emanate top-down. In fact, many if not most of the elements will emerge bottom-up from the many "intelligent agents" (i.e., people) that populate the organization. Top management's primary role, in this regard, is to make sense of all these activities and nurture or prune appropriately.

Before delving into decision processes more deeply, it is important to return briefly to an earlier point. Most managers will agree that the notion of achieving focus by adopting explicit decision processes seems quite logical. However, not as many managers value such processes. In numerous experiences with government agencies—both federal and state—and with nonprofit organizations, I have worked with senior managers who have learned to take advantage of ambiguity rather than attempt to lessen it.

When you have a wide range of stakeholders and various checks and balances, it is likely that there are, in effect, no decision makers. There are usually people with tremendous influence, who can articulate compelling visions that gain broadly based support, for example, John Kennedy's vision of going to the moon. However, most decisions involve compromises among interests in different programs, jobs, and money. A compromise in one direction on one issue may be made to achieve a compromise in another direction on a different issue.

Managers who are skilled at working in such environments often see explicit decision processes as very limiting. Their experience tells them that people will "game" an explicit process to the organization's disadvantage. They all see significant loss of discretion to work deals. Such deals may not be the best for the organization, in a purist sense, but they do keep resources flowing and adversaries at bay. People who are good at playing this type of game do not want explicit, public rules of decision making.

I raise this overall issue simply to caution possible optimism that explicit decision processes will cure all ills. The types of processes discussed in the remainder of this chapter work well when there are a modest number of types of stakeholders, there are people empowered to make decisions on the behalf of these stakeholders, and these decisions will, for the most part, be implemented and quite likely improved with experience but not constantly second guessed and consciously undermined. To the extent that your organization matches these characteristics, there are powerful methods and tools for helping to achieve focus.

Elements of Decision Making

For those decisions in which instinct and intuition—if used solely—are unlikely to provide a sound basis for good decisions, there is a collective wisdom accumulated over many decades, with roots going back much further. This wisdom is articulated somewhat differently by various pundits, but the essential elements are very much common across perspectives.

Good decision making—for the minority of situations for which formal decision making is warranted—begins with consideration of both near-term and long-term goals, for example, becoming profitable and then going public. These goals are then translated into measurable objectives, for example, revenues, profits, and market shares for each of the next 3 years.

Next is consideration of alternatives, which often includes the status quo, that is, what you are doing now, and several other courses of action. These may include alternative strategies, acquisitions, projects, and so forth. It is important to have a creative set of alternatives rather than, for example, just the status quo and the salient alternative that everyone already agrees about pursuing. Nontraditional alternatives, seriously considered, can result in very creative discussions and insights.

Alternatives should be characterized in terms of attributes, some of which are very likely to be the aforementioned objectives. Attributes stated in terms of objectives usually reflect the viability of alternatives in terms of benefits and costs. Additional attributes are likely to relate to acceptability and validity (Rouse, 1991, 1994). Acceptability attributes concern the extent to which alternatives fit in, that is, are compatible with overall strategies, provide synergies with other activities, and so forth. Validity attributes relate to the "correctness" of alternatives, for example, meet technical and regulatory requirements. Thus, the set of attributes of interest is usually significantly larger than the set of objectives.

An important element of decision making is the uncertainty associated with alternatives. The consequences of choosing an alternative are characterized in terms of the alternative's attributes. The actual values of these attributes that result are often uncertain. The uncertainties associated with attribute values, for each alternative, should be characterized either with data or, in the absence of data, with subjective estimates of probabilities, means, variances, and so forth.

Central to this line of reasoning is the assessment of decision makers' preferences relative to the set of uncertain attributes. This involves representing trade-offs among attributes, for example, revenues vs. profits, as well as characterizing decision makers' attitudes toward uncertainties. Risk-averse decision makers will prefer alternatives with more predictable attribute levels, that is, lower variance of outcomes. In contrast, risk-prone decision makers will prefer alternatives with more attractive mean attribute levels, despite larger variances.

In situations involving multiple types of stakeholders, identifying the real decision makers can be difficult. The board of directors or CEO may be empowered to make decisions on behalf of the shareholders. However, rarely can such decision makers blatantly focus on maximizing profits, for example, at the expense of customers, employees, and the public. Enlightened executives realize that shareholder value will only be maximized if he or she can find the "sweet spot" among the interests of shareholders, customers, employees, the public, and so forth. Thus, multi-stakeholder, multi-attribute attribute decision-making situations are quite common.

All of the foregoing serves the purpose of supporting decision making in the sense of assuring well-founded decisions. Methods and tools associated with the line of reasoning just elaborated—discussed in detail later in the chapter—serve to support decision making rather then determine decisions. Humans making decisions, supported by methods and tools, are central to gaining and maintaining support for decisions. Specifically, the underlying goal is to ensure that all key stakeholders understand the process whereby decisions were reached and, regardless of the resulting decisions, feel the process was well-informed, prudent, and fair.

Support and commitment of stakeholders are key to successful implementation of decisions. All too often, I have found that decisions are supposedly made but are either sluggishly implemented or never implemented. This can be due to lack of resources, but lack of support is just as common a reason. One or more stakeholders "signs up and salutes" but does not act. This may be due to lack of understanding, lack of agreement, or perhaps lack of consequences for not acting. In extreme cases, there may not be measurements available for determining whether or not anybody has acted!

The elements of good decision making just outlined are reflected in two recent books that provide insightful perspectives on decision making, as well as valuable methods and tools. Hammond, Keeney, and Raiffa (1999) emphasize eight key elements of good decision making, including problem definition, objectives clarification, alternative generation, consequence assessment, trade-off analysis, uncertainty quantification, risk accounting, and decision coordination for linked decisions. They suggest five steps for framing decisions, which, using the terminology introduced earlier, can be restated as follows:

- capture the concerns, considerations, and criteria to be addressed by the decision;
- convert general concerns into succinct objectives and organize them, both in terms of related concerns and perhaps as a hierarchy of concerns;
- separate ends from means to establish fundamental objectives—means may also have associated attributes, for example, for acceptability and validity;
- clarify the meaning of each objective and attribute, including how it can be measured; and
- test objectives to determine if their achievement successfully addresses the concerns, considerations, and criteria captured earlier.

Matheson and Matheson (1998) discuss decision making with particular emphasis on strategic R&D. The guidance presented is broadly applicable to a wide range of decision-making situations involving projects and portfolios of projects. They present 45 best practices gleaned from extensive studies of a large number of major companies. These best practices are presented in an overall framework, which can be restated in the earlier terminology as follows:

- Making quality decisions
  - decisions are well framed in terms of the key elements discussed above,
  - decisions are driven by long-term, market-oriented strategies,

- investments of resources are managed as a portfolio, and
- individual investments are managed to ensure value creation
- Organizing for decision quality
  - decision making processes are employed,
  - relationships with internal customers are explicitly managed,
  - relationships with external customers are explicitly managed, and
  - culture and values receive careful attention
- Improving decision quality
  - postproject audits provide lessons learned,
  - project effectiveness is explicitly measured,
  - frameworks for organizational learning are created, and
  - learning processes include learning from others

As discussed in Chapter 1, Eisenhardt (1999) sees strategy as synonymous with decision making or, in other words, addressing the challenge of focus. She suggests four tactics for approaching this challenge. Specifically, she argues that effective decision makers create strategy by

- building collective intuition that enhances the ability of a top-management team to see threats and opportunities sooner and more accurately;
- stimulating quick conflict to improve quality of strategic thinking without sacrificing significant time;
- maintaining a disciplined pace that drives the decision process to a timely conclusion; and
- defusing political behavior that creates unproductive conflict and wastes time.

This guidance clearly relates to the ways in which managers should address the key elements of decision making discussed earlier. In particular, these tactics can help to build commitment and ensure that decisions are implemented.

We revisit the nature of decision making in Chapter 6, which considers the challenge of the future, specifically in terms of long-term investment decision making. In the remainder of this section, we consider three decision-making issues: project selection, multistage decision processes, and portfolio management.

Project Selection

Selecting the projects in which to invest is a classic type of decision-making problem, the results of which define, if only by inference, the focus of the organization. Henriksen and Traynor (1999) review a wide range of methods and tools for project selection. Their analysis of these alternative approaches suggests six overall types of attributes:

- relevance,
- risk,
- reasonableness,
- basic research return,
- programmatic research return, and
- business return.

Specific attributes within these categories are usually combined into an overall value equation, which may be cast in computational form using generalized spreadsheet packages or incorporated in specialized software packages, some of which are discussed later in this chapter.

I have found these types of approaches to project selection to be quite common. What varies considerably, however, is how these approaches are integrated into decision making. Some organizations view the project "scores" that result as determinates of project funding, either yes/no or level of funding. Other organizations view these scores as just one component of the eventual investment decision. The former organizations seem to be able to justify their decisions fairly easily; the latter organizations have more difficulty justifying their decisions but often seem to make more creative decisions. The choice of one approach or the other—or, obviously, somewhere in between—appears to be related to the organizational environment and culture more than anything else.

Beyond selecting projects that score well in terms of the above types of attributes, there is also the issue of the likely success of the projects. Balachandra (1989) reports on an in-depth investigation of this issue. He identifies success and failure factors correlated with project outcomes:

- Success factors
  - profitability of company,
  - early external competition,
  - favorable internal competition,
  - top management support,

- project personnel commitment,
- chance event with positive impact,
- probability of success,
- presence of a project champion, and
- smoothness of technological route
- Failure factors
  - number of projects in portfolio,
  - number of expected end uses,
  - pressure on project leader, and
  - stage in product's life cycle

Some of these relationships are far from surprising. For example, the estimated probability of success of a project correlates positively with the actual success. Other factors are less obvious. For instance, the extent of management pressure on project leaders correlates negatively with project success. In other words, the more project leaders are pressured to succeed, the less likely it is that they will succeed.

Balachandra also discusses indicators of needs to stop projects. To the extent that probability of technical success decreases, continued existence of the market becomes questionable, availability of raw materials is no longer assured, and unfavorable government regulations emerge, one should seriously consider stopping projects. Beyond these "red light" signals, he suggests "yellow light" signals related to the project, organization, and environment that provide possible early warning mechanisms.

Balachandra and Friar (1997) consider how project success factors are affected by the context of projects. They suggest three contextual variables:

- nature of innovation—incremental vs. radical,
- nature of market—existing vs. new, and
- nature of technology—low vs. high.

The eight combinations of these variables yield very different levels of importance for market, technology, and organization factors in terms of their impact on project success. Thus, it is possible to refine the assessment process portrayed by the general factors listed earlier.

To determine how actual project termination decisions are made, Balachandra, Brockhoff, and Pearson (1996) surveyed R&D managers from almost 80 large firms. They found that all firms use some form of project monitoring procedures, with most, by far, being formal processes and some being informal. The most frequently monitored variables include time, technical success, probability of technical success, cost, market conditions, probability of market success, and extent to which technical and market-related objectives are met. The most frequent way of communicating termination decisions was through written information.

Project selection methods are well developed and pervasively used. The most useful attributes are summarized above. Of particular importance, these methods are used to both initiate projects and to stop projects. This is an essential distinction because the match of number of projects to resources available is critical to the success of an investment portfolio, as later discussion elaborates. For this match to be appropriate, it is critical that projects be both started and stopped. Unfortunately, as one executive told me, "It's almost impossible to put a stake through the heart of an idea. They just keep on coming back, again and again." This is one of the greatest weaknesses of idea-generating processes and also one of the greatest strengths!

Multistage Decision Processes

Project selection, management, and possible termination can be somewhat more complicated than the process just depicted. This is because project initiation often involves various uncertainties that are not resolved until the project progresses. Thus, there are usually several opportunities to continue or not continue a project and, hence, several decisions rather than one.

Cooper (1998) addresses such multistage decision making processes. He developed a process he has trademarked as the "stage-gate" process. A generalized version of this process, using terminology that is consistent with the foregoing discussion, is shown in Figure 4.1. This figure depicts how ideas, recall the 3,000:1 or 10,000:1 discussed in Chapter 3, go through a multistage decision-making "funnel" to become market innovations.

As might be expected, the decision-making attributes at each stage change to reflect criteria for investing larger amounts as projects proceed through the funnel. Earlier stages typically involve more subjective and broadly strategic

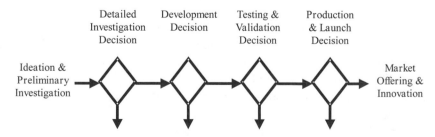

Figure 4.1. Multistage decision-making process

criteria than later stages in which firm, quantitative business criteria dominate. All along the funnel, projects exit as shown in Figure 4.1 as they fail to satisfy criteria for further investment and lose in the competition among projects to be the best investments to take forward.

In Cooper's ongoing studies of industry practices – discussed below – he finds that multistage decision processes are very common among major companies. The number and names of the stages may vary, and the particular criteria at each stage depend on the company. However, the overall processes are very similar.

One concern that cuts across most companies is how to manage the "fuzzy front end" of the funnel, where attributes are more subjective and few data are available for assessing likely success, risks, and so forth. There has been a variety of recently published reports on how a range of companies address this fuzzy front end.

O'Brien and Fadem (1999) discuss how DuPont decides what types of initiatives should fill the front end of the funnel. The process begins with looking at macro trends in the economy and society and the implied market issues of these trends. This analysis, in conjunction with consideration of technology trends, enables identifying potentially attractive markets. They thas employ a set of 25 criteria to evaluate the potential of new business initiatives for DuPont. Each criterion relates to one of seven categories:

- market factors,
- DuPont competencies,
- competitive issues,
- time factors,
- financial considerations,
- potential gaps, and
- fatal flaws.

They note that this approach results in 50–60 new business ideas in the evaluation pipeline at any time and 30 actively being managed by the Corporate New Business Development Division.

Smith, Herbein, and Morris (1999) discuss critical success factors in front-end innovation at Alcoa and the former AlliedSignal (now Honeywell). The components of this front-end process include

- identification of transitions in key markets and technologies,
- knowledge of relevant external scientific breakthroughs,

- competitors' patent activities and long-term business strategies,
- new business intelligence for evolving market gaps,
- technology/business core strengths and weaknesses, and
- understanding of cross-business opportunities.

The criteria they use to decide on the potential attractiveness of new initiatives include

- innovative technical vision,
- potential for proprietary position,
- alignment with corporate strategy,
- responsiveness to market trends,
- team composition and qualifications,
- literature and/or market search,
- risk/reward assessment, and
- anticipated speed of execution.
-

Montoya-Weiss and O'Driscoll (2000) discuss Nortel's (Northern Telecom) idea-to-opportunity front-end process. The four phases of this process include

- idea qualification,
- concept development,
- concept rating, and
- concept assessment.

Evaluation for each phase involves use of standard questions and rating forms, all embedded in a computer-based support system.

These published approaches by these four well-known technology-based companies serve to illustrate the pervasiveness of multistage decision processes. The need for such processes at the output end of the funnel is obvious—at this point, major investment decisions are being made. The need at the input end of the funnel is driven by needs for alternatives with strong strategic relevance and potential.

Portfolio Management

Thus far, the primary decision-making issue has been framed in terms of whether or not to invest in a particular project or, more generally, whether a particular alternative is worthy of continuing through the multistage decision process. However, quite often the primary question concerns which alternatives belong in the portfolio of investments and which do not.

Portfolio management is a fairly well-developed aspect of new product development (e.g., Cooper, Edgett, and Kleinschmidt, 1998 and Gill, Nelson, and Spring, 1988). Well-known and recent works on R&D/technology strategy pay significant attention to portfolio selection and management (e.g., Roussel, Saad, and Erickson, 1991; Matheson and Matheson, 1998; Boer, 1999; Allen, 2000; and Graves et al., 2000). Furthermore, the conceptual underpinnings of option pricing theory, which is discussed in Chapter 6, are based on notions of market portfolios (Amram and Kulatilaka, 1999).

Most approaches to portfolio evaluation include three particular elements:

- representations of the portfolio in terms of rewards vs. risks,
- scoring or ranking mechanisms to decide which investments to include, and
- means for dealing with correlated rewards and/or risks.

Figure 4.2 depicts a typical representation of rewards vs. risks. The line through W, X, Y, and Z represents the efficient frontier. Points on this line provide the most reward for a given risk (W vs. A) or the least risk for a given reward (Z vs. B). In general, one wants to select portfolio investments from alternatives on the efficient frontier; otherwise, one is accepting less reward than possible or more risk than necessary.

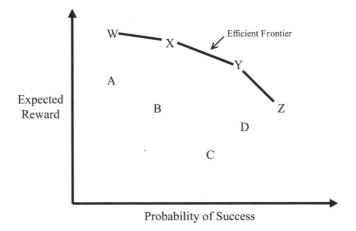

Figure 4.2. Rewards vs. risks and the efficient frontier

Cooper, Edgett, and Kleinschmidt (1998) and Allen (2000) discuss a range of alternative choices for axes of representations like Figure 4.2. Rewards are usually quantified in terms of net present value or economic value added. Risks may be characterized by probability of technical success, probability of market success, or volatility of expected rewards.

Scoring and ranking methods usually consider a broader range of attributes than just rewards and risks. Strategic alignment, match to company competencies, and sustainability of competitive advantages are good examples. To a great extent, these more subjective criteria are used to identify the feasible set of alternatives; the much more quantitative rewards vs. risks analyses serve as "sanity checks" for these alternatives.

A more sophisticated view of portfolio management considers interactions among alternatives (Boer, 1999; Allen, 2000). Synergies between two alternatives may make both of them more attractive. Correlated risks between two alternatives may make both of them less attractive. A good portfolio has an appropriate balance of synergies and risks. The *Decision Advisor*, discussed below, provides means for determining the impacts of alternatives with correlated rewards and/or risks.

Cooper, Edgett, and Kleinschmidt (1999, 2000) have conducted an ongoing assessment of industry practices in portfolio management. The earlier study found that roughly 70% of over 200 companies surveyed were using formal portfolio management processes. Those companies getting the best results from their investments were using financial, strategic, and scoring methods for portfolio evaluation. Interestingly, the companies using only financial methods experienced the poorest results.

Their subsequent study was limited to those companies using formal portfolio management processes. Typical problems with these processes included too many projects for resources available, too many projects making earlier hurdles, lack of information for making well-informed decisions, and too many minor projects clogging the funnel. They suggest that analysis of the output requirements of the funnel combined with analysis of the capacity of the funnel can enable determining an appropriate match between number and nature of projects.

SUPPORTING DECISION MAKING

The decision-making frameworks and processes discussed earlier are quite logical and, to an extent, fairly straightforward. They are straightforward in the sense that one can understand the basis for each step and relationships among the steps. On the other hand, it is not easy to behave consistently with these processes. Consequently, a variety of methods and tools have been developed for supporting use of these decision-making processes.

Product Planning Advisor

Rouse, Boff, and colleagues (1997, 1999) have developed a method for investment decision making that is based on multi-attribute utility theory as discussed in Chapter 3. This approach focuses on concerns, values, and perceptions of the multiple stakeholders typically involved in investment decisions. The steps of the process are as follows:

- identify stakeholders in alternative investments,
- define benefits and costs of alternatives in terms of attributes,
- determine utility functions for attributes (benefits and costs),
- decide how utility functions should be combined across stakeholders,
- assess parameters within utility models,
- forecast levels of attributes (benefits and costs), and
- calculate expected utility of alternative investments

This process is supported by the *Product Planning Advisor* (ESS, 2000) introduced in Chapter 3. Use of this tool in this manner is illustrated in Rouse, Boff, and Thomas (1997). Applications of this methodology to examples ranging from investments in aircraft cockpits to training simulators are provided by Rouse and Boff (1999).

Expert Choice

An alternative approach to multi-attribute utility theory is the analytical hierarchy process (Saaty, 1980). This approach involves interactive construction of a hierarchical decision tree based on managers' judgments regarding goals, criteria, and alternatives. Managers make pair-wise comparisons of alternatives in terms of criteria, from which are inferred quantitative weightings. The inferred weightings are then used to rate the alternatives relative to the criteria for goal achievement.

This process is embodied in another off-the-shelf software tool, *Expert Choice* (Expert Choice, 2000). This relatively easy-to-use tool enables users to construct and employ hierarchical preference models without having to understand the underlying mathematics involved in creating these models. This is the significant strength of this tool but also a weakness in that the results can seem a bit "magical" to users. Consequently, counterintuitive results may be difficult to understand and accept.

NewProd

When investment decisions involve new product development, another available tool is *NewProd* (Cooper, 1985; PDI, 2000). With this tool, proposals for new product initiatives are evaluated by managers using several using 0–1 scales. These ratings are combined to create an overall score that is compared to the scores of roughly 200 actual, historical new product development projects to predict probability of success. Limitations of this tool include the idiosyncrasies of historical linkages and the focus on a single attribute—probability of success.

Calantone and colleagues (1999) discuss use of both *Expert Choice* and *NewProd*, comparing their relative strengths and weaknesses. They conclude that the two tools are complementary, in part due to different theoretical and algorithmic approaches underlying these tools. The notion of using multiple tools is quite often reported in studies of best practices.

Decision Advisor

Another approach is provided by the *Decision Advisor* (Creswell, 2000; SDG, 2000). This tool is intended to support the frameworks and methods presented by Matheson and Matheson (1998) and by Allen (2000). It provides more comprehensive support than the other tools discussed above but also requires training for competent use. The following elements of support are provided:

- creation of influence diagrams to represent decisions,
- deterministic evaluation of business outcomes, for example, net present values,
- sensitivity analysis of outcomes relative to variations of input variables,
- probabilistic analysis of outcomes relative to high-sensitivity variables, and
- portrayal of results as cumulative probability charts that reflect overall risks.

The *Decision Advisor* also supports portfolio analysis across projects, including dependencies among projects. As noted earlier, such dependencies can significantly affect outcome variances and hence risks. This tool also includes knowledge-based coaches—one for influence diagrams, one for structuring the analysis, one for modeling costs, one for modeling commercial value assuming technical success, and one for guiding evaluation.

Balanced Scorecard

The above methods and tools are focused on individual investments or port-folios of investments. The balanced scorecard approach advocated by Kaplan and Norton (1996) provides a way for planning and monitoring overall enter-prise performance. They argue for four categories of measures of perform-ance:

- customer,
- financial,
- internal business processes, and
- learning and growth.

Typically, three or four metrics are defined in each category. The score-card is composed of four quadrants, one for each of the above categories. In each quadrant, objectives, measures, targets, and initiatives are defined for each metric. Scorecards are usually defined annually and reviewed quarterly.

I have found this approach to be quite stimulating. First, it drives serious discussion and consensus building about what really matters to the enter-prise's future success. The financial metrics are usually straightforward and the customer metrics are not too difficult. The other two categories, however, require much discussion and debate.

Quarterly reviews of scorecard results usually yield the following:

- for targets met, everyone celebrates the enterprise's success but also asks if the targets were too easy;
- for targets not met, initial discussion focuses on whether or not these targets were achievable;
- if they were achievable but not met, discussion then focuses on diagnosing the sources of the shortfalls;
- attention then shifts to possibly revising targets for the next period, which may involve reconsideration of metrics.

I have found that this process works best when the whole management team feels that they own the overall scorecard. Different people will inevitably be responsible for some initiatives more than others. Nevertheless, during the pe-riodic reviews it helps if everyone views the whole scorecard as "our respon-sibility" rather than simply a compilation of individual responsibilities and results.

Summary

The nature of the methods and tools discussed in this section suggest several cross-cutting needs:

- structuring methods and tools that enable decomposition of higher-level goals, strategies, and plans into lower-level subgoals and action plans;
- models that allow representation and evaluation of alternatives in terms of goal-plan hierarchies and their impacts on business outcomes;
- methods and tools to enable creation, portrayal, and update of scoring and ranking procedures, as well as balanced scorecards.

There is a wide range of methods, tools, and models that are potentially applicable to meeting these needs; see Sage and Rouse (1999) for an extensive compilation.

It is also important to emphasize that the types of methods and tools discussed here are intended to support decision making and, hence, achieve focus. In contrast, these tools are not intended to dictate decisions. In Chapter 9, which summarizes best practices, we discuss the findings of a study of over 2,000 managers regarding how they want tools to support their decision making (Rouse, 1998b). Their desires are quite specific as this later discussion reveals.

CONCLUSIONS

This chapter has addressed the challenge of focus and the need to make decisions to achieve focus. We considered various decision-making disabilities and the nature of decision making that underlies these disabilities, as well as decision-making proficiency. Frameworks for good decision making were discussed, including approaches to project selection, multistage decision processes, and portfolio management. Finally, we considered methods and tools for supporting decision making and achieving focus.

There is a variety of risk, resource, and organizational issues associated with the approaches to decision making discussed in this chapter. Of course, most of the methods and tools discussed here are concerned with allocating resources among risky alternatives. However, the risk of interest at this point concerns the risk of adopting explicit decision-making processes. Managing this risk also requires resources.

I have found that the types of processes discussed here are most acceptable when tailored to the specific nature and culture of an organization. To this end, the processes discussed here are best proposed as starting points, which the organization will vary as experience is gained. At the very least, you need to be open to changing labels, criteria, and so forth. Your may, for example, also want to add or delete stages from the typical multistage decision processes.

All in all, you need to spend the time and resources necessary to create understanding and raise comfort levels with processes that will become integral to the how the organization makes many of its most important decisions. Assuring this understanding and comfort may slow decision making at first, but, once they are achieved, processes should be easier, faster, and produce better results.

KEY QUESTIONS

To successfully address the challenge of focus, you should consider the following key questions. The concepts, principles, methods, and tools discussed in this chapter should provide the basis for exploring answers to these questions:

- Do you have a well articulated and well-understood process for making major decisions, especially those involving unfamiliar and infrequent elements?
- Does this process ensure consideration of several alternatives, ranging from status quo to incremental change to radical change?
- Does this process ensure that the number of investments matches the resources available and needed for these investments to succeed?
- Does this process have multiple stages that result in regular termination of investments that are not progressing as needed?
- Has this process resulted in your enterprise being focused on a few key investments that are receiving the attention and resources necessary for success?
- To the extent that your answers to the above questions are "no," are you pursuing development of the processes necessary for answering "yes"?

REFERENCES

Allen, M. S. (2000). *Business Portfolio Management: Valuation, Risk Assessment, and EVA Strategies*. New York: Wiley.

Amram, M., and Kulatilaka, N. (1999). *Real Options: Managing Strategic Investment in an Uncertain World*. Boston: Harvard Business School.

Argyris, C., and Schon, D. A. (1978). *Organizational Learning: A Theory of Action Perspective*. Reading, MA: Addison-Wesley.

Balachandra, R. (1989). *Early Warning Signals for R&D Projects: How to Pick the Winners and Make Your Investments Pay Off*. Lexington, MA: Lexington Books.

Balachandra, R., Brockhoff, K. K., and Pearson, A. W. (1996). R&D project termination decisions: processes, communication, and personnel changes. *Journal of Product Innovation Management* 13: 245–256.

Balachandra, R., and Friar, J. H. (1997). Factors for success in R&D projects and new product innovation: a contextual framework. *IEEE Transactions on Engineering Management* 44(3): 276–287.

Boer, F. P. (1999). *The Valuation of Technology: Business and Financial Issues in R&D*. New York: Wiley.

Calantone, R. J., Di Benedetto, C. A., and Schmidt, J. B. (1999). Using the analytic hierarchy process in new product screening. *Journal of Product Innovation Management* 16(1): 65–76.

Cooper, R. G. (1985). Selecting winning new product projects: using the NewProd system. *Journal of Product innovation Management* 2: 34–44.

Cooper, R. G. (1998). *Product Leadership: Creating and Launching Superior New Products*. Reading, MA: Perseus Books.

Cooper, R. G., Edgett, S. J., and Kleinschmidt, E. J. (1998). *Portfolio Management for New Products*. Reading, MA: Addison-Wesley.

Cooper, R. G., Edgett, S. J., and Kleinschmidt, E. J. (1999). New product portfolio management: practices and performance. *Journal of Product Innovation Management* 16(4): 333–351.

Cooper, R. G., Edgett, S. J., and Kleinschmidt, E. J. (2000). New problems, new solutions: making portfolio management more effective. *Research Technology Management* 43(2): 18–33.

Creswell, D. (2000). Decision Advisor--A knowledge-based decision system. *Information • Knowledge • Systems Management*, 2 (1, Spring).

Eisenhardt, K. M. (1999). Strategy as strategic decision making. *Sloan Management Review* Spring: 65–72.

ESS. (2000). *Product Planning Advisor*. http://ess-advisors.com/software.htm. Atlanta, GA: Enterprise Support Systems.

Expert Choice. (2000). *Expert Choice*. http://www.expertchoice.com/software. Pittsburgh, PA: Expert Choice.

Gill, B., Nelson, B., and Spring, S. (1996). Seven steps to new product development. In: *The PDMA Handbook of New Product Development*, edited by M. D. Rosenau, Jr. New York: Wiley, chapt. 2.

Graves, S. B., Ringuest, J. L., and Case, R. H. (2000). Formulating optimal R&D portfolios. *Research Technology Management* 43(3): 47–51.

Hammond, J. S., Keeney, R. L., and Raiffa, H. (1998). *Smart Choices: A Practical Guide to Making Better Decisions*. Boston, MA: Harvard Business School.

Henriksen, A. D., and Traynor, A. J. (1999). A practical R&D project selection scoring tool. *IEEE Transactions on Engineering Management* 46(2): 158–170.

Kahneman, D., Slovic, P., and Tversky, A. (Eds.). (1982). *Judgment Under Uncertainty: Heuristics and Biases*. Cambridge, UK: Cambridge University Press.

Kaplan, R. S., and Norton, D. P. (1996). Using the balanced scorecard as a strategic management tool. *Harvard Business Review* January–February: 75–85.

Klein, G. A. (1998). *Sources of Power: How People Make Decisions*. Cambridge, MA: MIT Press.

Klein, G. A., Orasanu, J., Calderwood, R., and Zsambok, C. E. (Eds.). (1993). *Decision Making in Action: Models and Methods*. Norwood, NJ: Ablex.

Magasin, M., and Gehlen, F. L. (1999). Unwise decisions and unanticipated consequences. *Sloan Management Review* 41(1): 47–60.

Markham, S. K., and Griffin, A. (1998). The breakfast of champions: associations between champions and product development environments, practices, and performance. *Journal of Product Innovation Management* 15(5): 436–454.

Matheson, D., and Matheson, J. (1998). *The Smart Organization: Creating Value Through Strategic R&D*. Boston, MA: Harvard Business School.

Mintzberg, H. (1975). The manager's job: folklore and fact. *Harvard Business Review* July–August: 49–61.

Mintzberg, H., and Van der Heyden, L. (1999). Organigraphs: drawing how companies really work. *Harvard Business Review* September–October: 87–94.

Montoya-Weiss, M. M., and O'Driscoll, T. M. (2000). Applying performance support technology in the fuzzy front end. *Journal of Product Innovation Management* 17(2): 143–161.

O'Brien, T. C., and Fadem, T. J. (1999). Identifying new business opportunities. *Research Technology Management* 42(5): 15–19.

PDI. (2000). *NewProd*. http://www.prod-dev.com. Hamilton, Ontario: Product Development Institute.

Rouse, W. B. (1991). *Design for Success: A Human-Centered Approach to Designing Successful Products and Systems*. New York: Wiley.

Rouse, W. B. (1993). *Catalysts for Change: Concepts and Principles for Enabling Innovation*. New York: Wiley.

Rouse, W. B. (1994). *Best Laid Plans*. Englewood Cliffs, NJ: Prentice-Hall.

Rouse, W. B. (1998a). *Don't Jump to Solutions: Thirteen Delusions That Undermine Strategic Thinking*. San Francisco, CA: Jossey-Bass.

Rouse, W. B. (1998b). Computer support of collaborative planning. *Journal of the American Society for Information Science* 49(9): 832–839.

Rouse, W. B., and Boff, K. R. (1994). *Technology Transfer From R&D to Applications*. Wright-Patterson AFB: Armstrong Research Laboratory.

Rouse, W. B., and Boff, K. R. (1999). Making the case for investments in human effectiveness. *Information • Knowledge • Systems Management* 1(3): 225–247.

Rouse, W. B., Boff, K. R., and Thomas, B. G. S. (1997). Assessing cost/benefits of R&D investments. *IEEE Transactions on Systems, Man, and Cybernetics, Part A* 27(4): 389–401.

Roussel, P. A., Saad, K. N., and Erickson, T. J. (1991). *Third Generation R&D: Managing the Link to Corporate Strategy*. Cambridge, MA: Harvard Business School.

Saaty, T. L. (1980). *The Analytic Hierarchy Process*. New York: McGraw-Hill.

Sage, A. P., and Rouse, W. B. (Eds.). (1999). *Handbook of Systems Engineering and Management*. New York: Wiley.

SDG. (2000). *Decision Advisor*. http://www.sdg.com/. Menlo Park, CA: Strategic Decisions Group.

Senge, P. M. (1990). *The Fifth Discipline: The Art and Practice of the Learning Organization*. New York: Doubleday/Currency.

Simon, H. A. (1957). *Models of Man: Social and Rational*. New York: Wiley.

Smith, G. R., Herbein, W. C., and Morris, R. C. (1999). Front-end innovation at AlliedSignal and Alcoa. *Research Technology Management* 42(6): 15–24.

CHAPTER FIVE

Change

Change has been a constant in our society for a long time—perhaps most visibly since the Industrial Revolution. All generations tend to see the changes that they are experiencing in current times as unprecedented when compared with the past. However, studies of past chronicles of change reveal similar observations by, for example, those who experienced the advent of steam power in the early 1800s or the onslaught of the railroads later in the 1800s (Rouse, 1996).

Change brings new opportunities for growth and rewards. However, it also challenges the status quo and established ways of doing business, making a living, and gaining recognition. Hard won and long honed skills can become less and less central to success. New skills easily learned by new market entrants can be difficult to gain for established players.

For managers of established businesses, this situation presents a fundamental challenge. You must keep the company you have running well, because that's where the cash flow is coming from, at the same time that you try to create the company you aspire to be, the company with new competencies and new growth opportunities. How much do you invest in maintaining the old business relative to creating the new business?

There are very strong pressures to keep the old business functioning, pressures that often consume all available resources. This is due to the simple fact that almost everyone in the current business is part of the status quo, hoping to continue prosperity and needing resources to pursue this goal. As the old business paradigm continues to falter, the status quo requires increasing attention. Although you should be focused on future business, you are trapped by current business.

You may also be plagued by the thought, and historical reality, that most businesses fail to transition from old paradigms to new (Rouse, 1996). New companies eventually and almost inevitably replace old companies. However, this is not easy. The vast majority of those striving to be the new players fail, but a few succeed, and most of the older players disappear.

As evidence of this, General Electric is the only current member of the Dow Jones Industrial Average (DJIA) that was a member in 1900. The rest of the major companies that were members have either disappeared or shrunk to whispers of their former prominence. "Newcomers" like Intel, Microsoft, Home Depot, and Wal-Mart have replaced the many railroads and commodity materials companies that formerly dominated the DJIA.

The overall process of creative destruction works quite well for the economy as a whole. It is not, however, quite so appealing to individual companies. Most companies invest enormous sums in attempts to survive and prosper, only to eventually disappear. However, some large, established companies are able to reinvent themselves and find new growth paths (Collins and Porras, 1994). Thus, the situation is not hopeless, but it does require well-founded strategic thinking and persistent effort to address the challenge of change successfully.

NATURE OF CHANGE

What aspects of change are difficult and why are they difficult? To answer these questions, it is useful to begin by considering several new business paradigms that companies have tried to adopt in recent years. The successes and failures of these attempts provide important insights into underlying difficulties.

Adopting New Paradigms

In the 1980s, large numbers of companies embraced and tried to adopt total quality management (Deming, 1986). There were many very visible successes such as Motorola's Six Sigma initiative. However, many companies struggled with this process-oriented approach. Furthermore, many companies were very slow in adopting the quality philosophy and practices.

Cole (1998) presents a case study of the quality movement and companies' decisions in this area. This behavioral, social, and organizational analysis of how change occurs—and does not occur—concludes that "The efficacy of evidence as a factor in changing management's working assumptions is much overrated." This observation fits quite well with the decision-making disabilities discussed in Chapter 4.

Cole's analysis focused on the extent to which managers are trapped by past experiences and successes. Consequently, many managers did not see the quality philosophy as significantly different from what they have always espoused, for example, "Zero Defects!" This misperception resulted in managers either doing nothing different or making insufficient investments to seriously adopt quality practices.

Total quality management was replaced, in the 1990s, as the reigning business panacea by business process reengineering (Hammer and Champy,

1993), causing a short-lived boom in the business card industry as thousands of consultants quickly relabeled their competencies. Rather than just adding measurement systems to processes and thereby attempting to continually improve them, reengineering advocated rethinking all processes.

Many companies benefited from this rethinking, often thinning their ranks significantly and swelling profits as a result. However, many more companies spent large sums on consultants and internal personnel who were tasked to reengineer the whole organization, with the primary results being confusion and disenchantment rather than significant business improvements (Davenport, 1995). They found that "cleaning the slate" was much easier than designing new processes and enabling employees to operate these processes with the promised efficiencies.

Lean thinking (Womack and Jones, 1996) is arguably an offshoot of the quality movement, perhaps seasoned a bit by reengineering. The primary emphasis of this concept is on identifying and eliminating waste; advocates of this approach have focused on manufacturing industries such as automobiles and airplanes. Lean thinking has resulted in substantial savings. However, as Kessler (1999) articulates, adopting this approach is a substantial undertaking that requires intense focus on value and how processes contribute—or do not contribute—to a company's value streams.

Dalton (1999) provides a similar assessment of open book management. This approach involves sharing detailed financial information with all employees and showing them how their work affects the numbers in financial statements, thereby getting them to improve their work to improve the numbers. She notes that, more than 15 years after the debut of this concept, only about 1% of companies fully embrace this idea.

Skeptical managers, apathetic employees, and costly training are hurdles that must be overcome for the idea to be embraced. For open book management to work, Dalton argues that companies need to educate employees about the meaning of the numbers and, most importantly, make them responsible for these numbers by linking them to their individual compensation. However, as with many good ideas, these concepts cannot simply be purchased and installed—much more investment is needed for success.

The examples of total quality management, business process reengineering, lean thinking, and open book management serve to emphasize three points:

- It can be quite difficult for management to understand the need for and value of new approaches.
- Once a new approach is embraced, it can be very difficult to manage expectations due to natural desires for panaceas.

- The levels of investment needed to fully succeed with new approaches are often substantially underestimated.

Thus, change can be difficult to initiate and, once initiated, often results in inflated expectations and is usually thought to be much easier than the actual experience. In the next section, we explore the underlying behavioral and organizational sources of these difficulties.

Underlying Difficulties

Day (1999) addresses the difficulties of creating market-driven organizations. He discusses the typical triggers of change processes, including market disruption, erosion of market alignment, strategic necessity, and intolerable opportunity costs. Note that all of these triggers are essentially external, involving either problems with existing market relationships or possible new market relationships. Thus, companies seldom decide to change without strong market signals of the necessity and/or desirability of change.

Day also considers persistent obstacles to change management success. These obstacles include absence of leadership, initiative burnout, stifling cultures, management turmoil, lack of urgency, and poor implementation. Note that these obstacles are almost totally internally determined. Thus, although change is usually demanded by the environment, the willingness and ability to change are determined by internal factors and forces.

Recognizing these underlying dynamics does not necessarily make change easier. Pfeffer and Sutton (1999) address the issue of why so much education and training, management consulting, organizational research, and so many books and articles produce so few changes in actual management practice. They characterize this phenomenon as a knowing-doing gap.

This gap is of fundamental importance to the whole notion of knowledge management, which is discussed in Chapter 7. Within the context of this chapter, this gap relates to the fact that inabilities to manage change effectively are only weakly related, at most, to lack of knowledge of best practices in change management. The hindrances relate more to inabilities to implement these practices due to underlying behavioral and social causes.

In *Don't Jump to Solutions* (Rouse, 1998), I discuss at length common individual and organizational delusions that hinder change. These persistent false beliefs, shown in Figure 5.1, keep managers from recognizing their true situations and dealing with them appropriately. Consequently, as Day (1999) indicates, it often requires major crises for the undermining effects of delusions to be circumvented.

Delusions 1–3 relate to incorrect, commonly held assumptions. Well-established, formerly successful enterprises are particularly prone to these de-

1. We Have a Great Plan
2. We Are Number One
3. We Own the Market
4. We Have Already Changed
5. We Know the Right Way
6. We Just Need One Big Win
7. We Have Consensus
8. We Have to Make the Numbers
9. We Have the Ducks Lined Up
10. We Have the Necessary Processes
11. We Just Have to Execute
12. We Found It Was Easy
13. We Succeeded as We Planned

Figure 5.1. Delusions that undermine abilities to change

lusions. They lead to, for example, putting Cadillac badges on Chevrolets and expecting customers to willingly pay many thousands of dollars for the honor of driving such cars.

Delusions 4–8 concern choices of goals. De facto, and usually unstated, goals often become preservation of the status quo and associated near-term objectives. Stated goals, in contrast, may herald change, new paradigms, and so forth. However, the ways that people spend their time will reflect what really matters.

Delusions 9–11 are associated with implementation of plans. New plans are often greeted with great fanfares. The fact is, however, that it is much easier to devise compelling plans than it is to implement them successfully. The inability to implement plans is a hallmark of many former CEOs (Charan and Colvin, 1999).

Delusions 12–13 relate to the reality of how plans succeed—seldom according to plan! Intense focus on plans succeeding exactly as originally devised is a sure recipe for missing opportunities to succeed in ways that far surpass original aspirations. These delusions can lead to excellent implementation of no longer valuable plans.

The above 13 delusions can completely undermine change efforts in particular and plans in general. At the very least, essential time is wasted as organizations wait for the evidence to become overwhelming before they decide to act. We return to the discussion of delusions later in this chapter when methods and tools for supporting change strategies are considered.

The above delusions provide a bit deeper explanation of the difficulties underlying change. To move deeper yet, we need to consider why these delusions emerge and persist. The needs-beliefs-perceptions model (Rouse, 1993), shown in Figure 5.2, provides useful insights into the sources of the delusions.

People's perceptions are usually viewed as being primarily influenced by their knowledge and information presented to them. With this view, knowledge gained via education and experience combines with the information available to yield perceptions. This perspective can lead you to explain others' misperceptions by their lack of understanding and requisite information. However, as indicated in Figure 5.2, misperceptions are likely to have other causes.

People's needs and beliefs affect what knowledge is gained, what facts are sought, and how both are interpreted. Thus, for example, people may need to feel that their competencies are important and valued. This leads them to believe that these competencies are critical elements of the company's competitive position. This prompts them to seek confirming information and perceive that the resulting "data" support their beliefs. Consequently, they advocate decisions to continue investments in competencies linked to fading markets.

Relationships among needs, beliefs, and perceptions can explain much of the difficulties associated with change. People believe that reigning paradigms are still valid and vital because they need to feel that they are still integral to the enterprise's future. They also may need to feel that their future is secure. Put simply, regardless of the validity of needs to change, this possibility may be significantly deficient relative to meeting people's needs. Consequently, they will believe that change is ill-advised and advocate sticking to the knitting.

Beyond providing a deeper explanation for resistance to change, the needs-beliefs-perceptions model also provides clear approaches to catalyzing

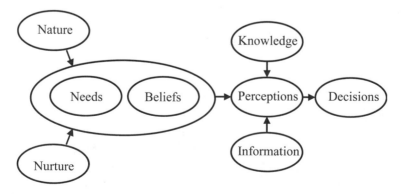

Figure 5.2. Needs-beliefs-perceptions model

change. These approaches focus on what information is provided to people, as well as how they are nurtured in the process of change. These catalysts are considered later in this chapter in the discussion of change strategies.

CHALLENGE OF CHANGE

Beyond the above underlying difficulties of change—which are inherent to much of life—this challenge is particularly problematic for companies because it concerns competing creatively while also maintaining continuity. Specifically, responding to changing market opportunities and threats often requires creative and possibly disruptive changes. However, successfully instituting these changes requires some degree of continuity to take advantage of the company you have in order to become the company you aspire to be. Striking a balance between these forces involves changing the organization to enhance competitive advantages and also building on existing competencies and inclinations. At one extreme, you can create chaos; at the other, you can be stymied by inertia (Rouse, 1999b).

A good example of where this challenge is likely to emerge in full force involves repositioning a company to address both current markets (e.g., defense electronics) and new markets (e.g., industrial electronics). This requires maintaining existing infrastructure and processes to satisfy current customers—and keep the cash flowing—while also creating new infrastructure and processes to enable the satisfaction of new customers. This becomes particularly problematic when the two sets of infrastructure and processes are incompatible. Worse yet are situations in which the same personnel have to work for both types of customers.

A related but somewhat less extreme example is reengineering processes to create a lean, agile organization. It is difficult to simultaneously foster new skills, retain critical existing skills, and discard obsolete existing skills. This is especially true when people with the soon-to-be obsolete skills are still needed to serve customers who, in the near term at least, will continue to provide significant cash flow. In situations like this, people almost always become very confused and uncertain as this process proceeds.

Another difficult aspect of the challenge of change is the need to engender and reward new competencies while old competencies continue to command center stage. For example, an engineering-oriented company that needs to become substantially more market oriented may have members of the engineering function finding it difficult to share the limelight. This is particularly problematic when most of senior management is steeped in the old competencies, with many long-standing loyalties to functional groups where these competencies are housed.

Yet another difficulty concerns incentives and rewards (Flannery, Hofrichter, and Platten, 1996; Weiss and Hartle, 1997). For substantial changes to have a chance of succeeding, it is often necessary to significantly modify the incentive and reward system. For example, it may be important to shift to a performance-based bonus system with base compensation that increases very slowly, if at all. If this is significantly different from the existing incentive and reward system, people may have difficulty adjusting, for instance, to the fact that a significant portion of their compensation is at risk.

Thus, change is a challenge in part because of inherent underlying behavioral and social difficulties associated with changes and in part because of the ways that changes have to be instituted in companies. The need to maintain both the old and the new simultaneously creates numerous problems beyond people's inherent reluctance to change.

Virtual Organizations

Thus far, we have focused on changes driven by market opportunities and threats. Other forces can also cause change. The best example in current times is the emergence of virtual organizations. Such organizations are envisioned as providing highly effective and efficient means for knowledge work and knowledge-based enterprises. Although the challenge of knowledge is considered in Chapter 7, it is important to consider at this point the challenges posed by the changes associated with virtual organizations.

The economic and social forces being experienced in many domains have caused reconsideration of the nature of organizations. This was initially prompted by needs to reduce costs by becoming leaner. More recently, it has become apparent that traditional organizational models are poor matches to emerging new ways of doing business. Furthermore, increased connectivity has enabled new organizational models.

There are three keys to prospering in an information-rich environment: speed, flexibility, and discretion. Speed means understanding a situation (e.g., a market opportunity), formulating a plan for pursuing this opportunity (e.g., a joint venture for a new product), and executing this plan (e.g., product available in stores), in this case all within a few weeks at most. The need for flexibility is obvious; otherwise, there would not be speed. However, flexibility is also crucial for reconfiguring and redesigning organizations and consequently reallocating resources. Functional walls must be quite portable, if they exist at all.

Discretion is what transforms flexibility into speed. Distributed organizations must be free to act. Although they may have to play by the rules of the game—at least the rules of the moment—they need to be able to avoid waiting for permission to proceed. Similarly, they need to be able to pull the plug when things are not working. In this way, resources are deployed quickly and results are monitored just as quickly. Resource investments that are not paying off in the expected time frame are quickly redeployed.

Loosely Structured Organizations

Speed, flexibility, and discretion are almost completely incompatible with traditional command and control hierarchies. The premium placed on these characteristics requires much more loosely structured organizations. In the past, structures in terms of organizations, jobs, and tasks determined human behaviors. Success was only possible by conforming to structural mandates.

Increasingly, however, we can see that behaviors now create structure. Organizational structures emerge from the behaviors that humans exhibit in response to opportunities, threats, and so forth. Emergent, and nondesigned, properties of organizations are becoming predominant. Managing emergent rather than designed properties involves considerable changes in how one thinks about the role of management.

The driving force in loosely structured organizations is economic gain. As indicated in earlier discussions, reengineering has been the executives' management tool of choice for several years, resulting in substantial cost cutting and impressive bottom lines. However, this tool is rapidly becoming less dominant. Inefficient loosely structured organizations are eliminated, not reengineered.

The focus, in contrast, is on top lines and value added. For bottom-line profits to grow continually, top-line revenues have to grow steadily. This requires providing value to customers, not just low cost. Fast and flexible distributed, collaborative organizations are formed to exploit economic, political, or military opportunities for the mutual gain of the collaborators. The goal is to create value and profits, monetary and otherwise, not cut costs.

Emergence of Virtual Organizations

The above considerations have fostered the emergence of "virtual organizations," which, as defined by the International Association of Virtual Organizations (IAVO), include "Any business, club, society, institution, governing body, or similar entity whose existence is dependent—either partially or entirely—on the emerging telecommunications technologies associated with the Internet, cable systems, phone systems, and others." (IAVO, 1999).

Virtual organizations may exist within or across traditional organizational boundaries. More importantly, enabled by computer and communications technologies, virtual organizations have the following characteristics (Voss, 1996):

- They have a shared vision and goal and/or a common protocol of cooperation.
- They cluster activities around their core competencies.
- They work jointly in teams of core-competence groups to implement their activities in one holistic approach throughout the value chain.
- They process and distribute information in real time throughout the entire network, which allows them to make decisions and coordinate actions quickly.
- They tend to delegate from the bottom up whenever economies of scale can be achieved, new conditions arise, or a specific competence is required for serving the needs of the whole group.

Other commentators associate virtual organizations with

- agility—dynamic assembly of core competencies from different corporations to react to a fast-changing marketplace that demands excellence and very flexible capabilities (Martin, 1996);
- integration—stitching together a business with partners that are treated as if they are inside the company (Magretta, 1998);
- focus—creating virtual organizations requires weakening the weaknesses of existing organizations and strengthening the strengths (Reinermann, 1996); and
- strategy—balancing customer interaction (virtual encounter), asset configuration (virtual sourcing), and knowledge leverage (virtual expertise) (Venkatraman and Henderson, 1998).

All of these characterizations depict loosely structured organizations as described earlier, potentially with little resemblance to traditional organizations. Designing and managing these new types of organizations present numerous challenges.

Benefits of Virtual Organizations

An immediate question, however, concerns why one would want to create a virtual organization. What are the benefits of virtual organizations? Broadly speaking, the benefits include

- enabling collaborative teamwork across organizational and geographic boundaries—work can be done in the home, a client's office, or on the road;
- providing ultimate flexibility and adaptability—they can provide anything, anytime, anywhere, anyhow;
- allowing companies to remain competitive with others and be able to respond to market changes quickly;
- giving companies an edge in hiring and keeping talented, highly motivated employees; and
- possibly leading to substantial cost reductions—many have reported lower fixed costs, higher productivity, and greater employee and customer satisfaction.

More specifically, most studies of the movement to virtual organizations report reduced costs and enhanced productivity as the initial drivers (Apgar, 1998; Davenport and Pearlson, 1998). Increased customer satisfaction, closer teamwork, greater flexibility, and retention of valued employees are also noted as motivations. It is nevertheless clear that reduced costs of real estate and infrastructure have thus far been the primary metrics in many decisions to "go virtual."

Reflecting on the benefits of virtual real estate, I have suggested that status symbols are now measured in megahertz and gigabytes, not square feet and horsepower (Rouse, 1997). Monies that were budgeted for investments in more space and higher-quality amenities might be better invested in enhancing people's virtual offices. There is likely to be much more payoff from putting computers and communications in people's hands rather than square feet beneath their feet.

Managing Virtual Organizations

The notion of a virtual organization has much intuitive appeal. However, realizing the benefits of this concept depends on adopting rather different approaches to management. These new approaches involve

- setting clear goals from the outset and agreeing on ways to monitor progress and measure performance,
- having open and spontaneous communication,
- having a significant level of trust,
- having self-disciplined employees who are capable of making decisions and judgment calls based on specific situations,

- outsourcing activities that are considered noncore or nonstrategic, and
- providing support (e.g., intranets and groupware) to facilitate communication and information sharing.

To assist in assessing the extent to which an organization has these characteristics, or is willing to adopt them, Apgar (1998) suggests several key questions:

- Are you committed to new ways of operating?
- Is your organization informational rather than industrial?
- Do you have an open culture and proactive managers?
- Can you establish clear lines between staff, functions, and time?
- Are you prepared for some pushback?
- Can you overcome external barriers?
- Will you invest in necessary tools, training, and techniques?

Davenport and Pearlson (1998) suggest several practices that will support moving to a virtual organizational design. With regard to managing people, they suggest that virtual organizations should assess virtual worker management and training programs to improve skills, provide training on personal work strategies in a virtual work environment, and foster dialogue and education on how to deal with changed family relationships. Information management within virtual organizations can be enhanced by instituting new information flows to replace those that are lost when workers leave offices and no longer have physical contact, ensuring that workers understand the strengths and weaknesses of various technologies for communicating in specific circumstances and educating workers on how to be more effective providers and consumers of information.

Many managers report that one of the most difficult aspects of adopting these recommended management practices concerns separating employees' time from their outcomes. Most organizations are used to paying suppliers for deliverables rather than time. However, paying employees for their time is very ingrained. Linking payment solely to outcomes presents several difficulties.

First and foremost, it requires that managers clearly specify the outcomes they want. If employees are only paid for outcomes, they are quite right to demand clear statements of the nature of the outcomes. Managers often note that such demands have led them to realize that, in the past, they may not have known what they wanted until they saw it.

However, if effort (or time) is not the metric that drives payment, then employees do not want to waste *their* time creating outcomes that will not be valued. This places substantial pressure on managers to formulate and clearly articulate goals, plans, and intermediate outcomes needed. Often, this pressure on managers is greater than the subsequent pressure on employees to deliver.

The obvious implication of this situation is to treat employees like suppliers. As reasonable as this sounds, what if employees can produce desired outcomes in much less than full time? Many managers say that they have difficulty accepting this. Worse yet, what if employees do not produce desired outcomes? Typically, managers will wonder if employees have really spent the time needed for success. Although they could penalize or dismiss employees who do not deliver, many managers have difficulty approaching this situation in such a manner.

Supporting Virtual Organizations
The support of virtual organizations includes assisting the transition to virtual operations as well as helping with ongoing activities. Voss (1996) suggests four key elements of supporting transitions:

- identifying and forming a shared understanding of the actual and target core competencies to trigger learning and people development;
- providing an infrastructure that supports knowledge sharing, communicating, and work on joint projects by dispersed teams;
- monitoring and measuring not only the "hard" facts of business performance but also the "soft" facts that indicate qualitative improvements of services and people; and
- shifting from a time-based pay system to rewarding and compensating individual and team improvement and performance by a variety of means, including financial ownership of the entity

It is clear from this guidance that becoming virtual is best not pursued in an ad hoc manner. Sustained success involves much more than providing people with laptops and modems and letting them work from home. From this perspective, technology investments may be a much smaller portion of the overall investments needed than previously imagined.

With regard to supporting teams with remote members, Davenport and Pearlson (1998) suggest that you encourage and train coaches rather than supervisors. They also argue for building processes to handle conflict resolution among remote workers. They further suggest providing explicit training on the use and benefits of groupware tools, including setting reasonable expectations for the impacts of these tools. The roles of such tools are discussed in more detail in Chapter 9, which summarizes best practices.

Summary

Virtual organizations represent the archetypal loosely structured organization. Although these types of organizations are becoming increasingly prevalent, our understanding of how to manage them is, as yet, rudimentary. This is due to the fundamental nature of loosely structured organizations, which precludes managing them in traditional ways. "Going virtual," therefore, has the potential for causing as much disruption as changing customers and competencies, as discussed earlier in this chapter.

CHANGE STRATEGIES

The general difficulties of change and the specific challenges for companies and other enterprises might suggest pessimism relative to any particular organization achieving substantial change. However, there are numerous success stories of change. Collins and Porras in *Built to Last* (1994) spotlight 18 visionary companies that have continually reinvented themselves over many decades; each is compared with a baseline company in the same market with similar longevity but not similar results. Slywotsky and Morrison in *The Profit Zone* (1997) discuss numerous examples of how companies have successfully dealt with change of market relationships and the nature of value provided. Thus, change, although it is a tremendous challenge, is possible.

It is important at the outset to recognize the different perspectives with which change can be addressed. Beer and Nohria (2000) contrast the continuum of perspectives as bounded by two differing theories of change:

- *Theory E* is based on economic value, with shareholder value being the only measure of success. Change driven by this theory usually involves major use of economic incentives, drastic layoffs, downsizing, and restructuring.

- *Theory O* is based on organizational capability, with organizational learning being the measure of success. Change driven by this theory focuses on building the organizational culture in terms of employees' behaviors, attitudes, capabilities, and commitment.

Where one chooses to be on the continuum between these two theories substantially influences how the elements of change strategies are pursued. In particular, the mixture of top-down and bottom-up initiatives changes substantially as one moves along this continuum. Beer and Nohria argue that the success of change is related to how one deals with the tension between these two perspectives and strikes an appropriate balance.

Organizational Baselines

An important starting point is understanding your current organization in terms of how it functions, makes decisions, and provides value to customers and other stakeholders. The organizational chart is often not much help here, as Mintzberg and Van der Heyden (1999) illustrate with their "organigraphs." They argue that seeing the organization the way it really works enables managers to determine how they can best serve the organization.

When developing descriptions for how business is captured, orders are processed, products are developed and manufactured, services are provided, and so on, you can see how information flows through the organization, where decisions are made, and how resources are consumed. In terms of business process reengineering or lean thinking, such process mapping also helps to identify waste and activities that should be eliminated.

However, efficiency is not the primary issue at this point. Instead, the concerns are focused on how the organization provides value, how and where information influences both the definition and provision of value, who makes critical decisions (ranging from operational to strategic), and how resources are allocated. It is also important to understand how the organization learns. This includes mechanisms for single-loop learning, whereby current ways of doing things are refined, but also mechanisms for double-loop learning, which enables redefinition of value and the processes whereby it is created and delivered (Argyris and Schon, 1978).

This base lining should consider possible organizational learning disabilities, such as those identified by Senge (1990):

- tendencies for people to see themselves in terms of their positions rather than their aptitudes, abilities, and skills;
- tendencies to blame the "enemy out there" as the source of problems—this relates to the discussion of attribution errors in Chapter 4;
- tendencies to fixate on events rather than ongoing trends that eventually lead to events;
- delusions of learning from experience, when consequences often cannot be related to decisions made years ago; and
- delusions that the management team is open to dealing with negative information and possibilities of conflict.

It is easy to see how these types of disabilities can lead to great difficulty accepting needs to change and implementing change. How these types of impediments can be identified and potentially remediated is discussed later.

Another important aspect of assessing organizational baselines concerns identifying organizational belief systems. The 10-step assessment methodology in *Catalysts for Change* (Rouse, 1993) can be used for creating an organization-specific needs-beliefs-perceptions model, which is depicted in Figure 5.2. In the next section, we consider how this model can be used to support organizational design.

Organizational baselines can provide essential foundations for change strategies. The process of making such baselines very explicit can help to overcome the types of organizational delusions discussed earlier. Otherwise, it is very common for organizations to assume, at least implicitly, that either fundamental change is unnecessary or that it has already been accomplished.

Organizational Design

Central issues in organizational design have tended to focus on structural alternatives such as functional hierarchies, product line organizations with functional departments, or matrix organizations. Design of the organizational chart often becomes the dominant task, and "who reports to who" becomes the dominant discussion. Of course, as virtual organizations become increasingly attractive alternatives, the whole notion of "reports" has to be reconsidered as discussed earlier.

An important legacy of the era of business processing reengineering (BPR) is the idea of business processes—coherent sets of interdependent activities that provide value to stakeholders. Processes do not necessarily align with traditional organizational structures. For example, the pricing process for systems such as aircraft or automobiles cuts across functional areas such as finance, marketing and sales, engineering, manufacturing, and so forth. This process should also cut across product lines so as to ensure a consistent process across the company and avoid unnecessary redundancies.

A particularly effective change strategy is to focus the organization on processes rather than traditional structural issues. Although learning disabilities and organizational delusions can make this shift of focus difficult, persistence can eventually result in the organization thinking about itself quite differently. Later in this chapter, we discuss a tool, *ProcessEdge*, that can be used to support becoming process oriented.

I hasten to note that a focus on processes carries with it, unfortunately, considerable baggage. BPR was often a primary means of downsizing or, more euphemistically, rightsizing organizations. Many people view process mapping as a first step toward a raft of pink slips. This perception is exacerbated by the fact that many companies undertook BPR to pull themselves out of crises in which diminishing profits were undermining stock market valuations.

A good way to avoid this perception is to *1*) proceed while the company is healthy if possible and *2*) use cross-functional teams of employees, perhaps assisted by experts, to map business processes. Such teams can also help identify and circumvent organizational delusions, which seem to be most rampant when one discipline and/or one level of management dominates discussions (Rouse, 1998). Cross-functionality is also important because, as noted earlier, most business processes cut across functions.

It is also important to give priority to redesigning incentive and reward systems. When an organization changes its directions and priorities, rarely is its current incentive and reward systems well matched with the new future. Nevertheless, most organizations delay consideration of incentives and rewards until they get everything else worked out. As a consequence, employees still march to old drummers. Change can be facilitated by focusing on incentives and rewards earlier rather than later.

Understanding and constructively changing belief systems within an organization is also an important aspect of organizational design. As discussed earlier, individual and organizational needs and beliefs have dominant effects on perceptions of the benefits and costs of change. Explicit portrayals of relationships among needs, beliefs, and perceptions can often resolve previous surface conflicts.

The 10-step methodology for developing needs-beliefs-perceptions models involves two principles that can be central elements of change strategies (Rouse, 1993):

- Understanding the relationships among needs, beliefs, and perceptions can be used to affect information provided to people. The central notion is to modify information content to satisfy needs without conflicting with beliefs. This presumes that needs and beliefs can be taken as givens, because it is usually very difficult to change needs and beliefs solely with information.

- Understanding the relationships among needs, beliefs, and perceptions can also be used to affect the way people are nurtured, which eventually may lead to modifications of their needs, beliefs, and perceptions. This might be accomplished via education, training, or changes of work situations that lead to satisfaction of basic needs, emphasis on higher-level needs, and eventual adoption of new beliefs.

These principles may seem rather abstract. However, the 10 case studies presented in *Catalysts for Change* (Rouse, 1993) show quite specifically how these principles can enable important elements of change strategies. For example, recognizing that the primacy of one discipline, for example, engineering, will be diminished by changing to a market-driven strategy can prompt creation of programs and opportunities for members of this discipline so that they believe that they are still central to the company's future but also accept the fact that they will have to share center stage with, for instance, marketing and finance.

Needs and beliefs, incentives and rewards, and teams may seem like secondary issues compared with who reports to who on the organizational chart. However, dealing with these issues well is central to formulating and implementing change strategies successfully. In contrast, the value of the organization chart may primarily be in terms of how needs and beliefs are supported for those whose names and pictures appear on this chart. Of course, this is also very important because leaders play central roles in the success of change strategies.

Role of Leadership

All commentators on organizational change agree that leadership plays a central role in success. In my experience, as discussed in Chapter 8 (on the challenge of time), sustained commitment by top management is key to almost every challenge of strategic management. Without committed leadership, energies for change dissipate and the status quo dominates. Another possibility is change becomes destructive, undermining the organization and perhaps even threatening its existence.

Collins and Porras in *Built to Last* (1994) provide what they call lessons of alignment for CEOs, managers, and entrepreneurs. They argue that a primary role of leaders is to align the organization with desired changes by

- painting the whole picture(how everything fits together),
- sweating the small stuff (details are how things get done),
- clustering, rather than shot gunning (coherency is important),
- swimming in your own current, even if it is against the tide (walk the walk),
- obliterating misalignments (consistency is essential), and
- keeping universal requirements while inventing new methods.

More recently, Collins (1999) discusses the notion of catalytic mechanisms for enabling or fostering change. He suggests such mechanisms have several common characteristics:

- produces desired results in unpredictable ways,
- distributes power for the benefit of the overall system, often to the great discomfort of those who traditionally hold power,
- has a sharp set of teeth,
- attracts the right people and ejects viruses, and
- produces an ongoing effect.

Note how both the earlier book and more recent article emphasize the role of leadership beyond coaching, mentoring, and cheerleading. Leaders set carefully thought-out and well-articulated standards and then ensure that the organization operates in accordance with these standards. Deviants are "obliterated" or "ejected." This is a far cry from an "anything goes as long as you meet your numbers" mentality. This role of leadership, the authors assert, is key to building companies that achieve sustained growth decade after decade.

Day (1999) discusses how to overcome obstacles to becoming market driven, which I have found is the most common form of change sought by companies. His six overlapping stages of change emphasize the role of leadership:

- demonstrating leadership commitment,
- understanding the need for change,
- shaping the vision,
- mobilizing commitment at all levels,
- aligning structures, systems, and incentives, and
- reinforcing the change.

This guidance is quite consistent with that of Collins and Porras. Indeed, there appears to be little disagreement among various pundits on the roles of leaders in achieving change. This immediately begs the question of why change initiatives are not more often successful.

Pfeffer and Sutton (1999) discuss this phenomenon in terms of a knowing-doing gap. As noted earlier, this gap has been the downfall of numerous high-profile top managers (Charan and Colvin, 1999). Bridging this gap, they argue, involves transforming knowledge of what needs to change into implementable programs of action. Their guidelines for action include

- why before how (philosophy is important),
- knowing comes from doing and teaching others how,
- action counts more than elegant plans and concepts,

- there is no doing without mistakes (what is the company's response?),
- fear fosters knowing-doing gaps, so drive out fear,
- beware of false analogies (fight the competition, not each other),
- measure what matters and what can help turn knowledge into action, and
- what leaders do, how they spend their time and how they allocate resources, matters.

Leaders do not only have to set the course. Grand strategy, no matter how compelling, is not enough. Leaders also have to ensure that there are programs of action that appropriately reflect the driving strategies. Leaders also have to ensure that these programs of action are implemented. Although command and control leadership is no longer the norm, laissez faire leadership is not the alternative. Sustained commitment and involvement are the keys. We return to this discussion in Chapter 8, which discusses the challenge of time and its relationship to leadership.

Change Strategies For Complex Systems

In Chapter 1, we discussed the nature of complex systems and how such systems change the ways in which strategies should be formulated and implemented. Due to the emergent nature of complex systems and the fact that no one entity is really "in charge," we concluded this discussion by characterizing management's strategic tasks as

- defining rules such as goals of the enterprise and boundaries within which these goals should be achieved; and
- allocating resources to proposals for succeeding within these rules, monitoring ongoing success, and reallocating resources as needed;

The rules are necessary so that people stay focused on strategic organizational goals and behave consistently with organizational values—in other words, pursuing the right things in the right ways. Otherwise, component organizations tend to "suboptimize" and focus solely on what's good for them. As straightforward as this sounds, many managers find it quite difficult to specify goals and boundaries rather than behaviors.

The challenge of change in complex systems raises additional strategy issues. Such systems cannot be unilaterally redesigned. Furthermore, the activities within such systems cannot be controlled or perhaps even monitored. Typically, one has only purview of inputs (resources) and outputs (results). Different outputs can be requested and then decisions made regarding the acceptability of different input requirements. Also, one can consider alternative participants in the overall organizational system.

Managers are quite used to this type of thinking when considering alternative suppliers of components of their widgets, for example. Requirements are usually quite concrete, and price, quality, and schedule are the primary decision attributes. However, when the alternatives involve suppliers of core competencies to the overall endeavor, defining rules and boundaries becomes more subtle. Best practices in this area have yet to be formulated, other than in terms of broad generalizations. However, the difficulties here are commonly acknowledged. Thus, at the very least, managers should be aware that "business as usual" practices are unlikely to be sufficient for accomplishing desires changes.

Summary

Formulation of successful change strategies involves a range of organizational design issues, the most important of which are process oriented rather than structural. Leadership by top management plays a central role in all aspects of successful change. Both organizational design and leadership become more complicated and subtle when pursued in the context of complex systems. There is substantial consensus on these issues among thought leaders in this area; nevertheless, successful change remains quite difficult.

SUPPORTING CHANGE STRATEGIES

There are a variety of tools available for supporting assessment, formulation, and implementation of the types of change strategies just discussed. In this section, we consider three tools—one for process modeling, another for organizational assessment, and one for addressing the delusions discussed earlier.

ProcessEdge

ProcessEdge is a computer-based tool for supporting the planning and measurement associated with design and evaluation of organizational processes (Madni, 2000; Intelligent Systems Technology, 2000). The underlying elements of this tool include an enterprise ontology (i.e., hierarchy of enterprise concepts and relationships among concepts), an enterprise process lifecycle model, and embedded business rules. *ProcessEdge* provides support for process definition, verification, visualization, analysis, and composition, as well as various utilities for comparing, importing, and exporting process designs.

The value of this type of tool is the ease with which processes can be depicted, evaluated, manipulated, and presented. This enables effective movement toward process-oriented thinking and away from traditional functional thinking. Because of embedded knowledge and intelligence in this type of tool, one can learn and become productive much more quickly than if one started by studying textbooks. Such computer-based tools also inherently support group use via large-screen projected displays.

TOP Modeler

TOP Modeler (Technology, Organization, and People Modeler) is a knowledge-based tool for assessing change requirements (gaps) based on knowledge compiled via an extensive consensus-building process that involved experts from several leading firms (Majchrzak and Gasser, 2000; TOP Integration, 2000). The nature of this knowledge base is such that organizations are described in terms of 14 feature sets:

- business objectives,
- process variances,
- organizational values,
- skills,
- reporting structure,
- norms,
- general technology,
- performance measures and rewards,
- information resources,
- production process,
- empowerment,
- employee values, and
- customer involvement.

Users of *TOP Modeler* describe their company's business strategy by choosing among given choices for

- business objectives,
- process variance control strategies, and
- organizational values.

They then describe their "as-is" organization in terms of the 11 other feature sets. The tool then compares "as-is" to best practices, identifying gaps that need to be addressed. The user is then supported in deciding which gaps to close first.

Majchrzak and Gasser (2000) present a series of case examples of use of *TOP Modeler* and summarize an extensive evaluation of the predictive validity of this tool. This type of evaluation effort is quite unusual, primarily because it is so difficult and labor intensive to do. Furthermore, in my experience, managers will never just accept what tools tell them, regardless of the validity "pedigrees" of the tools. Nevertheless, the impressive studies reported do certainly increase confidence in this particular tool.

Strategic Thinking

The abilities to both recognize needs to change and implement change strategies are often hindered by the organizational delusions discussed earlier in this chapter. The electronic version of *Don't Jump to Solutions* (Rouse, 1998) available in *Strategic Thinking* (Rouse, 1999a) provides a means for assessing the risks of these delusions. Use of this tool involves answering 70 key questions about your organization and its relationships with markets or, in general, constituencies. Figure 5.3 shows the screen that presents the assessments based on answers to the key questions.

Note that "just having to execute"—delusion number 11—is portrayed as having the greatest risk, followed closely by "having to make the numbers"— delusion number 8. The subset of the 70 questions related to delusion number 11 include

- How frequently does the "ball get dropped" in your organization?
- Do you have the people and financial resources to execute your plans successfully?
- Do near-term problems and opportunities frequently preempt long-term plans and undermine progress?
- Who are the champions for your organization's long-term plans, and are they focused on executing these plans?
- Have you done the hard work of answering the who, how, what, when, and why questions of plan execution?

Choices among standardized answers to these questions resulted in the risk assessment shown in Figure 5.3.

Management teams using this tool will typically quickly answer all 70 questions or perhaps only the questions related to the few delusions of interest. They then view the assessments, as shown in Figure 5.3. For high-risk delu-

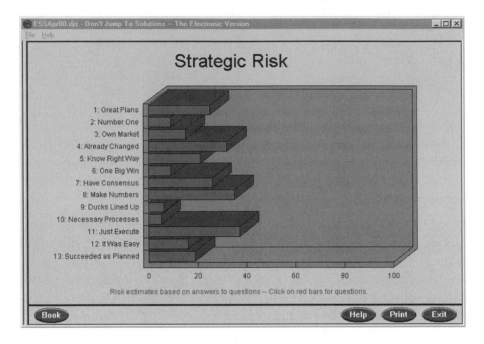

Figure 5.3. Risks of organizational delusions

sions, they may revisit the questions to see if they are still comfortable with their answers.

Attention will then shift to what they can do about their apparent delusions. One source of help is a set of principles associated with each delusion. For delusion number 11—"Just Having to Execute"—these principles are

- sustained and committed execution of plans can be very difficult to achieve;
- a common problem is overcommitment, which results in a lack of people and financial resources for execution;
- individual and organizational priorities dominated by near-term issues often preempt execution;
- lack of individual and organizational commitments to plans often hinders execution;
- without a champion, someone committed to a plan's success, plans almost always wither;
- dealing, in detail, with the who, how, what, when, and why questions of plan execution is the key to avoiding the delusion of "just" having to execute; and

- hard work is the only viable means of successfully linking plans to execution

To explore these principles in more depth, a link to a hypertext version of *Don't Jump to Solutions* is provided that illustrates delusions, explains principles, and provides examples of their implementation. Management teams might also, for example, link to the electronic version of the book via the types of examples of interest (e.g., computer industry) rather than by the delusions.

This assessment tool enables management teams to have discussions they might otherwise find difficult. The tool, with its outputs projected on large-screen displays, externalizes potentially threatening issues for the group to address as a team. Rather than argue with each other, they in effect argue with the tool. In the process, many perceptions emerge to justify answers to questions and provide interpretations of principles. Beyond providing opportunities to calibrate perceptions, this process often exposes underlying needs and beliefs that can be understood and addressed with the strategies discussed earlier.

CONCLUSIONS

Needs for change are inevitable. The central challenge involves whether or not organizations can adequately respond to these needs. Although there are numerous long-running success stories, change is inherently very difficult and most organizations fail to meet this challenge.

In this chapter, we have discussed both the general difficulties of change experienced in much of life and the specific difficulties faced by businesses. The history of companies attempting to adopt new business paradigms provides good illustrations of these difficulties. Underlying causes include organizational delusions and perceptions shaped by individual and organizational needs and beliefs.

The challenge for business is balancing desires for change with needs for continuity and consistency—keeping your current company running sufficiently smoothly to provide the cash flow to enable becoming the company you aspire to be. Strong socioeconomic trends, such as the emergence of virtual organizations, make this balancing even more difficult.

Fortunately, there is broad agreement about how to pursue change via baselining, organizational design, and leadership. There are also tools for supporting these strategies. Use of tools by management teams can assure that the right issues are addressed.

Despite available wisdom, there are innumerable ways to pursue change poorly. People become confused and disheartened. Performance suffers as discussions of ambiguity and disillusionment take center stage. To mitigate against these substantial risks, it is important to understand the needs and beliefs that underlie people's behaviors. Change should be planned and implemented in ways that support needs and does not conflict with beliefs unless, of course, you are prepared to invest in changing beliefs and thereby needs.

Change often involves redesigning the essence of an organization. This should be done carefully to ensure that you retain needed current competencies, discard no longer relevant competencies, and gain required new competencies. You need to do all this at the same time that you keep cash flowing to fuel your transition!

KEY QUESTIONS

Once you have successfully addressed the challenges of growth, value, and focus, you next must face the challenge of change—implementing your growth, value, and focus strategies. This is where "the rubber meets the road," and all too often strategic management hits roadblocks. Successfully circumventing these roadblocks involves answering several key questions, which draw on the concepts, principles, methods, and tools discussed in this chapter:

- Which delusions may be affecting your organization's abilities to recognize needs for change and develop appropriate change strategies?
- What individual and organizational needs and beliefs are likely to underlie any persistent delusions, and how might these hindrances be overcome?
- What is your organizational baseline in terms of the reality of how information flows, how decisions are made, and how resources are allocated?
- Are you prepared to lead change by demonstrating sustained commitment at all levels of change processes?
- Do you have the methods and tools needed to understand and characterize needed changes and overcome obstacles to achieving these changes?

ES

Apgar, M., IV. (1998). The alternative workplace: changing where and how people work. *Harvard Business Review* May–June: 121–136.

Argyris, C., and Schon, D. A. (1978). *Organizational Learning: A Theory of Action Perspective*. Reading, MA: Addison-Wesley.

Beer, M., and Nohria, N. (2000). Cracking the code of change. *Harvard Business Review* May–June: 133–141.

Charan, R., and Colvin, G. (1999). Why CEOs fail. *Fortune* June 21: 68–78.

Cole, R. E. (1998). Learning from the quality movement: what did and didn't happen and why. *California Management Review* 41(1): 43–73.

Collins, J. (1999). Turning goals into results: the power of catalytic mechanisms. *Harvard Business Review* July–August: 71–82.

Collins, J. C., and Porras, J. I. (1994). *Built to Last: Successful Habits of Visionary Companies*. New York: Harper Business.

Dalton, J. C. (1999). Between the lines: The hard truth about open-book management, *CFO* March: 58--64.

Davenport, T. H. (1995). The fad that people forgot. *Fast Company*. November.

Davenport, T. H., and Pearlson, K. (1998). Two cheers for the virtual office. *Sloan Management Review* Summer: 51–65.

Day, G. S. (1999). Creating a market-driven organization. *Sloan Management Review* 41(1): 11–22.

Deming, W. E. (1986). *Out of Crisis*. Cambridge, MA: MIT Press.

Flannery, T. P., Hofrichter, D. A., and Platten, P. E. (1996). *People, Performance, and Pay: Dynamic Compensation for Changing Organizations*. New York: Free Press.

Hammer, M., and Champy, J. (1993). *Reengineering the Corporation: A Manifesto for Business Revolution*. New York: Harper Business.

Intelligent Systems Technology. (2000). *ProcessEdge*. www.intelsystech.com. Santa Monica, CA: Intelligent Systems Technology.

International Association of Virtual Organizations. (1999). http://www.iavo.com.

Kessler, W. C. (1999). Implementing lean thinking. *Information • Knowledge • Systems Management* 1(2, Summer) 99-103.

Madni, A. (2000). Thriving on change through process support: the evolution of the ProcessEdge™ Enterprise Suite and TeamEdge™. *Information • Knowledge • Systems Management* 2(1, Spring).

Magretta, J. (1998). The power of virtual integration: an interview with Dell Computer's Michael Dell. *Harvard Business Review* March–April: 73–84.

Majchrzak, A., and Gasser, L. (2000). TOP Modeler: supporting complex strategic and operational decision making. *Information* • *Knowledge* • *Systems Management* 2(1, Spring).

Martin, J. (1996). *Cybercorp: The New Business Revolution*. New York: AMACOM.

Mintzberg, H., and Van der Heyden, L. (1999). Organigraphs: drawing how companies really work. *Harvard Business Review* September–October: 87–94.

Pfeffer, J., and Sutton, R. I. (1999). Knowing "what" to do is not enough: turning knowledge into action. *California Management Review* 42(1): 83–108.

Reinermann, H. (1996). Virtual organizations. *Informatika* 1 March: 12–19.

Rouse, W. B. (1993). *Catalysts for Change: Concepts and Principles for Enabling Innovation*. New York: Wiley.

Rouse, W. B. (1996). *Start Where You Are: Matching Your Strategy to Your Marketplace*. San Francisco, CA: Jossey-Bass.

Rouse, W. B. (1997). Real estate in a virtual world. *Competitive Edge!* March/April: 72.

Rouse, W. B. (1998). *Don't Jump to Solutions: Thirteen Delusions That Undermine Strategic Thinking*. San Francisco, CA: Jossey-Bass.

Rouse, W. B. (1999a). *Strategic Thinking*. Atlanta, GA: Enterprise Support Systems.

Rouse, W. B. (1999b). Connectivity, creativity, and chaos: challenges of loosely-structured organizations. *Information* • *Knowledge* • *Systems Management* 1(2): 117–131.

Rouse, W. B. (2000). Managing complexity: disease control as a complex adaptive system. *Information* • *Knowledge* • *Systems Management* 2(2).

Senge, P. M. (1990). *The Fifth Discipline: The Art and Practice of the Learning Organization*. New York: Doubleday/Currency.

Slywotsky, A. J., and Morrison, D. J. (1997). *The Profit Zone: How Strategic Business Design Will Lead You to Tomorrow's Profits*. New York: Times Books.

TOP Integration. (2000). *TOP Modeler*. www.topintegration.com. Urbana, IL: TOP Integration.

Venkatraman, N., and Henderseon, J. C. (1998). Real strategies for virtual organizing. *Sloan Management Review* Fall: 33–48.

Voss, H. (1996). Virtual organizations: the future is now. *Strategy and Leadership* July/August: 12–16.

Weiss, T. B., and Hartle, F. (1997). *Reengineering Performance Management: Breakthroughs in Achieving Strategy Through People*. Boca Raton, FL: St. Lucie Press.

Womack, J. P., and Jones, D. T. (1996). *Lean Thinking: Banish Waste and Create Wealth in Your Corporation*. New York: Simon & Schuster.

CHAPTER SIX

Future

Much of senior managers' time is devoted to the near term, ensuring for instance that this month's and this quarter's financial statements meet expectations. As another example, they may deal with crises with major customers, employee groups, or perhaps regulatory agencies. There often seems to be no end to daily fire drills.

Most managers will agree, however, that one of their primary responsibilities is the future. They see this responsibility as including anticipating future opportunities and threats, planning for dealing with these contingencies, and evolving the design of the enterprise so that these plans can be executed successfully.

An organization will, in general, be no more future oriented than its leadership. To the extent that senior management encourages and participates in discussions and debates concerning alternative futures, many others in the organization will be similarly future oriented. To the extent that senior management invests in researching alternative futures, others will become committed to these alternatives.

A central difficulty with the future is the often large uncertainties associated with the alternatives. How do you justify and then manage investments in alternatives that are unlikely to be fully realized for many years, may not payoff in the ways expected, or may not payoff at all? This chapter addresses this question.

CHALLENGE OF THE FUTURE

The future is a challenge because it involves investing in inherently unpredictable long-term outcomes. In particular, this challenge concerns economic justification of such investments. How do you justify unknown outcomes that are likely to benefit unknown product or service lines or, in general, unknown stakeholders?

This challenge is due, in part, to being unable to foresee the future. Who will be the customers, and what will these customers want? In a broad sense, answers to these questions are readily determined on the basis of demographics of today's younger population who will become the customers in 10–20 years. As Drucker (1997) notes, this future has already happened.

We can safely assume that these future customers will want many of the same things as current customers—for example, certainly homes, probably cars, and without doubt food. More specifically, you can reasonably project the proportion of people using cellular phones, for example, within each market segment. Then, using methodologies such as outlined by Barnett (1988), you can forecast total market demand for cellular phone *or substitutes*.

Given such forecasts, the challenge of the future shifts from the question of what will happen to the question of how you will successfully compete. In general, you would most likely aspire to be the preferred provider of attractive, easy to use, reasonably priced, state-of-the-art cellular phones *or substitutes*. Two of these characteristics have long lead times: state-of-the-art technology and substitute products and services. The future characteristics of your offerings are likely to require investment now.

The challenge now involves deciding on an investment portfolio and managing this portfolio. For the cellular phone example, this portfolio would involve R&D/technology investments (Rouse, Boff, and Thomas, 1997; Rouse and Boff, 1998). In other domains, the investments might involve training and organizational development to prepare future leaders. Many of these types of investments pay off, if at all, 5–10 years in the future.

The inherent difficulty of this challenge is profound. Not only are the magnitudes and timing of returns uncertain but the very nature of the returns are uncertain. As Burke (1996) ably illustrates, technology investments often yield returns in unexpected ways to unexpected beneficiaries. Furthermore, as discussed in Chapter 3, most large organizations have difficulty taking advantage of new technologies, even when they are due to these organizations' original investments (Christensen, 1997).

This challenge is further complicated by increasing pressures to base all investment decisions on financial metrics. With typical discount rates, the net present value or discounted cash flow, to cite just two metrics, of uncertain returns 10 or more years in the future often indicates negative values. If this one-dimensional perspective provides the sole basis for investment decisions, few if any investments would occur.

Implementation of this philosophy becomes even more difficult when the "value" provided is indirect and abstract. When anticipated benefits are not readily measurable in monetary units and only indirectly affect things amenable to monetary measurement, it can be very difficult to assess the worth of these benefits.

There are a wealth of examples of such situations. With any reasonable annual discount rate, the tangible discounted cash flow of benefits from investments in libraries and education, for example, would be so small that justification of societal investments in these institutions and activities would be difficult. Of course, we feel quite justified arguing for such investments. Thus, there obviously must be more involved in such an analysis than just discounted cash flow.

Such intangible issues are not solely the province of public or nonprofit enterprises. As Cooper, Edgett, and Kleinschmidt (1998) have found, companies must address qualitative issues such as strategic fit and sustainability of advantage if they are to gain the best returns from their investments. Thus, financial metrics become only one attribute of the overall utility model of a potential investment.

Some managers have told me that they use the qualitative filter, such as strategic fit and sustainable advantage, to determine whether alternatives make it into the feasible set. They then use financial metrics as "sanity tests" to determine whether alternative should remain in the set. One manager commented, "The numbers are not the drivers; nevertheless, you have to get the numbers right."

Boer (1998, 1999) addresses getting the numbers right in terms of typical mistakes made when valuing the future. These traps, pitfalls, and snares, as Boer terms them, include

- using "hurdle rates"—thresholds for rates of return—that are significantly higher than discount rates (costs of capital) to hedge against uncertainties;
- assuming that the status quo will prevail if long-term investments are not made and using this as a baseline, despite its inherent lack of sustainability;
- inappropriately calculating "horizon values"—the assumed value of the investment for years beyond the time horizon of the analysis;
- significantly undervaluing long-term investments because of their initial negative cash flows and highly discounted longer-term returns;
- confusing investment with operating expense—initial investments in technology, market development, and so forth can make initial expenses look quite high;
- ignoring linkages across investments involving technical dependencies, common risks, and possible synergies;
- neglecting the many ways in which an investment may pay off and just focusing on the original motivation for the investment; and
- not considering the options approach to valuation, which is discussed at length later in this chapter.

These types of valuation mistakes reflect inappropriate framing of investment problems in terms of not understanding intended and other possible impacts of investments, as well as relationships among investments.

Beyond getting the numbers right when valuing alternative investments in the future, there are, as mentioned earlier, additional attributes of interest. Cooper, Edgett, and Kleinschmidt (1998) found in their survey that the most popular metrics, in descending order of use, include

- strategic fit and ability to leverage core competencies,
- financial payoff,
- project risk and probability of success,
- market timing, and
- technological capability of business to undertake project.

Later in this chapter, we discuss how trade-offs among these and other attributes can be addressed in the process of creating and managing a portfolio of investments in the future.

In summary, the future is challenging for several reasons. First, you need to foresee the characteristics of the future. From a broad perspective, this is not too difficult, at least in terms of demographic characteristics. However, in terms of your specific products and services, there are many possible futures. To take advantage of this range of possibilities, you need to invest in a portfolio of alternative means for competing in the future. This is greatly complicated by the inherent uncertainties about what these investments will yield, when they will provide these returns, and how these results will help you to compete.

FUTURE STRATEGIES

There are many reasons and many ways to invest in the future. As noted earlier, education, training, and organizational development are investments we make in ourselves and our enterprises in anticipation that these investments will enable achieving future accomplishments. We might also invest in land, facilities, and possibly equipment for anticipated future expansion.

The remainder of this chapter focuses on one particular type of investment for the future, namely, research and development (R&D)/technology. We invest in R&D (activities) to yield technology (outcomes). These activities tend to be very expensive and time consuming, and the outcomes are very uncertain. The combination of these effects might lead you to wonder whether investing in R&D/technology is a wise decision.

Alternatively, you might conclude that such investments are important but should be made by somebody else, perhaps government or larger companies. In general, the government makes such investments when it is in the public interest and no one else can make these investments. Companies, on the other hand, invest in R&D/technology when future competitiveness depends on new proprietary technologies and their current market offerings provide sufficient margins to support long-term investments.

Hicks (1999) suggests six reasons to do long-term research. On the basis of a wide a variety of sources and supporting studies, these reasons are the following:

- Research eventually generates new sources of wealth.
- Technology applications make use of scientific results.
- Research opportunities facilitate recruiting.
- Research may yield big discoveries of proprietary value.
- Participation in the techno-scientific community provides benefits.
- Research tends to yield good financial return over time.

Although these reasons are far from mutually exclusive, they do portray a variety of benefits beyond direct support of planned future market offerings. Attracting good people, linkages to broader knowledge bases, and possible surprises are among these other benefits.

Mitchell (2000) discusses three trends that are profoundly influencing R&D/technology strategy:

- increase in industrial R&D intensity and shift toward information and health sectors, already amounting to two-thirds of expenditures, compared with earlier domination by chemical and manufacturing industries,
- use of the Internet to transform processes by which we acquire and develop technical knowledge, enabling expanding the organization beyond the organization—hence, collaboration is becoming the norm, and
- corporate management's growing recognition of technological innovation as an increasingly important factor in corporate growth and survival—hence, there are heightened expectations of R&D/technology.

Thus, the foci of most research investments are changing (e.g., away from airplanes and computer hardware toward biotechnology and computer software), the ways in which research is done are changing (i.e., away from insularity toward broad collaboration), and the expectations of research are changing (i.e., away from investing on faith toward strategic management of R&D/technology). In fact, these trends have been quite strong for some time, as evidenced by several books that have chronicled these changes as well as contributed to them (e.g., Roussel, Saad, and Erickson, 1991; Matheson and Matheson, 1998; Miller and Morris, 1999).

Scope of R&D

It is interesting to consider the scope of R&D activities across the numerous organizations involved. *Research Technology Management* (Whitely and Larson, 2000; Research Technology Management, 2000), published by the Industrial Research Institute, often includes compilations and analyses of various R&D funding forecasts. An annual forecast of R&D funding by Battelle is published by *R&D Magazine* (Studt, 2000, R&D, 2000). The American Association for the Advancement of Science (AAAS, 1999) also publishes an analysis of the federal budget.

This resource pool, as of 2000, includes government R&D budgets of almost $80 billion across all agencies. Industrial R&D budgets total over $140 billion across all companies and approximately $100 billion for the largest 100 spenders. Roughly one-third of this amount is due to spending by pharmaceutical and biotechnology companies, and another one-third is spent by electronics and information technology companies. Trends are toward increased industrial funding and slow growth, if at all, for government funding. This has resulted in industry's share of total US investment in R&D growing from 50% to over 70% in the near future, with emphasis on applied research and development rather than basic research.

There are marked differences in how various industries spend these resources. For mature industries such as automobiles and aircraft, a significant portion of investments goes to process technologies to reduce costs and improve quality. For information technology companies, much of investment is targeted at software development. Biotechnology and pharmaceutical companies devote a large portion of investments to research aimed at discovery. Thus, the full spectrum of activities that are labeled R&D includes quite a diverse set of undertakings.

Industrial R&D

Before discussing R&D strategies—a major element of many companies' future strategies—it is important to differentiate industrial R&D from academic research. University-based research has traditionally been focused on the pursuit of knowledge as an end in itself. This knowledge is made public via journals, conference proceedings, and so forth. The community at large can and has made use of this knowledge for a range of purposes, including as part of the process of creating proprietary competitive advantage.

Industrial R&D, in contrast, has always been much more focused on contributing to the competitive advantage of companies' products and processes. As such, resource allocations usually pragmatically reflect "little r and big D," with perhaps 3–5% of the overall R&D budget devoted to "big R." This orientation is far from recent, as evidenced by Moykr's (1990) analysis of centuries of technologically enabled economic progress. Burke's (1996) chronicle of technological innovations over the same period also reflects this orientation.

It is useful to note that, although the emphasis of industrial R&D has changed little over many years, the emphasis of academic research has shifted in recent years. With significant decline of defense R&D budgets, academia has aggressively pursued industrial support and, as part of the bargain, become in many cases more market driven and less open (Press and Washburn, 2000). At the same time, remaining defense R&D budgets, which still represent significant portions of overall national R&D expenditures, have become much more pragmatically focused.

The wave of business process reengineering discussed in earlier chapters combined with substantial shifts of government priorities, from defense to health-related research, has caused much reexamination of industrial R&D organizations. The roots of these types of organizations can be traced to Thomas Edison creating the archetype of industrial R&D organizations in the 1870s. Other notable events along this path include the formation of Bell Labs' in the 1920s, IBM Research in the 1940s, and Xerox PARC in the 1970s.

These premier R&D organizations faced difficult times when AT&T was split and IBM stumbled, both in the 1980s. However, as Buderi reports (1998, 1999), these organizations are refocused and flourishing. They are refocused in two ways. First, they are more directly linked to business units and product lines. Second, their portfolios have shifted from mostly physical science to much greater emphasis on software and networking.

From a strategic perspective, it is important to understand the ways in which such organizations contribute to discovery and innovation. William Brinkman (2000), currently the chief of Bells Labs, contrasts these processes: "One must be careful to distinguish innovation from discovery. You can only manage discovery by setting direction and hiring people to work in that direction with the hope of great discoveries. Innovation, the process of taking a discovery or idea to market, is something that must be managed carefully, and we work hard to do this." Thus, these processes are best viewed as significantly different and, therefore, managed in different ways.

Also important is recognizing the relative roles of discovery and innovation at any point in time. Joseph Miller (1997), chief technologist at DuPont, portrays how the balance between these roles has changed in 20-year cycles at DuPont. These cycles begin with discovery, transition to market innovation, and culminate in extensions and applications of the underlying technology. Thus, timing is also a very important aspect of R&D strategy.

The distinction between discovery and knowledge is also captured by a quote attributed to Bayer in Germany: "Research is the transformation of money into knowledge; innovation is the transformation of knowledge into money." Managing these two transformations in terms of timing, resource allocation, and transitions from one to another are essential elements of R&D strategy.

It is useful to reiterate Mitchell's (2000) assertion that top management has come to recognize technological innovation as an increasingly important factor in corporate growth and survival. This recognition has led to substantial investments in R&D at Microsoft, for example, and new major commitments to industrial R&D organizations such as Motorola Labs, as another example (Roberson, 2000). In this way, R&D strategy has become a central—and often *the* central—element of companies' future strategies.

R&D Strategies

Roussel, Saad, and Erickson (1991) pioneered generation typing of R&D strategies in their best-selling *Third Generation R&D: Managing the Link to Corporate Strategy*. They argue that the strategic role of R&D includes defending, supporting, and expanding existing business; driving new business; and broadening and deepening a company's technological capabilities. The way in which this role is filled depends on the philosophy toward R&D:

- First generation: Hire good people, leave them alone, and hope.
- Second generation: Manage costs and benefits of projects and monitor progress against objectives.
- Third generation: General managers and R&D managers work as partners to create the best portfolio of R&D activities for the corporation

First-generation R&D is similar to the typical academic philosophy. Second-generation R&D focuses on doing things right, whereas third-generation R&D emphasizes doing the right things. Roussel, Saad, and Erickson provide a set of key practices for managing third-generation R&D:

- Define and maintain a common vocabulary—very important for cross-functional teams, including engineering, marketing, manufacturing, and so forth.
- Adopt a process for clearly articulating mutually agreed-on objectives.
- Adopt a process for setting priorities and allocating scarce resources.
- Create a backlog of ideas—it is important to have more than one good idea when considering strategic fit, risk, and so forth.
- Adopt an approach to project design that addresses technical uncertainties early.
- Adopt an approach to project planning, reporting, measurement, and control.
- Employ project teams with appropriate structure, composition, and authority.

These practices are premised on each function being capable of providing important knowledge and skills. Cross-functional interaction is emphasized. However, the overall nature of the enterprise remains intact.

In contrast, Miller and Morris (1999), in *Fourth Generation R&D: Managing Knowledge, Technology, and Innovation*, argue for a broader perspective. Although third-generation R&D focuses on understanding customers' needs and targeting technology development of products and services to meet these needs, fourth-generation R&D is driven by synthesis of new knowledge across the enterprise and stakeholders. They advocate stakeholder involvement both for continuous feedback and as lead customers and participants in research. Such involvement clarifies and evolves needs and opportunities via mutual dependent learning.

They suggest the following key elements of managing fourth-generation R&D:

- management of knowledge from many diverse sources,
- expeditionary marketing through mutually dependent learning,
- integration of both explicit and tacit knowledge,
- robust competitive architectures and organizational capabilities,
- new organizational models,
- new approaches to finance, decision making, and accounting,
- management of technology represented as intellectual property,
- new innovation processes, and
- processes and tools through which these elements are merged.

The central theme throughout their elaboration of these elements is a broader view of the enterprise and its relationships with stakeholders. Boundaries are much fuzzier and collaboration across these boundaries is the norm. This provides opportunities for the types of loosely structured organizations discussed in earlier chapters, which, as noted, present management challenges in themselves.

Matheson and Matheson (1998) in *The Smart Organization: Creating Value Through Strategic R&D* present a more decision-oriented view of R&D strategy. On the basis of extensive industry benchmarking, they present 45 best practices for making quality decisions and organizing and improving decision quality. Their approach includes nine principles of smart R&D:

- value creation culture—maximize value created for customers and captured by the enterprise;
- creating alternatives—create several good alternatives and select the best one;
- continual learning—learn continually what creates value and how to deliver it;
- embracing uncertainty—understand and take advantage of the inherent lack of control of outcomes;
- outside-in strategic perspective—use the dynamics of industry and customers to determine the framing and evaluation of strategic decisions;
- systems thinking—address complex questions by thinking through cause-and-effect relationships in the context of the whole enterprise;
- open information flow—make all information available to whomever wants it, across organizational boundaries, to create value;
- alignment and empowerment—guide the organization through a shared understanding of your strategies for creating value; and
- disciplined decision making—identify strategic choices, engage the right people and information, and select the highest-value alternatives.

Rather than representing yet another generation of R&D, Matheson and Matheson provide a more analytical framework with which to ensure the best decisions are made and high-value outcomes are likely. This approach applies whether you adopt third- or fourth-generation thinking.

The approaches to R&D strategy discussed here have much in common. They all are driven by business objectives and fed with knowledge of customers and competitors. They all advocate explicit, structured processes and the discipline required to use and maintain these processes. They all deal with the inherent uncertainties of the future by dealing with them explicitly and continually.

Beyond the formulation of an overall R&D strategy, there are numerous R&D/technology management issues that need to be addressed. There has been a wealth of empirical studies of such issues for the purpose of identifying best practices for formulation of objectives, generation of projects, allocation of resources, transfer of technology, and design of the organization (Rouse and Boff, 1998). These studies, based almost solely on surveys and interviews, correlate business practices with technical and market success.

Measurement is, of course, central to gaining insights into what works and what does not. Werner and Souder (1997) provide a comprehensive review of efforts to measure R&D. They found that measures tend to fall in categories of inputs (e.g., budgets or headcount), outputs (e.g., number of patents filed or number of new products released), and ratios (e.g., revenue from new products divided by R&D costs or revenue from new products divided by total revenues). They suggest an integrated metric that includes ratios associated with the effectiveness, timeliness, and future potential of R&D efforts.

Donnelly (2000) discusses measurement from a financial perspective. He reports the results of a survey indicating the top 10 R&D metrics in use:

- R&D spending as a percent of sales,
- new products completed/released,
- number of approved projects ongoing,
- total patents filed/pending/awarded,
- current-year percent of sales due to new products released in past X years,
- percent of resources/investment dedicated,
- percent of increase/decrease in R&D head count,
- percent of resources/investment dedicated to sustaining products, and
- average development of cost per project/product.

Note that some of these metrics relate to current investments for possible future returns, whereas other relate to current returns from past investments. The time lags inherent in R&D, as well as the uncertainty about the nature of returns, present problems for all measurement schemes.

Thus, the challenge of the future must be approached with a balance of empirical and analytical approaches. Analysis can help to make the best decision based on what is known, or assumable, now. Measurements, however, may soon tell us things have changed. Future strategies should enable setting clear courses but also enable retaining the flexibility to change courses in response to such changes.

SUPPORTING FUTURE STRATEGIES

The approaches to developing future strategies outlined in the last section need two particular types of support: information and process. Information on economic, technological, and social trends are important to projecting opportunities and threats. Information on historical reactions to past trends and events are also valuable for benchmarking alternative strategies. Of course, internal information about strengths and weaknesses, as well as how these are changing, is central to formulating future strategies.

Processes are needed to organize strategy formulation, compile necessary information, represent and project outcomes, analyze trade-offs, and make well-informed decisions. Many of the methods and tools discussed in earlier chapters are useful for these purposes. In this section, we add to this toolkit.

Historical Benchmarks

We like to think that our times and our specific situations are fairly unique. However, this is far from true. I have experienced many common situations with thousands of managers. This includes opportunities and threats, both external and internal.

Knowledge of the nature of these situations, how they emerge, and alternative ways of addressing them should be central to formulating future strategies. Of course, a manager's ability to identify relevant elements of this knowledge base and adapt it to their particular situation is also critical. Blindly following off-the-shelf prescriptions is far from a best practice.

It is impossible to compile all you need to know from past experiences and package it as a "how to" method or tool. However, a small set of publications can provide a rich historical perspective, including a few useful methods and tools. My list of favorites—biased a bit—includes

- *The Lever of Riches* (Mokyr, 1990): historical view of the evolution of technology and its role in economic progress, including many vignettes of particular technologies from the Renaissance to Industrial Revolution to modern times.
- *The Pinball Effect* (Burke, 1996): traces hundreds of technologies and ideas from the Renaissance through the Industrial Revolution to current

times with emphasis on the unpredictable twists and turns that are inherent to innovation.

- *Invention & Technology*: published by Forbes; this quarterly magazine provides fascinating case studies of how particular inventions emerged and evolved to become, or not become, market innovations.
- *Start Where You Are* (Rouse, 1996): summarizes the evolution of the transportation, computer, and defense industries, describing the common patterns of changing relationships with markets, leading indicators of these changes, and typical organizational responses.
- *Built to Last* (Collins and Porras, 1994): describes business practices of 36 large, long-established contemporary companies, half of which are judged to be exemplary, with the other half serving as reference cases.
- *The Profit Zone* (Slywotsky and Morrison, 1997): describes how many large, well-known, contemporary companies have changed their business practices to adapt to changing markets by redefining how they provide value to customers.

Mokyr and Burke both cover about five centuries of technological innovation and economic progress. *Invention & Technology* and my book focus mainly on the 19th and 20th centuries, with the balance toward the latter. Collins, Porras, Slywotsky, and Morrison address 20th century case studies, with emphasis on recent decades.

At the very least, managers reading these books and journals will likely feel that they are treading well-worn paths and can benefit from chronicles of previous travelers. Beyond this rich perspective, *Start Where You Are*, *Built to Last*, and *The Profit Zone* provide specific guidance on how to employ experiences of others' to formulate future strategies for your enterprise.

Scenario Planning

With an informed historical perspective, you can consider the future more intelligently. Of course, the future cannot be described with the same certainty as the past. We need to rely on forecasts and other prognostications. Furthermore, some aspects of the future, as Drucker (1997) points out, are already determined.

In Chapter 2, which addressed the challenge of growth, we introduced competitive intelligence. We reconsider this topic again in Chapter 7 on the challenge of knowledge. Thus, at this point, we will assume that assorted types of future-oriented information have been compiled and analyzed.

Scenario planning provides a means for considering various possible implications of this information and your enterprise's alternative responses to these futures. Schwartz (1991) in his well-known *The Art of the Long View* provides a perspective for scenario planning based on his work with Shell and others. He suggests that scenario building blocks include

- driving forces,
- predetermined elements, and
- critical uncertainties.

Driving forces define what we care about in terms of trends in society, technology, economics, politics, and the environment. Predetermined elements concern things about which we are sure, such as the future demographics discussed by Drucker. Critical uncertainties include issues and variables that surround, in Schwartz' terms, our hopes and fears.

He provides several "standard" scenario plots with intriguing names such as winners and losers, challenge and response, evolution, revolution, cycles, infinite possibility, as well as several others, which provide excellent starting points for devising your own scenarios. I discuss the evolution scenario at length in *Start Where You Are* (Rouse, 1996) because this scenario often dominates in technology-driven strategies in which development and maturity tend to take much longer than anticipated.

Schoemaker (1995) suggests an excellent step-by-step process for developing and employing scenarios:

- define the scope—time frame and scope in terms of products, markets, geographic areas, and technologies;
- identify the major stakeholders—current roles, interests, and power positions and how these factors may change;
- identify basic trends—political, economic, societal, technological, legal, and industry trends;
- identify key uncertainties—political, economic, societal, technological, legal, and industry factors;
- construct scenario themes—identify extreme worlds by putting all trends and factors in positive and negative categories relative to current strategy;
- check for consistency and plausibility—determine compatibility of trends, internal consistency of outcomes, and reactions of stakeholders;
- develop learning scenarios—identify themes that are strategically relevant and organize outcomes and trends around them;
- identify research needs—determine areas where further study of trends and uncertainties are needed;

- develop quantitative models—investigate possibilities of creating formal models that embody scenarios; and
- evolve toward decision scenarios—converge on scenarios you will use to test your strategies and generate new ideas.

Fahey and Randall (1998) have compiled a notable set of expositions by leading thinkers in scenario planning, including Schwartz and Shoemaker. Chapters in this book address alternative processes for developing scenarios, integrating scenarios and strategy, and leading scenario development. Of particular note is Shoemaker's list of common pitfalls in scenario planning (Shoemaker, 1998):

- failing to gain top management support early on,
- lack of diverse inputs,
- poor balance of line and staff people,
- unrealistic goals and expectations,
- confusion about roles,
- failure to develop a clear road map,
- developing too many scenarios,
- insufficient time for learning scenarios,
- failing to link to the planning process,
- not tracking the scenarios via signposts,
- inappropriate time frame and scope,
- too limited range of outcomes,
- too much focus on trends,
- lack of diversity of viewpoints,
- internal inconsistencies in the scenarios,
- insufficient focus on drivers,
- not breaking out of the paradigm,
- failing to tell a dynamic story,
- failure to connect with managerial concerns, and
- failure to stimulate new strategic options.

Scenario planning is used to inform formulation and evaluation of future strategies. However, it can also provide the means for representing future strategies. Shaw, Brown, and Bromiley (1998) discuss how 3M uses strategic "stories" to represent plans. The rationale for this approach is compelling. Put simply, viewgraphs with bulleted lists and spreadsheets, no matter how colorful and graphically enhanced, tend to be rather dry and abstract.. They usually do not tell a story of where we are going and how we will get there.

In other words, traditional strategic plans present a train schedule and a rationale for why the train will be able to meet this schedule. Strategic stories, in contrast, portray what it will be like at the train's destination and the likely views along the way to this destination. The story format is much more readily understandable and tends to be more compelling. This approach also provides a means for integrating scenarios into the planning process and providing clear links to strategy, thereby avoiding several of the above pitfalls.

Investment Decision Making

In Chapter 4, we discussed the challenge of focus and approaches to decision making. The methods and tools considered in that chapter are very much relevant to framing and making decisions about investments in the future in general and R&D/technology in particular. Repeated studies have found that use of formal, quantitative, and multidimensional investment decision processes linked to long-term strategic goals provides the best returns (Rouse and Boff, 1998, 1999).

As noted earlier, it is important that the multiple dimensions chosen include both financial and nonfinancial metrics (Cooper, Edgett, and Kleinschmidt, 1998). Frequently used nonfinancial metrics include subjective assessments of the strategic fit of an investment and the sustainability of likely competitive advantages provided by outcomes. Multi-attribute models such as those discussed in Chapter 4 provide a goods means for addressing trade-offs among financial and nonfinancial dimensions of decisions.

It is also important to consider, select, and manage the set of alternative investments as a portfolio, as discussed in Chapter 4. Cooper, Edgett, and Kleinschmidt (1998) surveyed over 200 companies to assess their practices in managing R&D portfolios. Companies reported

- reasonable alignment between their portfolios and business strategies,
- portfolios with moderately high-value projects,
- investments that reflect priorities fairly well,
- gridlock with projects not being done on time,
- lack of balanced portfolios relative to time horizons and risk, and
- too many projects underway.

The top 20% of responding companies—in terms of returns on R&D investments—differed from the bottom 20% in terms of achieving the right balance of projects and having the right number of projects for resources available. The top 20% of firms also differed from the bottom 20% in terms of

- having an explicit, established method for portfolio management,
- management buying into the method and supporting it through their actions,
- the method having clear rules and procedures,
- projects being treated as a portfolio, and
- applying the method consistently across all projects.

Also of particular note, the top 20% of firms differed from the bottom 20% in terms of relying much less on financial models; poorer performers relied much more on these models. Top firms also rely much more on business strategy to drive allocations. As discussed earlier, the best practice appears to be to, first, use of strategic fit and competitive sustainability to define the feasible set of investment alternatives and, second, use of financial metrics to prioritize within this set or, at the very least, weed out alternatives that do not make financial sense.

My experiences with a wide range of companies support these survey results. Resources are often spread much too thinly across far too many projects. Portfolio management gets bogged down, coaxing under-resourced projects through the investment funnel only to achieve, at best, modest returns. In general, there is a tendency to bet on too many futures, resulting in the inability to fully commit to any particular future.

Option Pricing Models

It is important to appropriately characterize the financial nature of alternative investments. Many investments, particularly in R&D, are best characterized as purchases of options to later incorporate new technologies in market offerings. This approach enables use of option pricing models, which were originally developed in the early 1970s for establishing the value of stock and commodity options. They have only recently been adopted for valuation of technology investments that, as just noted, are often made to create the intellectual property and capabilities to subsequently decide whether or not to invest in launching new products or services. The initial investments amount to purchasing options to make future investments and earn subsequent returns. These options, of course, may or may not be exercised.

The use of option pricing models to analyze this type of investment situation has been widely discussed and advocated (Amram and Kulatilaka, 1999; Boer, 1998, 1999; Cetta, 2000; Coy, 1999; Lint and Pennings, 1998;

Luehrman, 1994, 1998). Option pricing models focus on establishing the value of an option to make an investment decision, in an uncertain environment, at a later date. The equations that follow summarize the basic calculations as outlined by Luehrman.

As shown below in the first equation, the net present value (NPV) quotient is formed as the ratio of the present asset value—that is, the traditional NPV of the free cash flow projected to result from exercising the option—and the present value of the investment required to acquire these assets, that is, the option exercise price (X). The second equation indicates that the latter present value decreases as the risk-free rate of return increases and/or the time increases until the option must be exercised or it expires.

$$\text{NPV quotient} = \text{present asset value}/\text{PV}(X)$$

$$\text{PV}(X) = \text{option exercise price}/(1 + r_f)^t$$

The use of a risk-free rate is premised on the assumption that $\text{PV}(X)$ will be invested now and accrue interest at rate (r_f) for time (t) periods so that the exercise price (X) will be available when the option can be exercised. The risk-free rate is used because these funds are not at risk until investors decide to exercise the option. If they choose to let the option expire, they retain X for other purposes.

Also important is the cumulative volatility expressed, as shown below, as the product of the standard deviation of returns per period times the square root of the number of periods.

$$\text{Cumulative volatility} = \sigma\sqrt{t}$$

where σ^2 is the variance of returns per time period and t equals the number of time periods. The inclusion of volatility in option pricing models is central to realistically representing investments for which it is seldom the case that future returns are certain.

The values of the NPV quotient and cumulative volatility are used to ascertain Black-Scholes values, which are computed from, not surprisingly, the Black-Scholes option pricing model (Black and Scholes, 1973). These values, expressed as percentages, increase with increasing NPV quotient and increasing cumulative volatility. This percentage is multiplied times the present asset value to determine the value of the option.

Thus, the value of an option to later decide on an investment would seem to increase with r_f, σ^2, and t. In particular, in the presence of high volatility and high risk-free returns, it would seem that the longer one can wait to decide the more valuable the option. However, the present asset value decreases with time. Thus, depending on the specific cash flow and investment projections, as well as the parameters chosen, the option value may increase, decrease, or possibly increase to a maximum and then decrease. Sensitivity analysis is a good way to gain an understanding of this range of possibilities.

The resulting option value is totally premised on the assumption that waiting does not preempt deciding later. In other words, the assumption is that the decision to exercise cannot be preempted by somebody else deciding earlier. In typical situations in which other actors (e.g., competitors) can affect possible returns, it is common to represent their impact in terms of changes of projected cash flows (Amram and Kulatilaka, 1999). In many cases, competitors acting first will decrease potential cash flows, which will decrease the option value. It is often possible to construct alternative competitive scenarios and determine an optimal exercise date.

Technology Investment Advisor

Options pricing models are central to the *Technology Investment Advisor* (Rouse et al., 2000; ESS, 2000), whose functionality is depicted in Figure 6.1. Note that this tool can be used in conjunction with the *Product Planning Advisor* discussed in Chapter 3.

The option pricing model needs as inputs the R&D investment over time and the subsequent, contingent investment, again over time, to launch the

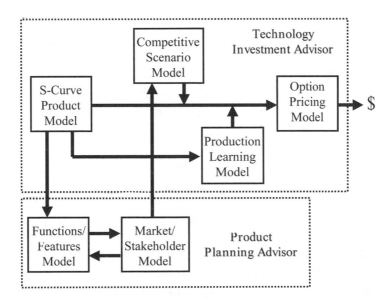

Figure 6.1. *Technology Investment Advisor* and *Product Planning Advisor*

technology in market offerings. The former investment represents purchasing an option, whereas the latter investment represents exercising the option. Also needed is the projected free cash flows resulting from both investments, which are usually minimal for the R&D investment and hopefully substantial for the market investment. The option pricing model can then compute the value of the options, which is often significantly higher than the necessary R&D investment, hence making the option quite attractive.

The other elements of Figure 6.1 represents models used to project the inputs for the options pricing model:

- S-curve models are used to project the maturity of market offerings and consequently revenues and, if appropriate, units sold (Roussel, 1984; Foster, 1986; Young, 1993; Meyer, 1994).
- Production learning models are used to project decreasing unit costs as the cumulative number of units produced increases (Lee, 1987; Hancock and Bayha, 1992; Heim and Compton, 1992).
- Competitive scenario models are used to guide projections of prices and margins, depending on market timing and relative technology and strategy advantages.
- Functions/features models are used to represent and evaluate the specific nature of each market launch, the timing of which is determined by the S-curve models.
- Market/stakeholder models are used to assess the relative market utilities of market offerings across stakeholders and competitors, thereby influencing competitive scenarios.

Thus, the combination of the *Technology Investment Advisor* and *Product Planning Advisor* includes models for options pricing, S-curve maturity, production learning, quality function deployment, and multi-attribute utility. Users can choose to employ any or all of these models for analysis of their investment portfolios. To the extent that useful data are already available—and, therefore, need not be projected—these data can be entered directly into the analysis spreadsheets.

Figure 6.2 shows example projections from S-curve models of a product line (*top left*) involving an initial product launch and subsequent derivative launches. These projections "feed" the option price valuation (*bottom right*). Extensive capabilities for sensitivity analysis and Monte Carlo analysis support exploration of such models and their interactions, enabling users to answer questions such as, "How wrong can I be and still have this investment make sense?"

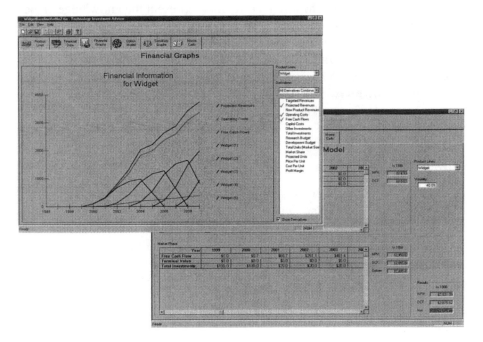

Figure 6.2. Example projections and option price valuation

Knowledge Management

Knowledge management is discussed at length in the next chapter. It is important, however, to indicate at this point an aspect of knowledge management that is of particular relevance to future strategies. One of the organizational delusions discussed in Chapter 5 concerned the persistent false belief that events and outcomes will—or, at least, should—follow the planned course. In fact, serendipity is often a key element of success.

Taking advantage of serendipity requires flexible planning processes that include mechanisms for recognizing and exploiting the unpredictable when it happens. (Rouse, 1998). This involves avoiding tunnel vision with regard to how emerging technologies, for example, might best be deployed. The best deployments might quite possibly be in areas other than those that prompted the original investments.

Some companies periodically and systematically review the results of their R&D investments with an eye for applications other those originally envisioned. They subsequently may pursue these new opportunities within their existing businesses or possibly license this intellectual property to companies that are already in the businesses in question.

This raises the issue of how to identify and represent the knowledge gained from R&D. One possibility is knowledge maps, whereby graphical representations of causes and effects are created and can be searchable relative to particular questions (Rouse, Thomas, and Boff, 1998). An interesting aspect of knowledge mapping concerns representing knowledge gained from ideas that failed. Knowing what does not work, and why it does not work, can be quite valuable. However, knowledge maps would be intractable if you attempt to incorporate knowledge of all the things that do not work.

Summary

In this section, we discussed a range of means for supporting formulation and implementation of future strategies. Historical benchmarks can be invaluable for taking advantage of lessons learned from past successes and failures. Scenario planning is very useful for making sense of alternative futures. Investment decision making is, of course, a central issue and should be supported with the methods and tools discussed in Chapter 4. Technology options provide a new and powerful way of thinking about the purpose and value of R&D investments. Finally, the knowledge resulting from these investments should be identified, managed, and leveraged.

CONCLUSIONS

The challenge of the future is fundamentally important to every organization. It is one of senior management's primary responsibilities. The inherent unpredictability and long-term nature of the future are central reasons for the difficulty of this challenge.

Alternatives futures and strategies for competing in these futures are essential questions. Competitive strategies for possible futures usually involve current investments. These investments often include R&D/technology investments, hopefully driven by a well-formulated R&D strategy.

To support making these investments intelligently, information and processes for utilizing this information are needed. Of particular importance is valuation of alternative investments. For financial metrics, it can be quite useful to think in terms of option pricing models. Both financial and nonfinancial metrics can be included in an overall multi-attribute portfolio model.

Future strategies are laced with cross-cutting issues related to risks, resources, organizations, and markets. The concepts, principles, methods, and tools discussed in this chapter are intended to address these issues rigorously and usefully.

KEY QUESTIONS

Addressing the challenge of future is all too easy to put off until tomorrow. It never demands attention today, although it often requires attention now. The following set of questions is intended to guide how you should pay attention to the future while you still have an opportunity to affect it, or at least affect your role in it and assure that this role is likely to provide the outcomes you seek:

- What is your forecast for the future of your markets 5–10 years from now?
- What are your alternative scenarios for how you might compete in this future?
- How might these scenarios be improved using historical benchmarks?
- What current long-term investments do these scenarios imply?
- What metrics do you use for valuation of long-term investments?
- Does the size of your investment portfolio match the resources available?
- How do you formulate, evaluate, implement, and review your future strategies?

REFERENCES

AAAS. (1999). *Research and Development: FY 2000*. Washington, DC: American Association for the Advancement of Science.

Amram, M., and Kulatilaka, N. (1999). *Real Options: Managing Strategic Investment in an Uncertain World*. Boston, MA: Harvard Business School.

Barnett, W. F. (1988). Four steps to forecast total market demand. *Harvard Business Review* July–August: 3–8.

Black, F., and Scholes, M. (1973). The pricing of options and corporate liabilities. *Journal of Political Economy* 81, 637–659.

Boer, F. P. (1998). Traps, pitfalls, and snares in the valuation of technology. *Research Technology Management* 41(5): 45–54.

Boer, F. P. (1999). *Valuation of Technology*. New York: Wiley.

Brinkman, W. F. (2000). Why Bell Labs sticks to the basics. *Business Week* March 20: 18F–H.

Buderi, R. (1998). Bell Labs is dead. Long live Bell Labs. *Technology Review* September/October: 50–57.

Buderi, R. (1999). Into the big blue yonder. *Technology Review* July/August: 46–53.

Burke, J. (1996). *The Pinball Effect: How Renaissance Water Gardens Made the Carburetor Possible and Other Journeys Through Knowledge*. Boston, MA: Little, Brown.

Cetta, J. (2000). Don't discount net present value. *Business Week* June 28: 10.

Christensen, C. M. (1997). *The Innovator's Dilemma: When New Technologies Cause Great Firms to Fail*. Boston, MA: Harvard Business School.

Collins, J. C., and Porras, J. I. (1994). *Built to Last: Successful Habits of Visionary Companies*. New York: Harper Business.

Cooper, R. G., Edgett, S. J., and Kleinschmidt, E. J. (1998). Best practices for managing R&D portfolios. *Research Technology Management* 41(4): 20–33.

Coy, P. (1999). Exploiting uncertainty: the real-options revolution in decision-making. *Business Week* June 7: 118–124.

Donnelly, G. (2000). A P&L for R&D. *CFO* February: 44–50

Drucker, P. F. (1997). The future that has already happened. *Harvard Business Review* September–October: 20–24.

ESS. (2000). *Technology Investment Advisor*. http://www.ess-advisors.com/software.htm. Atlanta, GA: Enterprise Support Systems.

Fahey, L., and Randall, R. M. (Eds.). (1998). *Learning From the Future: Competitive Foresight Scenarios*. New York: Wiley.

Foster, R. (1986). *Innovation: The Attacker's Advantage*. New York: Summit Books.

Hancock, W. M., and Bayha, F. H. (1992). The learning curve. In: *Handbook of Industrial Engineering*, edited by Salvendy, G. New York: Wiley, chapt. 61.

Heim, J. A., and Compton, W. D. (Eds.). (1992). *Manufacturing Systems: Foundations of World-Class Practice*. Washington, DC: National Academy.

Hicks, D. (1999). Six reasons to do long-term research. *Research Technology Management* 42(4): 8–11.

Lee, I. (1987). Design-to-cost. In; *Production Handbook*, edited by White J. A. New York: Wiley, chapt. 3.3.

Lint, O., and Pennings, E. (1998). R&D as an option on market introduction. *R&D Management* 28(4): 279–287.

Luehrman, T. A. (1994). *Capital Projects as Real Options: An Introduction* (paper no. 9-295-074). Boston, MA: Harvard Business School.

Luehrman, T. A. (1998). Investment opportunities as real options. *Harvard Business Review* July–August: 51–67.

Matheson, D., and Matheson, J. (1998). *The Smart Organization: Creating Value Through Strategic R&D*. Boston, MA: Harvard Business School.

Meyer, P. S. (1994). Bi-logistic growth. *Technological Forecasting and Social Change* 47: 89–102.

Miller, J. A. (1997). Basic research at DuPont. *Chemtech* April: 12–16.

Miller, W. L., and Morris, L. (1999). *Fourth Generation R&D: Managing Knowledge, Technology, and Innovation*. New York: Wiley.

Mitchell, G. R. (2000). Industrial R&D strategy for the early 21st century. *Research Technology Management* 43(1): 31–35.

Mokyr, J. (1990). *The Lever of Riches: Technological Creativity and Economic Progress*. New York: Oxford University Press.

Press, E., and Washburn, J. (2000). The kept university. *Atlantic Monthly* March: 39–54.

R&D Magazine (2000). www.rdmag.com.

Research Technology Management. (2000). www.onlinejournal.net/iri-rtm/.

Roberson, D. (2000). The genesis of Motorola Labs. *Information • Knowledge • Systems Management* 2.

Rouse, W. B. (1996). *Start Where You Are: Matching Your Strategy to your Marketplace*. San Francisco, CA: Jossey-Bass.

Rouse, W. B. (1998). *Don't Jump to Solutions: Thirteen Delusions That Undermine Strategic Thinking*. San Francisco, CA: Jossey-Bass.

Rouse, W. B., Boff, K. R., and Thomas, B. G. S. (1997). Assessing cost/benefits of R&D investments. *IEEE Transactions on Systems, Man, and Cybernetics* (Part A) 27(4): 389–401.

Rouse, W. B., and Boff, K. R. (1998). R&D/technology management: A framework for putting technology to work. *IEEE Transactions on Systems, Man, and Cybernetics* (Part C) 28(4): 501–515.

Rouse, W. B., and Boff, K. R. (1999). Making the case for investments in human effectiveness. *Information • Knowledge • Systems Management* 1(3): 225–247.

Rouse, W. B., Howard, C. H., Carns, W., and Prendergast, J. (2000). An options-based approach to technology strategy. *Information • Knowledge • Systems Management* 2 (1, Spring).

Rouse, W. B., Thomas, B. G. S., and Boff, K. R. (1998). Knowledge maps for knowledge mining: application to R&D/technology management. *IEEE Transactions on Systems, Man, and Cybernetics* (Part C) 28(3): 309–317.

Roussel, P. (1984). Technological maturity proves a valid and important concept. *Research Management* 27(1, January–February).

Roussel, P. A., Saad, K. N., and Erickson, T. J. (1991). *Third Generation R&D: Managing the Link to Corporate Strategy*. Cambridge, MA: Harvard Business School.

Schoemaker, P. J. H. (1995). Scenario planning: a tool for strategic thinking. *Sloan Management Review* Winter: 25–40.

Schoemaker, P. J. H. (1998). Twenty common pitfalls in scenario planning. In: *Learning From the Future: Competitive Foresight Scenarios*, edited by Fahey, L., and Randall, R. M. New York: Wiley, chapt. 25.

Schwartz, P. (1991). *The Art of the Long View: Planning for the Future in an Uncertain World*. New York: Doubleday/Currency.

Shaw, G., Brown, R., and Bromiley, P. (1998). Strategic stories: how 3M is rewriting business planning. *Harvard Business Review* May–June: 41–50.

Slywotsky, A. J., and Morrison, D. J. (1997). *The Profit Zone: How Strategic Business Design Will Lead You to Tomorrow's Profits*. New York: Times Books.

Studt, T. (2000). Industry spends big on development while feds focus on research. *R&D Magazine* January: S1–S11.

Werner, B. M., and Souder, W. E. (1997). Measuring R&D performance—state of the art. *Research-Technology Management* March–April: 34–42.

Whitely, R. L., and Larson, C. F. (2000). Industrial Research Institute's first annual R&D leadership board. *Research Technology Management* 43(1): 25–27.

Young, P. (1993). Technological growth curves: a competition of forecasting models. *Technological Forecasting and Social Change* 44: 375–389.

CHAPTER SEVEN

Knowledge

In Chapter 2, which considered the challenge of growth, the possibilities for growing electronically were discussed. These possibilities have fueled the transformation of many consulting companies to specialists in E-commerce, E-strategy, and so forth, as well as the emergence of numerous new players in this arena. Despite the hype, however, few companies feel that they can safely ignore the likely impacts of networking on their businesses.

The recognition of this threat and opportunity has caused many companies to reconsider their overall information strategies. The concept of information strategy has, in recent years, changed in two fundamental ways (Rouse and Sage, 1999). First, information strategy is no longer viewed as synonymous with information technology. Just as weapons systems enable military strategy, information technology is an enabler of information strategy, not the strategy itself. For many companies, this recognition has resulted in moving information strategy out of the information systems function and into the front office.

The second change has been the realization that investments in information technology should be driven by the company's overall information strategy. Furthermore, these investments should be focused on business processes in which the greatest impacts are needed. Consequently, in part because of the costs involved, many companies have moved away from automatically adopting the latest and greatest offerings of the information technology providers.

Succinctly, information strategy is no longer viewed as something you install. Investments are driven by focused business process needs. Three key business process issues receive the most attention:

- process integration,
- electronic commerce, and
- knowledge management.

Process integration is the focus of enterprise resource planning, with typical goals of dramatically increasing enterprise efficiency due to reengineering of processes, streamlining of information flows, and, as a consequence, reductions of process costs. Process integration investments are most common with large manufacturers.

Electronic commerce includes much more than just Internet-based retailing. It can include product support, purchasing spare parts, and even purchasing larger items such as automobiles. It can also include transactions with suppliers, for example, issuing requests for quotes (RFQs), receiving bids, notifying sources selected, and so forth. Obviously, the electronic commerce elements of a company's information strategy should dovetail with its process integration efforts.

Knowledge management involves a trade-off between capturing knowledge and making it available electronically and supporting employees who are key holders of knowledge. Companies tend toward the "capture" side of this trade-off when knowledge is crisply factual or can be proceduralized. The "support" side of the trade-off is emphasized when knowledge is more conceptual and requires explanation. Resolution of this trade-off for any particular company determines the attractiveness of, for example, market databases and data warehousing.

The marketing and sales function provides an excellent illustration of this trade-off. Knowledge of the demographics of large numbers of customers and the nature of their purchases can be used to target customers for upgrades, collateral products, and additional services. Customer databases, perhaps data warehouses, and doubtlessly contact management systems can provide essential support for doing this well. In contrast, when all market information can be maintained in a few salespeople's heads and need not be accessed by others, such investments are unlikely to pay off.

Information strategy involves defining the role information plays in the enterprise, that is, how it contributes to value, and determining an appropriate portfolio of investments in process integration, electronic commerce, and knowledge management. Figure 7.1 provides a framework for information strategy that has proven to be useful.

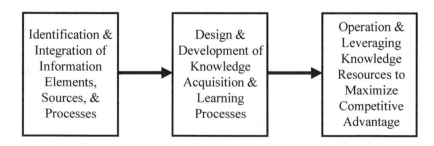

Figure 7.1. Framework for information strategy

This framework is value driven in that the first step involves determining information and knowledge requirements for improving the targeted value streams. These requirements then direct the identification of information and knowledge sources and processes. The second step involves designing and developing processes for the enterprise to acquire the targeted information and knowledge and for organizational learning to occur as a result. The third step in information strategy development concerns supporting use of information and knowledge for competitive advantage.

This chapter focuses on knowledge management and the challenge of defining the strategic role of knowledge in the organization, both as a competitive advantage and as a means for delivering value. Process integration and electronic commerce, in contrast, can no doubt be enormous undertakings but do not involve the conceptual difficulties of understanding, enhancing, and measuring knowledge assets and, in general, managing these assets. Unlike process integration and electronic commerce, you cannot simply buy and install—or possibly outsource—knowledge management. The nature of knowledge management, rather than its inherent cost, makes it a very significant strategic challenge.

KNOWLEDGE MANAGEMENT

Knowledge management is in vogue at the moment (e.g., see Brown and Duguid, 1998; Ungston and Trudel, 1999; Whitting, 1999). Abilities to create, compile, share, and apply knowledge are increasingly viewed as more valuable than the physical assets of an enterprise. The stock market valuation of many knowledge companies (e.g., software and biotech) reflects the broad consensus on this issue. If knowledge is an enterprise's primary asset, it makes sense that this asset should be managed.

The concept of knowledge management has been scoped in different ways:

- Knowledge management promotes an integrated approach to identifying, capturing, retrieving, sharing, and evaluating an enterprise's information assets. These information assets may include databases, documents, policies, and procedures, as well as the uncaptured tacit expertise and experience stored in individual workers' heads (Oracle, 1998).

- A knowledge management system should identify and link the organization's intellectual assets, accelerate the production of actionable information and knowledge, and accelerate the pace of both personal and organizational learning and exchange, even on a global scale (Coates, 1999).

- Knowledge differs from information in that it involves a human act, is the by-product of thinking, is created in the present, belongs to communities, and circulates within communities in many ways; new knowledge is created at boundaries of old (McDermott, 1999).

These three definitions range from an information-centric perspective to a management systems view to a more behavioral and social perspective. Definitions of knowledge capital, which is discussed later in this chapter, are strongly affected by which perspective one advocates.

One's choice among the range of possible perspectives of knowledge management has a strong effect on possible metrics. Davenport's human-centric view suggests measures such as improvements in strategic capabilities, contributions of hiring to strengthening capabilities, unit productivity per employee, contributions of learning to strengthening key capabilities, and retention of committed and engaged people in pivotal jobs (Davenport, 1999). Strassman (1998), in contrast, focuses on value-added of management and argues that this—as reflected in SG&A and R&D investments—is the cause of stock market valuations in excess of company book values.

Whiting (1999) argues that knowledge management is not as intuitively straightforward as it might seem. He suggests 10 myths of knowledge management to support this argument, as well as how the underlying issues should be realistically viewed:

- Knowledge management is something new—such systems emerged in the early 1980s.
- Knowledge management is a fad—the phrase may fade, but the practice is very real and will persist.
- Knowledge management is a technology—it is really about people, relationships, communities, and new ways of working.
- Knowledge management is the same as data warehousing—data warehousing enables data mining, which can be an important element of knowledge management.
- Getting employees to share their knowledge is extremely difficult—people will share if there is something in it for them.
- Knowledge management is mostly for capturing the knowledge of retiring or departing employees—maintaining connections to people is more useful.
- Knowledge management dramatically affects the bottom line—this is difficult to measure and may mainly be in terms of productivity rather than sales.

- To be successful, knowledge management must be implemented on an enterprise scale—it can succeed, or fail, on any scale.
- Knowledge management applies only within an organization— extended initiatives beyond organizational boundaries can be quite valuable although difficult to do.
- Knowledge management needs a chief knowledge officer (CKO)—it is difficult to have a CKO with sufficient authority to actually be "in charge."

Thus, the range of issues relevant to knowledge management is quite broad. Furthermore, these issues can interact in complicated ways, for example, culture, incentives, and environment interact to affect knowledge sharing. These issues and their interactions underlie the challenge of knowledge.

CHALLENGE OF KNOWLEDGE

Knowledge management is a challenge in terms of both identifying and capturing knowledge and in terms of disseminating and utilizing knowledge. O'Dell and Grayson (1998) discuss the typical difficulties that organizations encounter in the process of internal benchmarking—identifying, sharing, and using the knowledge and best practices within one's organization. These difficulties include

- ignorance about resources and others' needs,
- a culture that values personal expertise more than knowledge sharing, and
- lack of resources for implementation of best practices.

Such difficulties are exacerbated by alternative interpretations of the concept of knowledge and the extent to which knowledge can be captured. Cook and Brown (1999) contrast the epistemology of *possession* (i.e., knowledge) with the epistemology of *practice* (i.e., knowing). Their analysis framework includes dimensions of individual vs. group and explicit vs. tacit. This framework is used to classify four types of knowledge:

- individual and explicit, for example, concepts,
- individual and tacit, for example, skills,
- group and explicit, for example, stories, and
- group and tacit, for example, genre.

Given this breadth of possibilities, they conclude that training and educational programs "need to take as their aim both passing knowledge to individuals and creating situations that help groups develop practices (ways of knowing) that make use of knowledge in new, innovative, and productive ways." Thus, knowledge involves both things that can be archived in databases and things that reside solely in the heads of people.

This distinction has long been recognized as important. Polanyi (1958, 1966) explored the differences between tacit and explicit knowledge as well as the nature of "social knowledge." Much more recently, Nonaka and Takeuchi (1995) have considered these distinctions in the context of knowledge management. The implications of there differences for supporting knowledge strategies are discussed later.

Knowledge management is also a challenge because of the typical long path from data or experience to well-informed action. Knowledge management involves transforming data to information to insights to programs, as well as motivating and supporting the people who are often the repositories of knowledge. As discussed in Chapter 4, when considering the challenge of change, knowing "what" is not enough—you also need to know "how" (Pfeffer and Sutton, 1999).

There is an increasing wealth of available data and information; however, this information is seldom transformed into competitive knowledge and subsequent programs of action. Considerable emphasis is placed on creating the infrastructure to support information access and utilization. However, relatively little is invested in ensuring that this information is appropriately transformed to business value added. As McDermott (1999) argues, information technology is necessary but not sufficient for knowledge management because information and knowledge are complementary rather than identical constructs.

Good examples of the inherent difference between information and knowledge include the seemingly ever-expanding range of opportunities in electronic commerce (Evans and Wurster, 1997, 1999; Seybold, 1998; Shapiro and Varian, 1998; Venkatraman, 2000) and the revolution in database marketing and use of information for mass customization (Blattberg et al., 1994). Increasing portions of companies' capital expenditures are being invested in these types of computer and communications technologies. However, it is unclear how these investments are translating into increased knowledge assets for companies.

Managers' uncertainties are magnified by the simple fact that so many companies are making these investments. In perusing many recent business magazines, it would seem that investments in enterprise resource planning (ERP) or data warehousing should solve *all* of a company's problems. In truth, however, these investments only provide the basis for leveraging the company's knowledge assets—they do not inherently ensure that this leveraging happens.

The difficulty of transforming information to knowledge and action is often part of the fabric of the company. Large companies tend to become insular, with most people highly specialized in the context of existing market offerings—and everybody else managing these specialists. The result is a tendency to perceive that all leading edge, competitive knowledge is internal to the company (Rouse, 1998). Consequently, little need is felt to mine external sources for knowledge to inform innovation.

The challenges outlined in this section come together when trying to justify investments in knowledge management. As a point of reference, consider cost justification for ERP systems focused on enhancing process integration, one of the other three elements of information strategy introduced earlier in this chapter. It would seem much easier to justify return on investment (ROI) for more tangible systems like ERP than for more abstract notions like knowledge management.

However, as Fryer (1999) reports, at least 90% of ERP projects end up late or over budget, often taking 6–7 years or more to realize positive net present value. This tends to result in rather large "expectations gaps," often created by vendors of ERP systems. Fryer argues that a well-communicated *and* detailed ROI framework can help close the expectations gap. You need to determine what specifically will change with ERP, the projected savings due to these changes, how these savings will be captured, and how progress of the change process will be measured.

Inabilities to capture savings is a pervasive problem. Savings that should occur in principle often do not emerge in practice. Fryer reports change management, internal staff adequacy, and training as the biggest obstacles. Thus, you not only have to plan ERP implementation carefully. You also have to execute well, making sure, in particular, that people issues are addressed appropriately. Otherwise, the overall success statistics for ERP are rather disheartening.

Turning to knowledge management, Foster (1999) discusses experiences in justifying such investments. A central issue concerns translating intuitively understood benefits into tangible, measurable benefits. This is particularly difficult because people, information, and knowledge do not appear in traditional financial statements, other than as costs.

Foster argues for a traditional cost/benefit approach. The costs are usually much clearer than the benefits. However, as Foster's examples illustrate, careful analyses of time savings, productivity increases, and knowledge reuse increases can enable translation from intangible to tangible benefits. For intangible benefits inherently not translatable to monetary benefits, he suggests using a balanced scorecard, as discussed in Chapter 4.

To avoid making such a cost/benefit analysis overwhelming, you can begin this process by first focusing on potential impacts on tasks done frequently and/or done by many people, for example, order entry. Next, or in parallel, focus on very time-consuming and/or expensive tasks, for example, proposal preparation. Assess the likely benefits of improving these tasks, sum up the savings, and determine if the costs of the proposed knowledge management solution can be justified solely on the basis of these benefits. If not, broaden the scope of tasks analyzed, keeping in mind that the goal is to justify the investment, not analyze every task performed by every person in the organization.

The difficulties of justifying investments in knowledge management are, to a great extent, due to knowledge being viewed as a means to create assets, not an asset in itself. Thus, we have to find ways to translate this means to financial ends. However, if knowledge assets were important elements of companies' balance sheets, then we could directly link investments in knowledge management to balance sheet assets. In the next section, we consider a recent proposal for how knowledge assets could become a standard financial metric.

KNOWLEDGE STRATEGIES

Many companies are aggressively pursuing the challenge of knowledge, as illustrated by NCR's formation of a knowledge lab (Carter, 1999) and British Telecom Laboratories development of a knowledge management network (Warren and Davies, 2000). Likely best practices are beginning to emerge, but few, if any, have been empirically evaluated. In this section, we consider emerging best practices in the following areas:

- linkages to corporate strategy—carefully linking knowledge management investments to focused, measurable business objectives, for example, increased ROI;
- choices among alternative models—focused investments executed well provide better returns than broad investments intended to improve everything in general;
- knowledge sharing—knowledge reuse is central to realizing returns on identifying, capturing, and disseminating knowledge;
- knowledge capital—measuring the asset value of knowledge is key and possible metrics are emerging; and

- competitive intelligence—introduced in Chapter 2, this endeavor should be a key source of content for knowledge management.

Linkages to Corporate Strategy

There is a general tendency of management to want to "install" pervasive solutions to perceived problems. Recently, I was asked by a large corporation to recommend what software solutions would most improve their knowledge management practices. My response was to ask, "What is your biggest business problem, and how would timely access to knowledge help to solve this problem?"

Within a few hours, we had honed in on their sales organization for one major product line for which sales shortfalls relative to projections had become chronic. By interviewing a few senior sales people, we identified where timely access to knowledge would likely enhance the sales process—faster and higher probability of success—and also ensure that sales projections were not overly biased by unrealistic wishful thinking.

In this process, we also identified areas where knowing—using Cook and Brown's term—rather than knowledge was a central asset. In each of these cases, this asset resided in one person who, despite apparent willingness to share, had no mechanisms or processes to accomplish this sharing. Our assessment was that these situations put the corporation at risk relative to several major international accounts.

In general, knowledge acquisition should be driven by business issues and the resulting knowledge shared across stakeholders in these issues. For example, a company may determine that inaccuracies in demand forecasting are costly in terms of excess inventories of raw materials and finished goods and/or unacceptable delays in filling customer orders. By focusing on the knowledge needed to resolve this problem and then the information needed to provide this knowledge, the company can estimate the value of information and justify (or not) the investment in gaining access to this information. Companies such as Proctor & Gamble and Wal-Mart provide good examples of this practice.

Figure 7.2 provides a view of the potential strategic impacts of knowledge assets. Creation and/or acquisition of knowledge assets enable design and development of proprietary products and services. If this is combined with relatively low levels of physical assets and low costs of goods sold, for example, software and pharmaceuticals, high-profit margins result.

High-profit margins result in high market valuation. This enables acquisition of knowledge assets for stock rather than cash. High-profit margins also enable high investments in R&D and, thereby, creation of knowledge assets.

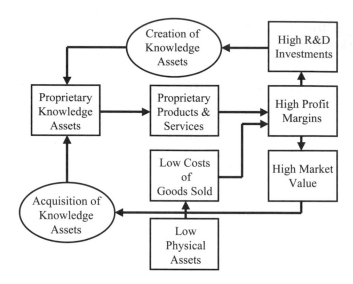

Figure 7.2. Strategic impacts of knowledge assets

Getting the process depicted in Figure 7.2 to work well results in creation of a wealth engine, as companies such as Cisco, Intel, and Microsoft have demonstrated.

Of course, not all companies enjoy low physical capital intensity and high knowledge capital intensity. However, these considerations can be addressed relative to the markets of interest.

Alternative Models

Knowledge management strategies have received considerable recent attention. Zack (1999a) contrasts conservative vs. aggressive knowledge management strategies in terms of focus (i.e., internal, external, unbounded) vs. mode (i.e., exploiter, explorer, innovator). Internal exploiters are the most conservative, and unbounded innovators are the most aggressive. Conservative firms tend to focus on protecting knowledge, attempting to create barriers to diffusion or transfer of knowledge outside the firm. Aggressive firms seek to obsolete their own knowledge, always staying one step ahead of the competition. For the former, Zack considers integrative knowledge management applications that exhibit a sequential flow of explicit knowledge into and out of a repository, although the latter are likely to be better served by interactive applications that focus primarily on supporting interaction among people with tacit knowledge (Zack, 1999b).

The breadth of Zack's framework illustrates one of the difficulties of formulating management strategies—there are simply too many ways one might proceed. As indicated earlier, corporate strategy should drive choices among these many alternatives. However, strategy is more useful for determining the specific objectives to be achieved via knowledge management and the business value of achieving this objectives. Strategy is less useful for identifying the best means for accomplishing these ends.

Figure 7.3 summarizes possibilities for content, scope, and approaches to knowledge management. Content ranges from factual knowledge to procedural knowledge, as well as the knowledge needed to capture, retrieve, evaluate, share, train, and produce knowledge. Scope could include knowledge internal to an organization, additional knowledge from particular external markets, and possibly knowledge from the global wealth of ideas, trends, and so forth. Internal, factual knowledge is certainly a good starting point, but it may be that returns on knowledge management investments will depend on broader perspectives.

Approaches range from centralized, codified repositories to decentralized, interactive support of "knowing" workers rather than knowledge bases. The choice along this continuum depends in part on content and scope. Factual databases are more easily hosted and maintained centrally, albeit with remote ac-

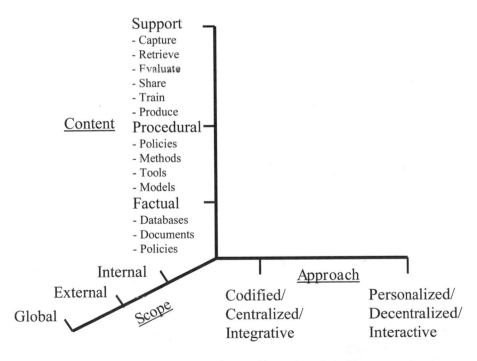

Figure 7.3. Content, scope, and approaches to knowledge management

cess, than procedural models for proposal preparation in, for example, developing countries. As another example, shared "knowing" is better facilitated by decentralized, interactive approaches.

Distinctions among approaches to knowledge management have been explored in recent studies of consulting companies. The comparison by Hansen, Nohria, and Tierney (1999) considers codification at Andersen and Ernst & Young vs. personalization at McKinsey, Bain, and the Boston Consulting Group. Sarvary (1999) provides a similar analysis, comparing centralization at Ernst & Young and decentralization at McKinsey. Apostolou and Mentzas (1999) outline four central knowledge management processes—generating, organizing, developing, and distributing—and compare 10 consulting firms, 6 in detail.

These articles discuss the differences among consulting companies' ways of doing business and the implications of these differences for approaches to knowledge management. On the one hand, you can attempt to capture and codify knowledge for subsequent communication to "knowledge workers." On the other hand, you can view the workers as the repositories of knowledge and invest in the means to foster communication and collaboration among workers. The choice between these alternatives, or along the continuum between these extremes, depends on the nature of the organization's culture and core competencies, as well as the content and scope of knowledge of interest as discussed earlier.

The feasible choices in Figure 7.3 also depend on the extent of support provided as depicted on the content axis. To the extent that online expertise, tutorials, and so forth are feasible and available, people need less direct access to other people with this knowledge. Thus, choosing a knowledge management model involves defining what knowledge will be managed and what other knowledge about this knowledge will also be provided.

Knowledge Sharing

The value of any approach to knowledge management is highly influenced by abilities and inclinations of people to share knowledge. A common failing is investing substantially in the requisite knowledge but not investing sufficiently in the mechanisms to get this knowledge in the hands of people who need it to resolve the issues at hand (Ottum and Moore, 1997). An important aspect of such mechanisms concerns creating means and incentives to share knowledge.

Ives, Torrey, and Gordon (1998) discuss factors that impact knowledge sharing. An overriding factor is the extent to which knowledge management reflects and is integrated into the business context. Organizational performance factors that affect sharing include how people are organized to support performance, the processes they are supposed to carry out, the social and political factors that affect performance, and the physical environment in which people perform. Individual performance factors that influence sharing include the guidance people receive, how they are measured, availability of tools to enhance performance, existence of skills to enable performance, and motivation to perform. These factors have to be aligned, the authors argue, to optimize knowledge sharing.

Cross and Baird (2000) consider aspects of knowledge management that go beyond technology. These aspects include determining which experiences are worth learning from, creating structures that encourage reflection and sharing, and embedding lessons of experience into databases, work processes, and support systems, as well as products and services. Thus, one should not assume that knowledge sharing will just happen naturally once the technology infrastructure is in place. The overall approach chosen for knowledge management should include mechanisms to foster and motivate sharing.

It is important to note that knowledge sharing cannot be assured solely by top-down management dictates (Brown and Duguid, 2000a, 2000b). Knowledge generation is predominantly a bottom-up process. Without the support of the knowledge workers, there is not much knowledge to manage. Thus, management's role is to create appropriate mechanisms and good environments for knowledge generation, dissemination, and management. This can involve sophisticated technological support. However, it more often involves ensuring that incentives and other rules of the game foster communication and collaboration among people who are, ultimately, the knowledge sources

Knowledge Capital

Regardless of the approach to knowledge management adopted, all managers would undoubtedly agree that the overall goal is to increase and leverage the knowledge capital of the organization. This leads to the obvious questions of defining and measuring knowledge capital. These questions were initially raised in Chapter 3, which discussed the challenge of value. In this section, possible answers are discussed.

Mintz (1998), drawing on the work of Baruch Lev, argues that knowledge capital can be determined by first estimating knowledge earnings, which he defines as "normalized" earnings minus earnings from tangible and financial assets. Dividing knowledge earnings by a knowledge capital discount rate yields an estimate of knowledge capital. He uses this metric to illustrate compelling differences between earnings of chemical and pharmaceutical companies.

Tangible assets and financial assets usually yield returns that are important elements of a company's overall earnings. It is often the case, however, that earnings far exceed what might be expected from these "hard" assets. For example, companies in the software, biotechnology, and pharmaceutical industries typically have much higher earnings than companies with similar hard assets in the aerospace, appliance, and automobile industries, to name just a few. It can be argued that these higher earnings are due to greater knowledge capital among, for example, software companies.

However, because knowledge capital does not appear on financial statements, it is very difficult to identify and, better yet, project knowledge earnings. A recent pair of articles by Mintz (1998, 2000) summarizes a method developed by Baruch Lev for estimating knowledge capital and earnings. The original article in *CFO* drew sufficient attention to be discussed in *The Economist* (1999) and to be reviewed by Strassman (1999). In general, both reviews applauded the progress represented by Mintz's article but also noted the shortcomings of the proposed metrics.

The key, Mintz and Lev argue, is to partition earnings into knowledge earnings and hard asset earnings. The equations below accomplish this by first projecting normalized annual earnings from an average of three past years and estimates for three future years using readily available information for publicly listed companies. Earnings from tangible and financial assets are calculated from reported asset values using industry averages of 7% and 4.5% for tangible and financial assets, respectively. Knowledge capital is then estimated by dividing knowledge earnings by a knowledge capital discount rate as shown below. On the basis of an analysis of several knowledge-intensive industries, Mintz and Lev use 10.5% for this discount rate.

Knowledge earnings = normalized annual earnings – earnings from tangible assets – earnings from financial assets

Knowledge capital = knowledge earnings/knowledge capital discount rate

Using this approach to calculating knowledge capital, Mintz compares 20 pharmaceutical companies to 27 chemical companies. He determines, for example, a knowledge capital-to-book value ratio of 2.45 for pharmaceutical companies and 1.42 for chemical companies. Similarly, the market value-to-book value ratio is 8.85 for pharmaceutical companies and 3.53 for chemical companies. In considering the correlation between knowledge capital and market value, Strassman (1999) points out that Mintz's estimates do not fully explain the full excess of market values over book values. Mintz's more recent article (2000) provides a knowledge capital scoreboard across 20 industries.

The key issue within this overall approach is being able to partition earnings. Although earnings from financial assets should be readily identifiable, the distinction between tangible and knowledge assets can be problematic. Furthermore, using industry average return rates to attribute earnings to tangible assets does not allow for the significant possibility of the tangible assets for any particular company having little or no earnings potential. Finally, of course, simply attributing all earnings "leftover" to knowledge assets amounts to giving knowledge assets credit for everything that cannot be explained by traditional financial methods.

Nevertheless, the knowledge capital construct appears to have potential application to investments such as R&D or training and development. The purpose of these two types of investments seems to obviously be that of increasing knowledge capital. Furthermore, companies that make investments for this purpose do seem to create more knowledge capital. The key when employing the knowledge capital construct is being able to project investment returns in terms of knowledge capital and, in turn, project earnings and separate these earnings into knowledge earnings and hard earnings. Furthermore, one needs to be able to do this for specific investment opportunities, not just the company as a whole.

Competitive Intelligence

In Chapter 2, the notion of competitive intelligence was introduced in the context of gaining information to support formulation and pursuit of growth strategies. In this section, this topic is discussed as a means for identifying, capturing, and compiling external competitive knowledge.

It is important to emphasize the external focus of competitive intelligence. As Herring (1999) indicates, the goal is to develop insights relative to strategic decisions and issues, early warning topics, and key players in the marketplace. More specifically, the company's vision, mission, and strategies—and especially key assumptions—drive the search for trends and events that portend changes of threats and opportunities.

This search involves publications databases, patent applications, websites, regulatory-required filings, newspapers and magazines, and so forth. For key players in the market, as an example, these sources of information are used to characterize competitors in terms of organizational structure, global presence, products and methodologies, operations, research and development, market image, growth strategy, and management (Settecase, 1999). Such knowledge enables formulation of strategies to compete with the adversary of the future rather than just the adversary of today.

John Pepper, former CEO of Proctor & Gamble, characterizes competitive intelligence at Proctor & Gamble as being focused on external benchmarking to achieve the company's goals of stretch, innovation, and speed (Pepper, 1999). This includes assessing emerging communications technologies for the purpose of enhancing the use of knowledge. Thus, knowledge management is not only a means of competitive intelligence it is also a target of this activity.

Use of technology to enhance knowledge management is a strong trend in itself. Shaker and Gembicki (1999) discuss major trends affecting competitive intelligence, including the dominance of information technology in general and the use of "knowbots" for searching online sources in particular. These autonomous agents prowl the Internet, looking for sources that satisfy their focused criteria for interesting information (e.g., see Watts, Porter and Courseault, 1999). After you react to what they have found, they modify their criteria and continue prowling.

The foci of these knowbots, or their much more ubiquitous human counterparts, are not solely on today's products, technologies, and competitors (Sharp, 2000). Alternative ways of providing the benefits of today's products and services and likely future market needs that cannot be met by today's products and services are likely topics. Also of interest are demographic trends and, for example, projections of size, weight, speed, and power consumption of various technologies.

The use of competitive intelligence to identify, capture, and compile knowledge of the sorts just discussed may seem so straightforward that it hardly deserves mention. However, I have frequently found that major corporations do this quite poorly. Furthermore, to the extent that external knowledge is gained, it often is not shared or, if shared, not used.

There appear to be several sources of this problem. In large, growing, and publicly listed companies, most managers are extremely time pressured to meet objectives, ensure quarterly revenues and earnings, and keep share prices rising. There is little time for reflection on the future. Time pressure is discussed in depth in Chapter 8.

Lack of external perspective can also be attributed to the increasing insularity that often accompanies successful growth (Rouse, 1998). This may be due, at least in part, to the increasing complexity of the growing organization, which makes keeping up with internal knowledge a substantial task in itself. It also appears to relate to the hubris that can emerge with success.

One solution to this problem is to make the external knowledge gained from competitive intelligence very easy to access. For example, associated with the *Technology Investment Advisor*, discussed in Chapter 6, is the *TIA Data Viewer*, which provides users the latest analyses and comparisons of their company to competitors and other companies of interest (ESS, 2000). The Internet is used to distribute updates of this competitive knowledge.

Use of the *TIA Data Viewer* is integrated within the task of technology strategy formulation and evaluation supported by the *Technology Investment Advisor*. Thus, knowledge is provided when and where it is needed, all with a mouse click or two. This type of support is often essential to ensuring that up-to-date knowledge is accessed and utilized for the purposes for which it is intended.

Summary

In this section, we have considered the importance of linking knowledge management strategies to overall corporate strategies. Alternative models for knowledge management were discussed. We also outlined issues associated with effective knowledge sharing, summarized the notion of knowledge capital, and considered the role of competitive intelligence in knowledge management. We now consider how these elements of knowledge strategies can be supported.

SUPPORTING KNOWLEDGE STRATEGIES

The alternative knowledge strategies outlined thus far inherently require a wide range of methods and tools for identifying, capturing, representing, and disseminating knowledge, as well as supporting knowledge management in general. These methods and tools vary depending on the content, scope, and approaches chosen from Figure 7.3. This section illustrates the types of support that span the gamut of alternatives in Figure 7.3.

Knowledge Capture

At first glance, it might seem that knowledge capture "simply" involves documenting knowledge elements and storing them in databases—or knowledge bases. Although this is sometimes the case, more often there are transformations required from data to information to knowledge. Data are just numbers; they have no meaning. Analysis and interpretation of these numbers yield information. When associated with a task context (i.e., goals, plans, etc.), information becomes knowledge.

Thus, for example, the data might be temperature measurements over the past 24 hours. The statistical properties of this time series would constitute information. The use of these properties in models for predicting tomorrow's temperatures would result in knowledge, albeit inherently uncertain. Thus, knowledge management is quite different from data management.

Methods and tools for supporting knowledge capture, therefore, include modeling tools, forecasting techniques, and risk analysis methods, to name just a few (Sage and Rouse, 1999). A good example of the role of these types of methods and tools for knowledge management is the mathematical models of customer and market purchasing behaviors for product planning, which were used by Gensch, Aversa, and Moore (1990).

There is also a range of knowledge available that only needs to be captured rather than transformed from data and information. This type of knowledge mainly concerns past promising ideas and results associated with these ideas, for example, evaluative data. Hargadon and Sutton (2000) argue that capturing and eventually reusing such ideas can provide the basis for an "innovation factory." They outline a four-step knowledge brokering cycle that includes capturing good ideas, keeping ideas alive, imagining new uses for old ideas, and putting promising concepts to the test. They suggest Thomas Edison's Menlo Park laboratory as the archetype of an innovation factory and IDEO and Idealab! as contemporary examples.

Knowledge Maps

Technologies for user-tailored information access and portrayal are also keys to helping users understand and use knowledge. We have found interactive knowledge maps to be quite useful in this regard (Rouse, Thomas and Boff, 1998). In particular, we found that the knowledge gained from a wide range of empirical studies of management practices could be represented using the following five elements:

- increases, decreases, presence, estimates of
- independent variable and class
- affects, increases, decreases, correlates, does not correlate
- dependent variable and class for
- population.

Use of this construct resulted in a large number of assertions of the form, "Perceived decreases of A result in measured increases of B for population C according to source D." On the basis of queries regarding A and B, for example, the relevant assertions could be used to construct graphical knowledge maps of the set of relationships.

Beyond the particulars of this approach, it is important to note the general need to capture and represent what has been learned—and hence is now known—from investments in creating knowledge. Creation of knowledge maps involves determining what can be asserted as a result of an investment, codifying these assertions, and then depicting the relationships among sets of assertions relevant to a specific query. This greatly enhances the ability to share knowledge beyond those originally involved in its creation.

Ernie

As mentioned earlier, Ernst & Young has adopted a centralized approach to knowledge management that involves an impressive compilation of consulting knowledge delivered via the Internet (Ernst & Young, 2000). *Ernie* allows users to start an electronic dialogue with a consulting professional on a variety of business topics and receive substantive responses delivered directly to them online. Business issues covered include strategic business planning, corporate finance, accounting, human resources, information technology, personal finance, real estate, and taxes.

Users of *Ernie* also have full access to a previously asked questions database, which provides instant answers to business questions. A feature called Trendwatch enables users to compare their experiences and projections with similar companies. Also provided are various business tools and numerous case studies. Overall, *Ernie* provides a very economical way for companies to gain access to premier consulting services that they otherwise might not be able to afford.

Ernie provides an interesting model of knowledge management. The goal is to disseminate best practices to as many people as possible, in an economical and user-friendly way. It is easy to imagine *Ernie*-like systems replacing companies' employee manuals or the help desk.

Of course, the costs of designing, developing, and maintaining such systems are likely to be rather significant, especially in terms of keeping the content up to date. Furthermore, the benefits of a significantly better-informed workforce may be difficult to estimate. Nevertheless, it seems reasonable to argue that systems like *Ernie* will be considered best practices in the future.

IKSM*Online*

This online publication is the electronic edition of the hardcopy management journal *Information • Knowledge • Systems Management* (IKSM, 2000). These publications are focused on systems-oriented senior managers. The typical subscriber is an individual who has received a PhD in electrical engineering or chemistry 20 or more years ago and now works as a vice president for marketing or engineering in a major technology-oriented company.

This online publication provides access to the full-text articles appearing in its hardcopy sibling publication, as well as full-text articles from other selected journals. Subscribers also complete an interest profile that is used to provide regular E-mail recommendations of specific articles from over 30 top management journals and magazines. There are also recommended websites, including reviews of websites. Interviews of top managers and thought leaders appear regularly, as do book reviews.

IKSM*Online* first appeared in the Fall of 1999. As of this writing, its 8 months of service have resulted in several useful lessons learned. First, the use of interest profiles has resulted in providing subscribers with reading recommendations that they judge highly in terms of matching their interests. These interest profiles also result in a much more comprehensive screening of relevant literature than subscribers would normally do themselves.

However, subscribers' actual use of this knowledge is highly related to its immediate relevance. Numerous subscribers have commented that the recommended articles were great matches to their interests and that "some day" they would read these articles. On the other hand, when a recommendation happened to coincide with a current high-priority issue, people accessed the material immediately.

As an experiment, we added, for selected subscribers, a service that attempted to more closely match their current needs. This resulted in E-mails, in this case to a CEO, like the following:

> "In preparing for your Board of Directors meeting next Tuesday, take a look at p. 117 of the May–June issue of *Harvard Business Review*. The table shown there will help in making the point we discussed last week."

The feedback we received from this experiment was that this is exactly the type of help managers want. They want targeted, timely, and easy to consume recommendations. IKSM*Online* scores fairly well on these attributes but not as well as a service that knows the subscribers' issues of the day. There are ongoing efforts to create mechanisms within IKSM*Online* to improve along these attributes, including means for subscribers to easily represent and update their issues and concerns.

Collaboration

The types of support discussed thus far assume that knowledge is captured, represented, and disseminated. These methods and tools are premised on being able to externalize and document knowledge. However, many types of knowledge, especially "knowing," are not amenable to externalization, capture, and dissemination.

For such tacit knowledge, the best approach to knowledge management is to link the people who have the knowledge to the people who need it (Hargadon and Sutton, 2000). E-mail is one mechanism for creating such links. Lotus Notes provides a more sophisticated means of addressing similar needs. In Chapter 9, we discuss managers' expressed desires for these types of support.

Aside from the technology, several compelling constructs have emerged in recent years for supporting collaboration among knowledge sources and users. The concept of communities of practice originated at Xerox (see, for example, Brown and Duguid 2000a, 2000b). Communities of practice are groups of people informally bound together by shared expertise and passion for joint enterprise (Wenger and Snyder, 2000).

The "classic"' example of a community of practice is the maintenance employees who service and repair Xerox photocopying machines at customers' sites (Brown and Duguid, 2000a, 2000b). This community shares troubleshooting experiences and identifies candidate best practices emerging from these experiences. In this way, both knowledge and knowing improve for all members of the community.

Using examples drawn from many companies, Wenger and Snyder (2000) conclude that communities of practice add value by

- helping to drive strategy,
- starting new lines of business,
- solving problems quickly,
- transferring best practices,
- developing professional skills, and
- helping to recruit and retain talent.

They also suggest ways to get communities going and sustain them over time, including the following:

- Identify potential communities that will enhance the company's strategic capabilities.
- Provide the infrastructure that will support such communities and enable them to apply their expertise effectively.
- Use nontraditional methods to assess the value of the company's communities of practice.

Thus, communities do not emerge, or at least do not function with maximum effectiveness, without organizational support. Furthermore, thcy should be judged using knowledge-relevant metrics rather than traditional operational metrics.

Another collaboration construct pioneered by Xerox is strategic communities (Storck and Hill, 2000). Such communities differ from communities of practice in that they are not voluntary groups of people who do similar work. Storck and Hill illustrate this concept in the context of a large, strategically critical information technology infrastructure project at Xerox.

They conclude that principles of effective strategic communities include the following:

- Design an interaction format that promotes openness and allows for serendipity.
- Build a common organizational culture.
- Demonstrate the existence of mutual interests after initial success at resolving issues and achieving corporate goals.
- Leverage those aspects of the organizational culture that respect the value of collective learning.
- Embed knowledge-sharing practices into the work processes of the group.
- Establish an environment in which knowledge sharing is based on processes and cultural norms defined by the community rather than other parts of the organization.

These principles relate to creating an effective—and usually distributed—team to pursue a strategic undertaking for a limited amount of time. It is important that such teams learn to function effectively quite quickly. Simply recognizing that they are, or should be, a strategic community is a very important first step.

Communities of practice focus on collaboration among people who do similar work. Strategic communities emphasize collaboration among people who do different work but have shared overall goals. The next logical step in the collaborative chain is coevolution. Eisenhardt and Galunic (2000) define coevolution in terms of two or more ecologically interdependent but unique species whose evolutionary trajectories become intertwined over time. As these species adapt to their environment, they also adapt to one another. The result is an ecosystem of partially interdependent species that adapt together.

On the basis of examples of the benefits of coevolution drawn from a wide range of companies, they suggest several steps to "kick-start" coevolution:

- Establish at least monthly, must-attend meetings among business unit heads to enable them to get to know one another.
- Keep the conversation focused on real-time information about operating basics to build intuition and business roles.
- Get rid of "good people collaborate, bad people don't" thinking by rewarding self-interested pursuit of individual business performance.
- When collaborative opportunities arise, remember that many managers get stuck on their first idea—brainstorm to expand the range of possibilities.

- Realistically analyze the costs and benefits of the most promising options.
- Fine-tune as you go. Up-front analysis is never a substitute for real-time learning.
- Avoid collaborative creep. Take the time to cut stale links.

The notion of coevolution is far from new. Universities have long co-evolved with sponsors and government since World War II; however, industry has adopted this notion more recently (Economist, 1997). What is different, however, is the idea of coevolution being the norm for relationships among companies. The possibility of both independence and interdependence being a desired organizational relationship, rather than just a transitional phase, is a relatively new way to think about business affiliations. Of course, this idea fits quite nicely with the notion of loosely structured organizations and virtual organizations, as discussed in Chapter 5.

Summary

The range of types of supports discussed in this section illustrate the richness of approaches to knowledge management and the wealth of choices of methods and tools possible. Striking the right balance between centralized and distributed approaches is critical, as is providing appropriate support mechanisms to ensure that knowledge management is more than just the latest management fad.

CONCLUSIONS

This chapter began with a discussion of the elements of information strategy—process integration, electronic commerce, and knowledge management. Alternative views of knowledge management were discussed, including misconceptions or myths about knowledge management. The underlying difficulties that cause knowledge to be a challenge were also considered.

Alternative knowledge strategies were characterized in terms of links to corporate strategy, choices among the wealth of possible models, enhancing knowledge sharing, measuring knowledge capital, and integrating competitive intelligence. Ways to support these strategies were discussed, including approaches to knowledge capture, knowledge maps, knowledge dissemination, and collaboration.

It is important to recognize the substantial risks associated with knowledge strategies. In recent years, companies have invested enormous sums in process integration, electronic commerce, and knowledge management. In many cases, the returns do not justify the investments. It is very easy to spend large amounts of money poorly in this area.

Those who have been successful drive their investment decisions by specific business issues for which needed outcomes are clear and measurable. They also deal explicitly and well with the many people issues associated with the success of such investments. Overall, risks and resources have to be very carefully managed. This is much easier to do with a well-founded and clearly articulated knowledge strategy in place.

KEY QUESTIONS

Successfully addressing the challenge of knowledge involves answering several key questions, as indicated below. The concepts, principles, methods, and tools discussed in this chapter will support pursuing answers to these questions:

- What business issues drive your organization's information strategy?
- What does knowledge management mean within your organization?
- Does your organization know what it knows?
- How do you measure the value of knowledge in your organization?
- What is your knowledge strategy in terms of content, scope, and approaches?
- How do you support your knowledge strategy?

REFERENCES

Apostolou, D., and Mentzas, G. (1999). Managing corporate knowledge: a comparative analysis of experiences in consulting firms. *Knowledge and Process Management* 6(3): 129–138.

Blattberg, R. C., Glazer, R., and Little, J. D. C. (Eds.). (1994). *The Marketing Information Revolution*. Boston, MA: Harvard Business School.

Brown, J. S., and Duguid, P. (1998). Organizing knowledge. *California Management Review* 40 (1): 90–111.

Brown, J. S., and Duguid, P. (2000a). *The Social Life of Information*. Boston, MA: Harvard Business School.

Brown, J. S., and Duguid, P. (2000b). Balancing act: how to capture knowledge without killing it. *Harvard Business Review* May–June: 73–80.

Carter, M. (1999). The knowledge lab. *Technology Review* 102(5): 84–89.

Coates, J. F. (1999). The inevitability of knowledge management. *Research Technology Management* 42(4): 6–7.

Cook, S. D. N., and Brown, J. S. (1999). Bridging epistemologies: the generative dance between organizational knowledge and organizational knowing. *Organization Science* 10(4): 381–400.

Cross, R., and Baird, L. (2000). Technology is not enough: improving performance by building organizational memory. *Sloan Management Review* 41(3): 69–78.

Davenport, T. O. (1999). *Human Capital: What It Is and Why People Invest It.* San Francisco, CA: Jossey-Bass.

Economist. (1997). The knowledge factory: a survey of universities. *The Economist* October 4: 1–22.

Economist. (1999). A price on the priceless: measuring intangible assets. *The Economist* June 12: 61–62.

Eisenhardt, K. M., and Galunic, D. C. (2000). Coevolving: at last, a way to make synergies work. *Harvard Business Review* January–February: 91–101.

Ernst & Young. (2000). Ernie. ernie.ey.com.

ESS. (2000). Technology Investment Advisor. http://www.ess-advisors.com. Atlanta, GA: Enterprise Support Systems.

Evans, P. B., and Wurster, T. S. (1997). Strategy and the new economics of information. *Harvard Business Review* September–October: 71–82.

Evans, P., and Wurster, T. S. (1999). Getting real about virtual commerce. *Harvard Business Review* 77(6): 85–94.

Foster, F. (1999). Justifying knowledge management investments. *Knowledge and Process Management* 6(1): 154–157.

Fryer, B. (1999). The ROI challenge: can you produce a positive return on investment from ERP? *CFO* September: 85–90.

Gensch, D. H., Aversa, N., and Moore, S. P. (1990). A choice-modeling market information system that enabled ABB Electric to expand its market share. *Interfaces* 20: 6–25.

Hansen, M. T., Nohria, N., and Tierney, T. (1999). What's your strategy for managing knowledge? *Harvard Business Review* March–April: 106–116.

Hargadon, A., and Sutton, R. I. (2000). Building an innovation factory. *Harvard Business Review* May–June: 157–166.

Herring, J. P. (1999). Key intelligence topics: a process to identify and define intelligence needs. *Competitive Intelligence Review* 10(2): 4–14.

IKSM. (2000). www.IKSM*Online*.com.

Ives, W., Torrey, B., and Gordon, C. (1998). Thought leadership. *Knowledge Management* (April/May). http://www.ac.com/services/knowledge/knowlshar.html.

McDermott, R. (1999). Why information technology inspired but cannot deliver knowledge management. *California Management Review* 41(4): 103–117.

Mintz, S. L. (1998). A better approach to estimating knowledge capital. *CFO* February: 29–37.

Mintz, S. L. (2000). A knowing glance: the second annual knowledge capital scoreboard. *CFO* February: 52–62.

Nonaka, I., and Takeuchi, H. (1995). *The Knowledge Creating Company*. New York: Oxford University Press.

O'Dell, C, and Grayson, C. J. (1998). If we only knew what we knew. *California Management Review* 40(3): 154–174.

Oracle. (1998). Special issue on knowledge management in the information age. *Oracle Magazine* 12(3, May/June).

Ottum, B., and Moore, W. L. (1997). The role of market information in new product success/failure. *Journal of Product Innovation Management* 14: 258–273.

Pepper, J. E. (1999). Competitive intelligence at Proctor & Gamble. *Competitive Intelligence Review* 10(4): 4–9.

Pfeffer, J., and Sutton, R. I. (1999). Knowing "what" to do is not enough: turning knowledge into action. *California Management Review* 42(1): 83–108.

Polanyi, M. P. (1958). *Personal Knowledge: Towards a Post-Critical Philosophy*. Chicago, IL: University of Chicago Press.

Polanyi, M. P. (1966). *The Tacit Dimension*. New York: Doubleday.

Rouse, W. B. (1998). *Don't Jump to Solutions: Thirteen Delusions That Undermine Strategic Thinking*. San Francisco, CA: Jossey-Bass.

Rouse, W. B., and Sage, A. P. (1999). Information technology and knowledge management. In: *Handbook of Systems Engineering and Management*, edited by Sage, A. P., and Rouse, W. B.. New York: Wiley, chapt. 30.

Rouse, W. B., Thomas, B. G. S., and Boff, K. R. (1998). Knowledge maps for knowledge mining: application to R&D/technology management. *IEEE Transactions on Systems, Man, and Cybernetics* (Part C) 28(3): 309–317.

Sage, A. P., and Rouse, W. B. (Eds.). (1999). *Handbook of Systems Engineering and Management*. New York: Wiley.

Sarvary, M. (1999). Knowledge management and competition in the consulting industry. *California Management Review* 41(2): 95–107.

Settecase, M. (1999). The competitiveness assessment model: a thought-structuring approach to analysis. *Competitive Intelligence Review* 10(3): 43–50.

Seybold, P. B. (1998). *Customers.com: How to Create a Profitable Business Strategy for the Internet and Beyond*. New York: Times Business.

Shaker, S. M. and Gembicki, M. P. (1999). Competitive intelligence: a futurist's perspective. *Competitive Intelligence Magazine* January–March: 24–27.

Shapiro, C, and Varian, H. R. (1998). *Information Rules: A Strategic Guide to the Network Economy*. Boston, MA: Harvard Business School.

Sharp, S. (2000). Ten myths that cripple competitive intelligence. *Competitive Intelligence Magazine* January–March: 37–40.

Storck, J., and Hill, P. A. (2000). Knowledge diffusion through "strategic communities." *Sloan Management Review* 41(2): 63–74.

Strassman, P. A. (1998). The value of knowledge capital. *American Programmer* March: 3–10.

Strassman, P. A. (1999). Does knowledge capital explain market/book valuations? *Knowledge Management* September. www.strassman.com/pubs/km.

Ungston, G. R., and Trudel, J. D. (1999). The emerging knowledge-based economy. *IEEE Spectrum* May: 60–65.

Venkatraman, N. (2000). Five steps to a dot-com strategy: how to find your footing on the web. *Sloan Management Review* 41(3): 15–28.

Warren, P., and Davies, G. (2000). Knowledge management at BT Labs. *Research Technology Management* 43(3): 12–23.

Watts, R. J., Porter, A. L., and Courseault, C. (1999). Functional analysis: deriving systems knowledge from bibliographic information resources. *Information • Knowledge • Systems Management* 1(1): 45–61.

Wenger, E. C., and Snyder, W. M. (2000). Communities of practice: the organizational frontier. *Harvard Business Review* January–February: 139–145.

Whiting, R. (1999). Knowledge Management: myths and realities. *Information Week* November 22: 42–54.

Zack, M. H. (1999a). Developing a knowledge strategy. *California Management Review* 41(3): 125–145.

Zack, M. H. (1999b). Managing codified knowledge. *Sloan Management Review* 40(4): 45–58.

CHAPTER EIGHT

Time

When managers talk about scarce resources, they usually focus on money in terms of shortfalls in revenues and/or overruns in costs and tight budgets due to either or both of these problems. In boom times, resource discussions also often focus on people and problems in recruiting people with needed skills. Senior managers usually devote much of their time to addressing these money and people issues.

I have found, however, that an organization's scarcest resource usually is the time of senior management. There is always the possibility of more money, but the collective time of the management team is inherently limited. A typical top management team includes roughly 10 or, perhaps, up to 20 people. Assuming 2,000 work hours per year, this team has 20,000–40,000 hours to devote to the essential challenges of strategic management discussed in this book, as well as a sundry of other tasks.

In contrast, the 10–20,000 employees of the company have 20,000–40,000,000 hours to invest in designing, developing, selling, servicing, and accounting for the company's products and services. If the 40,000 management hours are not invested appropriately, many of the 40,000,000 hours will be poorly spent, perhaps providing little or no return.

Appropriate allocation of senior management time is a significant challenge. The primary motivation for successfully addressing this challenge is not simply to minimize wasted time. Instead, the driving force is the recognition that how senior managers spend their time defines the substance and style of the leadership of the organization. Inappropriate allocations of time not only do not get the right work done but such misallocations send wrong messages that propagate throughout the organization.

CHALLENGE OF TIME

The difficulty of this challenge stems from two strong forces. First and foremost, the compensation plans of most senior managers are highly linked to relatively short-term results. Failure to meet these goals can result in substantial economic penalties and, perhaps, the ultimate penalty of being replaced. This force often prompts micromanagement.

The second force is more subtle. Today's events demand attention. They also provide more concrete and immediate feedback. Tomorrow's goals are often more abstract and inherently provide much more delayed feedback. Senior managers have typically succeeded—achieved their current positions—because they delivered short-term, concrete results. Perhaps, for example, they proved themselves by ensuring that the savings expected from business process reengineering were actually realized. Managers who have succeeded in such assignments are often very impatient with abstractions and any delay in gratification of having solved a problem or made a decision.

Obvious examples of this phenomenon are often complete absorption in ensuring this month's sales and this quarter's earnings per share. Less obvious examples include time devoted to dealing with day-to-day people problems. Consequently, many lower-level managers report that one of their biggest problems is too much help from higher-level managers.

This, often excessive, attention stems from top management's very appropriate concern with making sure that plans get executed successfully. Indeed, lack of execution, or poor execution, appears to be the most common reason that top managers fail (Charan and Colvin, 1999; Bennis and O'Toole, 2000). Furthermore, the perceived need to micromanage often leads to executives being overextended (Economist, 1999).

Thus, to address the challenge of time, it is necessary to overcome strong and natural tendencies of top management to become completely absorbed by today's press of events. A recent study that we performed for a major United States corporation clearly illustrates some of the sources of these difficulties. This study was prompted by ongoing, periodic interviews of members of the management team that repeatedly indicated time management to be a nagging problem.

The study was organized around a version of Stephen Covey's well-known chart of the importance vs. urgency of management tasks (Covey, 1989). The version of this chart that was created for this study is shown in Figure 8.1.

The third habit of Covey's highly regarded seven habits is "put first things first." This habit is most often undermined by urgent but unimportant tasks that demand attention and then tend to get it, thereby diminishing attention to nonurgent but important tasks.

With the use of Figure 8.1 as the starting point, the following interview question was posed to 10 executives (including the president of the company), as well as 5 executive secretaries supporting these executives and having supported a total of almost 40 executives since becoming executive secretaries.

> Can you provide examples of situations where you—or the executives that you support or have supported—have felt trapped by the urgent, but not important?

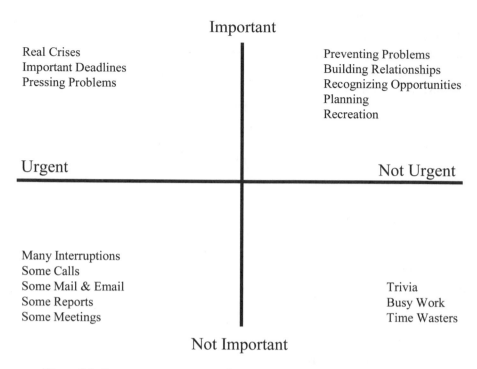

Figure 8.1. Importance vs. urgency of management tasks (based on Covey, 1989)

The results of this assessment indicated that executives were most often trapped by the urgent but unimportant in the following ways:

- too much email—84 per day estimated by executives vs. 59 per day estimated by their secretaries,
- too many poorly planned meetings without conclusions,
- too many subordinates asking for permission and delegating upward, and
- too many fire drills for corporate, sector, and unions,

The average executive time trapped was 41% for executives' self estimates and 42% for secretaries' estimates. The rather surprising closeness of the two independent estimates of time lost by executives supports the shared perception of there being a time management problem. These statistics are also in general agreement with study results reported by Covey (1989) and Miller and Morris (1999). Roughly speaking, executives perceive that about half of their time is wasted.

Pursuit of the underlying causes of difficulties delegating tasks and keeping them delegated led to the following:

- Instructions/expectations were inadequate.
- Training and/or coaching was inadequate.
- Error avoidance was more important than performance.
- Micromanagement preempted lower levels.
- Incentives/rewards were not linked to performance.
- Wrong people were chosen for the tasks to be done.

These are, for the most part, leadership problems that cause time management problems. We discuss leadership issues in the next section. Note also that the full recommendations that emerged from this study are discussed later in this chapter when support of time strategies is considered.

The types of time-related issues that emerged from this study are neither novel nor unique to contemporary organizations. Roughly 25 years ago, Oncken and Wass (1974) and Mintzberg (1975) explored these issues. Revisiting these classic papers makes it very clear that we cannot blame the time challenge on the remnants of TQM, BPR, and, more recently, "Internet time." The challenge has probably been with us for as long as there have been managers.

Oncken and Wass' 1974 classic "Who's got the monkey" article begins by outlining the types of time demands on managers, which include

- boss-imposed time,
- system-imposed time,
- subordinate-imposed time,
- self-imposed time, and
- discretionary time.

Subordinate-imposed time robs self-imposed and discretionary time by subordinates taking monkeys (tasks and responsibilities) off their backs and shifting these burdens to their boss' backs. Oncken and Wass argue that, when accepting monkeys, managers voluntarily assume positions subordinate to their subordinates.

Thus, delegation has long been a problem. Their prescription for dealing with the resulting monkeys are expressed in terms of rules for care and feeding of monkeys:

- Feed a monkey or shoot it.
- Keep the monkey population below the number that can be fed in budgeted time.

- Feed monkeys by appointment only.
- Feed monkeys face to face or by telephone, never in writing.
- Assign monkeys their next feeding time.

Thus, managers should help subordinates take responsibility for their monkeys, but carefully avoid ending up with the monkeys. However, as Covey (1999) indicates in his commentary on the republication of the Oncken and Wass article, many managers are actually eager to take on subordinates' monkeys. Covey also notes the difficulty of delegation in this era of empowerment, which was less the case during Oncken and Wass' era.

The other classic article from the same period is Mintzberg's (1975) treatment of the facts and folklore surrounding how managers spend their time. (This article is also discussed in Chapter 1.) Mintzberg discusses four myths and compares them with the facts emerging from his studies of what managers really do. These four myths include the following:

- Myth: managers are reflective, systematic planners. Fact: managers simply respond to the pressures of the job, with plans often existing only in their heads.
- Myth: effective managers have no regular duties to perform. Fact: there are many rituals, ceremonies, negotiations, and processing of "soft" information that are performed.
- Myth: senior managers need aggregated information, which is best provided by a formal management information system. Fact: managers favor verbal media, telephone calls, and meeting over documents; timely tidbits are important to them.
- Myth: management is, or is quickly becoming, a science and profession. Fact: managers' programs for scheduling time, processing information, and making decisions remain locked deep in their brains.

Mintzberg outlines a framework for thinking about managers' roles, including interpersonal roles (figurehead, leader, and liaison), informational roles (monitor, disseminator, and spokesperson), and decisional roles (entrepreneur, disturbance handler, resource allocator, and negotiator). He discusses rough percentages of time spent in each of these roles.

His overall conclusions are well captured by, "The pressures of the job drive the manager to take on too much work, encourage interruption, respond quickly to every stimulus, seek the tangible and avoid the abstract, make decisions in small increments, and do everything abruptly." (Mintzberg, 1975). Three other quotes that fit squarely with the themes of this chapter include

- "Perhaps the most important resource the manager allocates is his or her own time."
- "Managers have the information and authority; analysts have the time and the technology."
- "Free time is made, not found."

In a recent book, Miller and Morris (1999) summarize several studies, indicating the skewed percentage of time managers devote to operational issues and the relatively small percentage of time devoted to longer-term issues for which managers may be uniquely positioned to influence outcomes. They argue that "Behavior focused exclusively on operations is marginally effective, while efforts made upstream can provide leverage and compound benefits to long-term results." They advocate the following allocation: 50% to the game (day-to-day work), 30% to practice (improving capability), and 20% to discovery (future practice).

The classic articles of Oncken and Wass (1974) and Mintzberg (1975), as well as the more recent summary of Miller and Morris (1999), provide ample explanation for my frequent experiences when discussing the challenges presented in this book with management teams in a wide variety of companies. Almost always, executives and senior managers latch onto the challenge of time. They usually can relate to the other challenges and recognize their importance, at least intellectually. However, the challenge of time strikes deeper chords. Most managers are plagued by this challenge.

TIME AND LEADERSHIP

In several of my recent books (e.g., Rouse 1994, 1996, and 1998), I summarize lessons learned in terms of likely success factors for creating and implementing plans, repositioning companies in changing markets, and avoiding organizational delusions. In one of my many seminars on these topics, a participant asked, "I've read several of your books and noted with interest the success factors you have compiled. If you could only recommend paying attention to one factor, across all of the issues you discuss, what one factor would you recommend as the most important factor in success?"

After I reflected on this question—and quickly scanned the mental versions of my lists—the answer was readily apparent. Sustained commitment by an organization's leaders is the most important single factor in success. If leaders do not demonstrably commit themselves and this commitment is not visibly sustained, most best-laid plans will go awry.

A key indicator of committed leadership is time. Leaders provide attention to the things of most importance to them. Thus, to the extent that the challenges discussed in this book receive attention from your leaders, you can conclude that strategic management is important to these leaders. Similarly, to the extent that these challenges never seem to make it to the head of the queue, you can reach the opposite conclusion.

These two possibilities beg the question of why leaders would not be concerned with strategic issues. One strong possibility is that they are too busy managing to lead. It may be that they view management as synonymous with leadership. For these reasons, appropriately addressing the challenge of time requires that we consider the nature of leadership.

Nature of Leadership

The topic of leadership has received significant attention for a very long time, originally in the context of political and military leadership and, more recently, in terms of managers as leaders. This body of material cannot possibly be reviewed here. However, it is possible to delve sufficiently into this topic to show clear linkages between leaderships and how managers allocate their time.

Kouzes and Posner (1987), in their best-selling book on leadership, suggest five fundamental practices of exemplary leaders:

- Leaders challenge the process—they search for opportunities to change the status quo, and they experiment and take risks during this search.
- Leaders inspire a shared vision—they envision the future and enlist others in pursuit of this vision.
- Leaders enable others to act—they foster collaboration, actively involve others, and strengthen others, making each person feel capable and powerful.
- Leaders model the way—they create standards of excellence and then set an example for others to follow, planning small wins along the way.
- Leaders encourage the heart—they recognize contributions that individuals make, celebrate accomplishments, and make everyone feel like heroes.

Relative to the challenge of time, these practices have two things in common. First, if done well, they are time consuming. Second, they cannot be delegated. This does not mean, however, that they are always done well. One reason is that they tend to fall in the important but nonurgent quadrant of Figure 8.1. It is difficult to pay full attention to leadership responsibilities when you are spending half your time dealing with urgent but unimportant demands.

More broadly, leadership responsibilities are often preempted by management tasks. Maccoby (2000) contrasts management as a function—planning, budgeting, evaluating, and facilitating—with leadership as a relationship—selecting talent, motivating, coaching, and building trust. Management functions are much easier to delegate than leadership relationships. However, as noted earlier, delegation is difficult for many managers. Thus, they spend their time managing rather than leading.

Focusing on organizational change, Shields and colleagues (1999a, 1999b) stress the importance of consistent leadership at the top for achieving successful change. They assert that the leader's role is to give voice to the vision, motivate employees to participate, and serve as behavioral role models. Contrasting management and leadership, they conclude that "Managers maintain organizations; leaders transform them" (1999b).

Leadership style is also an important factor in the effectiveness of leaders. Building on the pioneering work of McClelland (1987), Goleman (2000) discusses the impacts of leadership styles on organizational climate. Styles associated with positive impacts include authoritative (not authoritarian), affiliative, democratic, and coaching. Style associated with negative impacts are coercive and pacesetting.

Pacesetting leaders are highly competent and know best how to do everything. If they are also coercive, they force others to do things the way they would. In my experience, followers of pacesetters often wait for the leader to decide what he or she wants, rather than propose or advocate other ideas. Such leaders often find the monkeys repeatedly returning to their backs.

Pacesetting leaders are often trying to save time. They know exactly what to do and they simply want followers to do it. After all, why discuss and debate the issue if the right answer is already obvious? Why waste the time? If such leaders are also coercive, other ideas have less than a whisper of a chance of getting attention.

I am reminded of a 5-day course I took many years ago for CEOs of small, growing companies. With four seasoned instructors and only 13 students, all CEOs, it was an intense experience. The lead instructor, addressing delegation issues, commented, "When you look around the table at your top management team—the senior managers of marketing, sales, finance, engineering, manufacturing, etc.,—if you feel that you could do any of these people's jobs better than they are, if you had the time, replace them. All of your top managers should be better at their jobs than you could be even if you had the time."

Here lies an important factor underlying delegation problems. Pacesetting leaders micromanage because they are not confident in their subordinates.

Such leaders want to make sure things are done right. Not having developed their subordinates sufficiently, they intervene and command—or coerce— these people to do what they, the pacesetters, know is the right way. Thus, unable to delegate management tasks, they steal time from leadership tasks.

The view of leadership portrayed thus far has been emerging for several decades—it is far from novel. Furthermore, the concept of leadership continues to evolve. In Chapter 1, I briefly discussed Peter Drucker's (1997) commentary on the demise of command and control management. Put simply, as we move toward a network economy, rather than an employee economy, with associated diseconomies of scale, command and control are being replaced by more flexible relationships in which no one controls and no one commands.

Wheatley (1992) has also heralded the changing nature of leadership. Her "new science" view emphasizes "the importance of simple governing principles: guiding visions, strong values, organizational beliefs—the few rules that individuals can use to shape their own behavior. The leader's task is to communicate them, to keep them ever-present and clear, and then allow individuals in the system their random sometimes chaotic-looking meanderings."

Both Drucker's and Wheatley's perspectives suggest a further shift in the balance from management toward leadership. As explicated in Chapter 5, increasing trends toward loosely structured and perhaps virtual organizations suggest that traditional management functions will be distributed—that is, people will manage themselves—and centralized leadership, as defined above, will be the glue that keeps the venture together and moving forward.

Shifting to a specific example of the role of leadership, consider new product development, a topic that was discussed at length in Chapter 3. Jassawalla and Sashittal (2000) summarize the literature on leadership of product development teams. They conclude that effective team leaders should

- clearly communicate the organization's expectations,
- foster high levels of communication and create a climate that raises morale and energizes the team,
- take responsibility for the team's goals, guide and share burdens, and interface with key external constituents,
- enjoy high levels of autonomy and support from superiors,
- involve all functional groups from the initiating stages, and
- balance both technical and human interaction issues and reduce destructive conflict.

These conclusions, many of which are empirically based, are completely consistent with the broader definitions of leadership discussed earlier in this section.

Jassawalla and Sashittal used these results as the basis for conducting interviews of 40 managers in 10 high-tech companies. The results of these interviews suggested that carefully selected team leaders endowed with high levels of autonomy are likely to

- ensure commitment,
- build transparency,
- function as facilitators,
- strengthen human relations, and
- foster learning.

Again, we see consistency with the broader, earlier discussions.

As another specific example, consider leadership in technological innovation, which was discussed in Chapters 3 and 6. A recent issue of *Research Technology Management* (RTM, 2000) included brief commentaries by eight previous winners of major Industrial Research Institute awards. Their collective views of the roles of leaders align very well with the foregoing in this section.

The consistency of best practices across broad and more focused treatises on leadership lead to a central conclusion of this chapter and, indeed, the whole book. Effective leadership, as defined in this chapter, is critical for successfully addressing all the essential challenges of strategic management. More specifically, successfully addressing these challenges requires the time of top leaders, which dictates that the challenge of time be successfully addressed.

Recruiting Leaders

Not surprisingly, finding good leaders is a major issue for most organizations. Leadership gurus Warren Bennis and James O'Toole (2000) discuss this issue in the context of the impacts of choosing the wrong CEO. They provide a set of questions to keep in mind when interviewing CEO candidates:

- Does the candidate lead consistently in a way that inspires followers to trust him?
- Does the candidate hold people accountable for their performance and promises?
- Is the candidate comfortable delegating important tasks to others?
- How much time does the candidate spend developing other leaders?

- How much time does the candidate spend communicating vision, purpose, and values? Do people down the line apply this vision to their day-to-day work?
- How comfortable is the candidate sharing information, resources, praise, and credit?
- Does the candidate energize others?
- Does the candidate consistently demonstrate respect for followers?
- Does the candidate really listen?

Notice how factors such as time, delegation, and empowering others are laced throughout these questions.

Relative to several well-known successes as CEOs, Bennis and O'Toole conclude that they "are great because they demonstrate integrity, provide meaning, generate trust, and communicate values. In doing so, they energize their followers, humanely push people to meet challenging business goals, and all the while develop leadership skills in others. Real leaders, in a phrase, move the human heart."

Well-known executive recruiters Thomas Neff and James Citrin, in an interview with Jennifer Reingold (1999), suggest six principles of effective leadership:

- Live with integrity, lead by example.
- Develop a winning strategy or "big idea."
- Build a great management team.
- Inspire employees to greatness.
- Create a flexible, responsive organization.
- Use reinforcing management systems.

The implications for how leaders should spend their time are quite clear. They need to embody the practices advocated by Kouzes and Posner and delegate management tasks to the extent that they take away from time spent leading.

Leaders and Time

Coming full circle, it is important to consider what leadership experts say specifically about how leaders spend their time. Kouzes and Posner (1987) make the following points:

- Quoting Warren Bennis, they indicate that "routine work drives out non-routine work."

- "It seems that situations and people conspire to make leaders into bureaucrats."
- With regard to how leaders spend their time, they suggest, "Time is the truest test of what the leader really thinks is important."

Peter Senge, the well-known proponent of learning organizations, as explicated in *The Fifth Discipline* (1990) and other publications, reflects on how manages allocate their time:

- "Apparently, the 'ready, fire, aim' atmosphere of American corporations has been fully assimilated and internalized by those who live in that atmosphere."
- "The way each of us and each of our close colleagues go about managing our own time will say a good deal about out commitment to learning."

More recently, as discussed in Chapter 8, Pfeffer and Sutton (1999) consider an essential issue in knowledge management—the difficulties of transforming knowing "what" to knowing "how" and doing it. They conclude that successful organizational change in this area is highly related to what leaders do, how they spend their time, and how they allocate resources.

Summary

The challenge of time has both immediate, practical aspects and longer-term, far-ranging aspects. Losing control of one's time means that it tends to be spent poorly, regardless of preferences and priorities. Gaining control of one's time offers the potential for allocating this time for maximum personal and organizational advantage. Time strategies need to address both gaining control and allocating appropriately. The next section addresses these needs.

Beyond these practical needs, there is the essential issue of how allocations of time reflect on leaders. Leaders need to understand that their allocations of time reflect their real priorities. Some would assert that "How you spend your time is who you are." This assertion may be too strong. However, there are certainly merits in the argument that this view significantly affects followers' perceptions.

Leaders also need to understand that their allocations of time send strong messages to their followers. Regardless of "official" goals, strategies, and plans, how leaders spend their time usually reflects the true organizational agenda. Thus, for example, economic growth or saving more lives may be the stated goals, but leaders' behaviors may reflect higher priorities on maintaining control and assuring continuity.

Because all of us are followers in at least some aspects of life, it is also useful to consider how leaders spend their time from this perspective. Followers should pay attention to how their leaders allocate their time, because this allocation, rather than their words, reflects their real priorities. If words and deeds are inconsistent, you may want to point out this inconsistency and help to ameliorate it, seek opportunities with greater consistency, or possibly simply live with it, knowing that the organization will never achieve the advertised goals because top management is not really committed to them.

TIME STRATEGIES

Time is a critically scarce resource for top management. Although, at least in principle, financial resources can be continually increased, this is not the case for time. Certainly, you can add senior staff and delegate more and more management tasks to staff members. However, as noted earlier, you cannot delegate leadership. Thus, your time, and perhaps that of other members of the leadership team, is a constrained resource.

In Chapter 4, we discussed the challenge of focus, including methods and tools for deciding where to allocate resources. If one could determine the impacts of varying allocations of time on key outcome variables, one certainly could apply these methods and tools to the problem of allocating time. However, such relationships between allocations of time and outcomes would be very difficult to specify. Furthermore, the time allocation problem can be approached on another level.

The strategies for growth, value, and so forth that have emerged from challenges addressed in the previous chapters constitute a strategic agenda. Analysis of this agenda can help to define your time strategy in terms of where leadership is central to successful implementation of the strategies embodied in the agenda. This should determine your priorities.

As indicated in earlier discussions of leadership, the first and foremost responsibility is to articulate and communicate the strategic agenda, as well as motivate participation and enthusiasm. Beyond this overarching responsibility, there are likely to be particular elements of the agenda that require leaders to play specific roles. These roles imply, of course, allocations of time.

Thinking this through can be assisted by consideration of the following questions and issues:

- For each element of the strategic agenda, what factors are critical to successful implementation of the strategy embodied in this element?

- Who is responsible for each of these success factors, and what is your role in helping them succeed?
- To the extent that no one is responsible, either you are or you have to recruit some one; otherwise, the element does not belong on the agenda.
- How can you best fill your role—resource development, networking, recruiting, mentoring, coaching, cheerleading?
- What allocation of time is implied by your role and is this allocation reasonable and sustainable across all your roles?
- How can time be managed to ensure this intended allocation becomes the actual allocation of your time?

The type of analysis reflected by these questions is not too difficult—assuming that your strategic agenda is clear! The time strategy that results is a first step in successfully addressing the challenge of time. The next step is implementing this strategy.

At this point, you have to convince your superiors and subordinates to let you implement this time strategy. It helps if all the parties agree that the strategy reflects how you should be spending your time. Disagreements are likely to require some discussion and perhaps modification of your strategy.

Once you have reasonable agreement, it is up to you to change your behaviors, to the extent necessary, to conform to your chosen strategic allocation of time. This can require considerable self-discipline. However, if you do not "walk the walk," your superiors and subordinates will conclude that your time strategy was all just words.

A variation of this approach to developing and implementing a time strategy involves addressing this challenge for the whole management team. Keep in mind that this team, from your perspective, mainly includes your direct reports in the organization you manage, regardless of where in the overall corporate hierarchy your organization fits.

Consider using a tailored version of Covey's chart, such as shown in Figure 8.1, to motivate and structure the discussion of time strategies. Next, review the strategic agenda—again, assuming one exists—discussing the roles of each member of the management team. Have each member individually address the questions listed above and report their conclusions back to the team.

The results of this dialogue are likely to include several straightforward changes. Others may dictate some organizational development investments, especially if delegation is an underlying problem. People may also want help with time management methods, tools for which are discussed in the next section.

SUPPORTING TIME STRATEGIES

There are two aspects of supporting time strategies. First, you need to gain control of your time, keeping monkeys in their places and avoiding being trapped by the urgent but unimportant. Second, you need to make sure that your time is being allocated to the right things. Becoming a very efficient micromanager is not a good path to effective leadership. Thus, supporting time strategies involves methods and tools for improving both the efficiency and effectiveness of allocations of time.

Time Management

Gaining control of your time can be supported by a variety of time management systems, ranging from hardcopy specialized calendars and more elaborate "organizers" to computer-based calendars and organizers. As useful as these supports may be, their value depends totally on your commitment to improving time management.

Many senior managers that I have worked with learned the gospel of time management from Stephen Covey's *The Seven Habits of Highly Effective People* (1989). His third habit—put first things first—has been the topic of many one-on-one discussions with managers. Importance-urgency charts, such as Figure 8.1, have been scratched on many napkins and used to support much personal strategizing.

This awakening is a good start. However, time management, in itself, does not inherently address important issues such as the substantial shifts in priorities needed to move important but nonurgent tasks to the front on the queue and completely eliminate many urgent but nonimportant tasks. Time management methods also do not inherently address leadership style issues, although other aspects of Covey's best-seller does treat these issues.

I have also found that computer-based contact management systems can be useful adjuncts to time management, not only for sales' tasks—the original intent of most of these systems—but also for managing relationship information in general. One of the most popular of these systems is ACT! (Symantec, 2000), with which I have considerable experience.

ACT! helps you to define the key characteristics of your relationships, including contact information, previous contacts and transactions, and planned contacts and transactions. Using ACT! while making contacts, especially telephone and E-mail contacts, provides easy access to interactions leading up to the contact at the moment as well as planned future interactions.

ACT! can be used to manage your overall schedule for each week and detailed agenda for each day. At a glance, I know who I intend to contact, when and why I am contacting them, and how to contact them (phone number or

E-mail address is shown). With the shared database version of ACT!, you also know who else in your organization has made contact with people, when, for what purpose, and with what results.

The data captured by ACT! can also be used to analyze transactions with contacts and learn things such as

- how many contacts are made per week, per person and total,
- types of contacts made per week (i.e., meetings, deliverables, etc.),
- average times between events (e.g., initial contact and first meeting), and
- correlations of number of contacts with outcomes (e.g., repeat sales).

Analyses of these types of metrics can help determine whether individuals and organizations are managing time efficiently and effectively. On the other hand, these types of analyses do not provide much insights into things that you are not doing.

Several time management needs emerged from the interview study discussed earlier in this chapter. One need involved reaching an agreement on E-mail etiquette. Processing E-mail can become a major task in itself, especially if you get hundreds of E-mails per day. However, typically, a large proportion of these E-mails are for information only, particularly those received via cc (carbon copy). An E-mail etiquette that requires specifying in the message title the purpose of the message—for example, action required or information only—can dramatically reduce the amount of time devoted to E-mail.

Another need was to establish meeting norms. These norms relate to clear objectives, prepared agendas, fixed meeting lengths, and conventions to ensure that everyone gets to speak. The goal, obviously, is to avoid meetings that serve vague purposes, wander across topics, drag on interminably, and become dominated by a few participants. Meeting norms can make a substantial difference if senior managers have the discipline and commitment to make sure that they are observed.

Not surprisingly—in light of the data presented earlier—another need was to substantially improve delegation. This issue was discussed in some depth earlier in this chapter. Pervasive reasons for this problem is lack of clarity of goals and instructions, lack of selection of the right personnel and provision of needed training, and tendencies to preempt initiatives of subordinates via micromanagement. This issue often needs careful attention but also seldom gets serious treatment.

Strategic Thinking Time

Once you have control of your time, the next consideration is ensuring that your time is allocated to the right things. One important but nonurgent task

that is often undernourished in terms of time involves long-term strategic issues. Thoughtful, reflective consideration of where markets, technologies,
and your enterprise appear to be headed is a primary responsibility of top management. However, as discussed earlier, this responsibility is frequently
preempted by other tasks.

This situation can cause strategic thinking skills to become rusty, sometime
causing top management teams to appear to lack strategic thinking aptitudes.
However, I have found that these aptitudes are usually present—although
often well hidden—and skills can be regained with practice. The problem is
stealing time away from other tasks to focus on long-term strategy.

One approach is executive training and development programs. Such programs often create immersion experiences in which executives are completely
divorced from day-to-day demands. Participants must address long-term strategic issues to succeed in the exercises at hand. Debriefings after these exercises foster discussions of perceptions of what was happening and why
decisions were made.

Another approach involves carefully designed strategic thinking opportunities so that the senior management team has frequent (e.g., monthly or quarterly) experiences of addressing long-term issues. I have found that these
opportunities work best when they are focused on one strategic issue. It is also
important to reach some degree of closure on the topic, for example, an agreed
to next step.

For one large company, we developed a series called Futures Forums, each
of which addressed a single long-term strategic issue such as technology strategy, virtual organizations, and leading change. An outside expert began each
forum with a 30-minute talk on trends within the designated topic. After the
talk, a 60– to 90–minute facilitated discussion focused on what these trends
meant for the company. Over the whole series of these forums, the management team created an impressive list of strategic insights.

Also useful are methods and tools for taking senior managers out of the fray
and enabling them to see themselves in broader contexts. I have found experiences ranging from hikes in the mountains to immersion in foreign cultures
can achieve this end, especially if these experiences are well planned and
laced with opportunities for reflection (Rouse, 1994). It may soon be possible
to create such experiences in simulated business "microworlds" (Casti, 1997).

Impact of Tools

Throughout the earlier chapters, various computer-based tools for supporting
strategy formulation and implementation have been discussed. Such tools can
help address the challenge of time. Enormous progress can be made on important issues with 1–2 days of intense effort using these tools to frame issues,

create models, test plans via models, and determine sensitivity to key variables.

This can increase efficiency, both during and after meetings, because of creation of shared mental models. Such shared models tend to increase sharing of information, without necessarily increasing the time devoted to communication. This also enables creating and managing expectations, which tends to keep monkeys where they belong.

As an aside, I have found that these types of meetings are ideally 2 days in length. By the end of the first day, the team usually has achieved a high level of momentum. On the second day, they harvest this momentum, often teeing up and resolving issues and trade-offs quite quickly. By the end of the second day, people are usually exhausted, making a third day impossible or at least quite unproductive.

Managers often say that they cannot possibly spend 2 days on one topic. They ask if we cannot keep it to 1 day or perhaps a half day. In almost all cases in which we have accommodated this request, these managers have concluded that a second day was needed to take full advantage of the momentum gained during the first day. Furthermore, the productivity of the team during such sessions easily justifies stealing the 2 days away from other, less-strategic issues.

CONCLUSIONS

Senior management time tends to be the scarcest resource in the organization. The challenge of this scarcity is of great concern to many managers, both organizationally and personally. One aspect of this concern is finding the time to address the many tasks on most managers' plates. Another aspect is making sure that important but nonurgent tasks get any attention at all.

Fundamental to this challenge is the very strong tendency for management tasks to consume all available time, thus leaving little, if any, time for leadership tasks. However, effective leadership is critical for successfully addressing all the essential challenges of strategic management discussed in this book. And, effective leadership requires attention—it requires time.

An overarching strategy for addressing the challenge of time is to drive the allocation of senior management time by the organization's strategic agenda—the goals, strategies, and plans associated with addressing the strategic challenges. Careful analysis of the roles of senior managers relative to the elements of the strategic agenda can provide the basis for appropriate allocation of senior managers' time.

Translating desired allocations of time to actual allocations can be supported by methods and tools of time management. It is also very important to increase the priority given to various long-term strategic tasks, which all too often suffer from demands for time from near-term operational tasks. This increase in priority, and consequent reallocation of time, can be supported with various methods and tools for enhancing strategic thinking.

The challenge of time has many associated risks. Most crucial is the fact that people are often much too busy to take the time to address this challenge. As one senior manager told me, "I'm much too busy under-performing to be able to devote the time to get good at these tasks." Thus, although managers often mention this challenge, they seldom seem to seriously address it.

This risk carries over to the other challenges. Without enough time to think strategically about growth, value, and so forth, these challenges are also not addressed adequately. Organizations are misguided and resources are wasted because managers are trapped by management responsibilities and unable to fulfill their leadership responsibilities. If you do not deal well with the challenge of time, everything suffers.

KEY QUESTIONS

The challenge of time seems very straightforward, yet it is so often addressed poorly. Consideration of the key questions shown below—either by yourself or with your team—are intended to help you deal successfully with this essential challenge:

- What percent of your time is trapped by the urgent but unimportant?
- How is your time allocated between management and leadership?
- How is your time strategy linked to your strategic agenda?
- What methods and tools do you use to support your time strategy?
- How would you assess your management team's strategic thinking skills?
- How often does your team have significant strategic thinking opportunities?

REFERENCES

Bennis, W., and O'Toole, J. (2000). Don't hire the wrong CEO. *Harvard Business Review* May–June: 171–176.

Casti, J. L. (1997). *Would-Be Worlds: How Simulation is Changing the Frontiers of Science*. New York: Wiley.

Charan, R., and Colvin, G. (1999). Why CEOs fail. *Fortune* June 21: 69–78.

Covey, S. R. (1989). *The Seven Habits of Highly Effective People*. New York: Simon & Schuster.

Covey, S. R. (1999). Making time for gorillas. *Harvard Business Review*, November–December: 185.

Drucker, P. F. (1997). Toward the new organization. *Leader to Leader* Winter: 6–8.

Economist (1999). Overworked and overpaid: the American manager. *The Economist* January 30: 55-56.

Goleman, D. (2000). Leadership that gets results. *Harvard Business Review*, March–April: 78–90.

Jassawalla, A. R. R., and Sashittal, H. C. (2000). Strategies of effective new product team leaders. *California Management Review* 42(2): 34–51.

Kouzes, J. M., and Posner, B. Z. (1987). *The Leadership Challenge: How to Get Extraordinary Things Done in Organizations*. San Francisco, CA: Jossey-Bass.

Maccoby, M. (2000). Understanding the difference between management and leadership. *Research Technology Management* 43(1): 57–59.

McClellend, D. C. (1987). *Human Motivation*. Cambridge, UK: Cambridge University Press.

Miller, W. L., and Morris, L. (1999). *Fourth Generation R&D*. New York: Wiley.

Mintzberg, H. (1975). The manager's job: folklore and fact. *Harvard Business Review* July–August: 49-61.

Oncken, W., Jr., and Wass, D. L. (1974). Management time: who's got the monkey. *Harvard Business Review* November–December.

Pfeffer, J., and Sutton, R. I. (1999). Knowing "what" to do is not enough: turning knowledge into action. *California Management Review* 42(1): 83–108.

Reingold, J. (1999). In search of leadership. *Business Week*, November 15: 172–176.

Rouse, W. B. (1994). *Best Laid Plans*. New York: Prentice-Hall.

Rouse, W. B. (1996). *Start Where You Are: Matching Your Strategy to Your Marketplace*. San Francisco, CA: Jossey-Bass.

Rouse, W. B. (1998). *Don't Jump to Solutions: Thirteen Delusions That Undermine Strategic Thinking*. San Francisco, CA: Jossey-Bass.

RTM. (2000). Succeeding in technological innovation. *Research Technology Management* 43(3): 24–38.

Senge, P. M. (1990). *The Fifth Discipline: The Art and Practice of the Learning Organization*. New York: Doubleday/Currency.

Shields, J. L. (1999a). Transforming organizations: methods for accelerating culture change processes. *Information • Knowledge • Systems Management* 1(2): 105–115.

Shields, J. L., Harris, C. S., and Hart, B. K. (1999b). Culture, leadership, and organizational change. In: *Handbook of Systems Engineering and Management*, edited by Sage, A. P., and Rouse, W. B. New York: Wiley, chapt. 20.

Symantec. (2000). ACT!. www.symantec.com.

Wheatley, M. J. (1992). *Leadership and the New Science: Learning About Organization From an Orderly Universe.* San Francisco, CA: Berrett-Koehler.

CHAPTER NINE

Best Practices

When discussing the challenges addressed in this book with a wide range of top management teams, I have found that most managers immediately recognize one or more challenges that are keeping them awake at night. This recognition quickly leads to the question, "How do other people deal with these challenges?" They are usually eager to understand the best practices across a range of enterprises.

It is important to explore the intentions behind this question. When managers ask about best practices, they are not looking for—in formal terms—provably optimal solutions to their problems. They would be extremely skeptical if someone was to argue that a particular practice has been proven to be the one and only way to proceed.

The basis of such reactions would be managers' experiences with the complexity and variety of most businesses. They would ask, "How can someone who knows nothing about my particular business know exactly what I should do?" Thus, with the possible exception of purely technical issues such as routing trucks among distribution centers, balancing loads on computer networks, or pricing airline seats, best practices touted as optimal solutions would be rejected.

In contrast, best practices when presented as good ideas that have some intuitive merit and have benefited other organizations tend to meet considerable interest on the part of many managers. Then their questions are more like, "How have they assessed that these practices were the actual causes of these benefits?" This question is more methodological than confrontational.

As discussed in Chapter 1, in some cases a practice has been rigorously and empirically evaluated relative to competing approaches and shown to provide the greatest benefit, for example, highest probability of profitability. In other cases, a practice has become a de facto standard approach among widely admired companies, although there has been no rigorous evaluation to assess the merits of this practice.

In many cases, a practice has yet to be widely employed but makes considerable sense and all results to date are supportive of its likely merits. In some of these cases, there are published works explaining and arguing the benefits of a practice. In a few cases, there is only experiential support for a practice.

In all cases, of course, managers have to decide the relevance of a practice to their enterprises and the sufficiency of the support for the merits of the practice.

In this chapter, I first provide a broad review of the best practices discussed in the earlier chapters. Methods and tools for supporting best practices are then reviewed. This review provides a basis for discussing the roles of tools in general. Finally, a method is outlined for deciding which challenges to address and how to address them.

BEST PRACTICES

In the course of investigating the essential challenges in the earlier chapters, numerous best practices were identified and discussed. If viewed broadly, these practices can be summarized as follows.

To address the challenge of growth, the basic three practices are buying growth via strategic acquisitions and mergers, wringing growth from existing market offerings via enhanced productivity, and creating growth via innovative new products, including brand extensions. All three of these practices involve significant risks and limitations. Abilities to execute well are, therefore, central to deciding which of these practices are best in a particular context.

Achieving growth requires providing value, which is best pursued by directly addressing the nature of value in your markets. All businesses want to recover costs plus acceptable margins, but this is not a primary concern of most markets. Thus, you should focus on the benefits sought by these markets and use these market forces to determine your business processes. This includes designing your cost accounting system to align budgets and expenditures with value streams.

Given a growth strategy and value proposition, the next challenge is to focus or decide what things to invest in and, equally important, those things to be avoided or stopped. Focus is much easier when desired outcomes are clearly articulated and behaviors needed to achieve these outcomes are clearly specified. Resulting decisions are better implemented when choices are clearly linked to organizational goals, strategies, and plans. Multi-stage decision processes and portfolio management methods can help with such linkages.

Successfully addressing the challenge of focus often results in growth and value strategies that require significant organizational change. Once this is recognized and accepted, most organizations have found that cross-functional teams are good mechanisms for planning and implementing significant changes. Another very important practice concerns redesigning incentive and reward systems to ensure that people align their behaviors with desired new directions.

Strategic management inherently involves the future, especially the long-term future. The long-term typically involves much uncertainty and considerable risks. Investing in the future is, therefore, a significant challenge. Those who do this best, as evidenced by their investment returns, employ formal and quantitative investment decision processes, often with multiple stages involving portfolios of investments . Furthermore, because the future often involves surprises, companies try to create mechanisms for recognizing and exploiting unpredictable outcomes.

Knowledge is central to addressing strategic challenges. However, this does not mean that all knowledge is useful. Instead, knowledge acquisition and sharing should be driven by business issues in which knowledge has been determined to make a difference. Competitive intelligence activities in general and market/customer modeling in particular provide valuable means for identifying and compiling this knowledge. Knowledge management also provides a means for access and sharing knowledge.

Successfully addressing the essential challenges of strategic management depends totally on commitment and leadership by top management. This requires that top management devote time to these challenges, which, in turn, requires that the challenge of time be successfully addressed. This can be accomplished through a combination of improved time management, executive training and development programs, and provision of increased strategic thinking opportunities.

As evidenced by this brief section, the overall set of best practices can be summarized quite succinctly. Of course, each chapter in this book has shown that there are a variety of ways to put such practices to work. Indeed, this book is laced with numerous pundits' lists of guidelines, rules of thumb, success factors, and so forth. Much of this guidance applies to one particular challenge; in some cases, such guidance crosses challenges. There is much wisdom in many of these lists, especially for those elements that are common across lists.

Knowledge of best practices is a necessary starting point. However, supporting these best practices is often essential to realizing the potential offered by these practices. The next section summarizes the ranges of support mechanisms discussed in this book.

SUPPORTING BEST PRACTICES

There is a substantial difference between knowing about best practices and actually putting them to work. This difference is clearly reflected in the set of challenges. For example, successfully addressing the challenges of growth and value depends on also successfully addressing the challenges of focus, change, and time. Otherwise, your energies will be too disperse, your organization will not fit your goals, and you will be too busy to pay attention to implementing your growth and value strategies.

The methods and tools for supporting best practices introduced in the earlier chapters are intended to ease the transition from knowing about practices to putting them to work. The 28 methods and tools discussed earlier are listed in Table 9.1. In this section, we briefly review the purposes of each of the items in this table.

TABLE 9.1. Methods and Tools Discussed in Earlier Chapters

Challenges	Methods & Tools
Growth	Competitive intelligence
Growth	*Situation Assessment Advisor*
Value	Human-centered design
Value	Multi-attribute utility models
Value	Quality function deployment
Value	*Product Planning Advisor*
Value	Activity-based cost accounting
Focus	*Product Planning Advisor*
Focus	*Expert Choice*
Focus	*NewProd*
Focus	*Decision Advisor*
Focus	Balanced scorecard
Change	*ProcessEdge*
Change	*TOP-Modeler*
Change	*Strategic Thinking*
Future	Historical benchmarks
Future	Scenario planning
Future	Investment decision making
Future	Option pricing models
Future	*Technology Investment Advisor*
Future	Knowledge management
Knowledge	Knowledge capture
Knowledge	Knowledge maps
Knowledge	*Ernie*
Knowledge	IKSM*Online*
Knowledge	Collaboration
Time	Time management, e.g., *ACT!*
Time	Strategic thinking time, e.g., Futures Forums

The methods and tools suggested for supporting formulation of growth strategies include competitive intelligence and the *Situation Assessment Advisor*. Competitive intelligence supports information gathering, hypothesis formation and testing, model building, and so forth relative to external trends and events that may affect the competitive position of an organization. The *Situation Assessment Advisor* uses such information, expressed in terms of current and leading indicators, to assess the current and likely future competitive positions of an organization, as well as provide advice on how to address this situation.

Several methods and tools are available for supporting formulation of a value strategy. Human-centered design is a methodology that focuses on the multi-attribute, multi-stakeholder nature of value in most domains. Multi-attribute utility models provide the analytical components of this methodology, while also being broadly applicable to other frameworks. Quality function deployment provides a means for representing relationships and trade-offs among elements of value and alternative product or service attributes. Multi-attribute utility theory and quality function deployment come together in the *Product Planning Advisor*, which embodies the human-centered design methodology. Finally, activity-based cost accounting provides a means for linking budgets and expenditures to value streams.

Focus is concerned with decision making. Four tools and one method were discussed for supporting decision making. The *Product Planning Advisor* provides a multi-attribute decision analysis framework. *Expert Choice* embodies the analytic hierarchy process to develop decision models based on choices in a range of paired comparisons. *NewProd* emphasizes benchmark projects to assess likely success. *Decision Advisor* employs influence diagrams and probabilistic models to show the impacts of uncertainties on the attractiveness of alternative decisions. The balanced scorecard is a method for constructing a multidimensional measurement template for assessing organizational effectiveness.

Addressing the challenge of change can be supported by several tools. *ProcessEdge* supports process modeling and evaluation. *TOP Modeler* helps to assess the compatibility of processes with stated goals and provides advice on filling gaps between "as is" and "to be." The suite of tools provided by *Strategic Thinking* includes one for assessing the presence of organizational delusions and also helping to deal with these delusions.

There are a rich set of alternative tools for supporting pursuit of the challenge of the future. Several sources are recommended for historical benchmarks to enable learning from past successes and failures. Scenario planning methods provide structured ways of constructing and evaluating alternative futures. Investment decision-making methods include many of those discussed for addressing the challenge of focus, with particular emphasis on port-folio management models. Option pricing models provide a means for representing contingent futures in which initial investments, in effect, purchase options for future investments, which may or may not be exercised. The *Technology Investment Advisor* integrates option pricing models with maturity models, production learning models, and competitive scenarios. Finally, knowledge management concerns methods for capturing benchmarks, scenarios, and so forth and mechanisms for recognizing when unpredictable events portend opportunities and threats.

Addressing the challenge of knowledge can be supported by methods for capturing and representing—or mapping—knowledge in terms of databases, knowledge bases, models, and interactive queries and knowledge displays. With regard to knowledge dissemination, *Ernie* is an online consultant that provides access to a wealth of business knowledge. IKSM*Online* provides access to a wide range of business books, journals, magazines, and websites, including analyses and recommendations regarding best matches to subscribers' needs. Collaboration is also an important approach to knowledge dissemination, especially when knowledge is not easily codified.

The challenge of time poses two problems—gaining control of your time and allocating your time appropriately. Time management helps with the first problem. Tools such as *ACT!* help to schedule and track time, as well as assess outcomes of time expenditures. Managers not only need to seek efficiency in use of their time they also need to make sure that their time is allocated to effective leadership. This, in part, involves investing time in the important but usually nonurgent task of strategic thinking. This often requires dedicated events or opportunities such as Futures Forums.

I do not suggest that any particular management team employ all of the methods and tools in Table 9.1. This list is much too long for any one team to gain competency in all these methods and tools. In fact, this list could be much longer if we were to consider the full range of systems engineering and management tools (Sage and Rouse, 1999). However, it is important to keep in perspective the roles and purposes of management tools.

ROLES OF METHODS AND TOOLS

In a recent article (Rouse, 1998a), I discuss the insights gained from of a series of observations of cross-functional planning teams in a wide variety of enterprises using computer-based tools such as discussed in this book. These observations involved over 2,000 managers in 100 planning efforts over a period of 6 years. These efforts focused on planning of new products or processes, development of strategic business plans, and consensus building around planned organizational changes.

The experiences gained with this large number of groups led to a strong sense of what such groups want from computer-based tools. In particular, we asked members of these groups what they really wanted and expected from tools, as well as what roles they saw for such tools. Four types of support were identified. Table 9.2 summarizes the nature of these desires.

Regarding the first desire indicated in Table 9.2, it is important to note that the planning activities discussed in Rouse (1998a) were performed in groups. Individuals may have prepared background materials and initial analyses before group activity. However, most problems were formulated and decisions were made in group settings. In such settings, groups often want a structured process that provides a nominal path for proceeding. Succinctly, managers want a clear and straightforward process that can guide their discussions, with a clear mandate to depart from this process whenever they choose. In this regard, they do like to be required to perform all steps of a process to gain any return for their efforts.

A second desire expressed by groups involves capturing the information compiled, decisions made, and the linkages between these inputs and outputs. Managers want such an audit trail so that they can justify decisions and sometimes reconstruct decision processes. The former need usually arises when plans are presented to top management or investors. The latter occurs when external forces dictate changes and it is necessary to determine how plans got to be as they are. Furthermore, because groups may not all be together at the same time, they want group members to be able to asynchronously access the audit trail to understand what went on since they were last involved.

TABLE 9.2. What Support Managers Want from Computer-Based Tools

Support	Description
Process	A clear and straightforward process to guide their decisions and discussions, with a clear mandate to depart from this process whenever they choose.
Information	Capture of information compiled and decisions made and linkages between these inputs and outputs so that they can communicate and justify their decisions, as well as reconstruct decision processes.
Facilitation	Computer-aided facilitation of group processes via management of the nominal decision making process using computer-based tools and large-screen displays.
Surprises	Tools that digest the information that they input, see patterns or trends, and then provide advice or guidance that the group perceives they would not have thought of without the tools.

A third desire is for facilitation of the group's process. Human facilitation is often a key element in such group settings. However, computer-based tools can also provide elements of facilitation. For example, large screen displays linked to computer-based tools can present and manage the nominal process, provide prompts in terms of questions, and give advice based on what has transpired thus far. The neutrality of this type of facilitation—the computer has no explicit stake in the proceedings—is often quite compelling. Groups often comment that this type of facilitation provides a clear means of short circuiting tangents and getting back on track.

There appear to be a couple of reasons why this happens. First, large screens can be very compelling. When a particular question or type of analysis is displayed, there is a strong tendency to pursue this question or analysis, assuming of course that it is relevant. Second, most tools tend to provide substantial support if the group stays within the envelope of the methodology embodied in the tool. For example, sensitivity and "what if" analyses provide the means for quickly exploring the effects of assumptions. Groups tend to want these types of support and, consequently, tend to stay within this envelope. This inherently avoids frequent tangents.

A fourth desire that managers have of such tools is for the tools to tell them something that they did not know—to surprise them. Although structured processes, audit trails, and facilitation are greatly valued, they may involve inputting much information to the computer. This process may result in considerable sharing of information among group members. However, inherently, at least one of the group members already knew this information. Why should they invest the effort necessary to provide the tool for this information?

The answer has to be that the tool is able to digest this information, see patterns or trends, and then provide advice or guidance that the group perceives they would not have thought of without the tool. This is accomplished in a variety of ways in the range of tools discussed in this book. In general, however, these types of advice and guidance have to be such that they are not viewed as magic. Thus, the tools have to be able to explain the sources of their suggestions. Managers have to be able to explore the basis of tools' outputs until they can realign their intuitions with these results. Otherwise, they are not likely to accept the advice or guidance. In particular, groups frequently mentioned the importance of tools providing the means to determine the underlying sources of the advice provided.

Considering these four desires, it is quite clear that the "number crunching" roles of tools are far from their dominant roles. Instead, the development and manipulation of shared problem representations, capture of information and decisions, and support of group processes are the major roles. Managers want the number crunching to be correct, but the essential challenges of strategic management are seldom driven by calculation issues. Collaboration and communication, facilitated by appropriate methods and tools, are much more key to addressing the essential challenges successfully.

ADDRESSING YOUR CHALLENGES

I have presented much of the material in this book many times, typically at strategic offsite meetings of top management teams. Usually, managers find all the challenges of interest—especially, as noted in Chapter 8, the personal and organizational challenge of time. They also often find one or two challenges that they want to pursue in more depth during their strategic discussions.

Some management teams like to consider systematically the full set of challenges to determine which challenges should be their highest priorities and how they should address them. In this section, I discuss an approach to considering the full set of challenges and determining both where and how to begin to address your most important challenges.

The first step is to review the questions associated with each challenge that appear at the end of each chapter. For convenience, the full set of questions appears in the Appendix after this chapter. Considering each question, ask yourself or your team members if you have an answer to the question and are comfortable with this answer. For any challenge for which you either do not have answers to two or more questions, or are uncomfortable with your answers, consider this challenge to be a potential priority.

Once you have reviewed all the challenges, consider the number of challenges that are potential priorities. If this number is greater than two or three, tighten the criteria for being considered a priority challenge. For example, only place priorities on challenges where you do not have answers to three or more questions or are uncomfortable with your answers.

Once you have narrowed to three or less priority challenges, review the chapters that addresses these challenges in terms of the following characteristics:

- nature of challenge,
- examples,
- difficulty of challenge,
- best practices, and
- methods and tools.

Typically, this review results in team members suggesting other, often internal, examples and case stories. They also usually discuss the underlying difficulties that they have encountered. Overall, this review usually results in tailoring challenges to the particular organization associated with the management team.

Once this review is complete, consider the best practices discussed in each chapter and summarized earlier in this chapter, Rate each of the best practices using the following scheme:

1. Current competency of this organization
2. Current need receiving adequate attention
3. Important need not currently receiving adequate attention
4. Irrelevant practice for this organization

Best practices rated with twos and threes are candidates for subsequent attention. Discussion and debate usually focus on the adequacy of ongoing efforts. Metrics of progress are reported, proposed, and/or argued. At the very least, the team evolves to a shared sense of how things are going.

After this process is repeated across the priority challenges, two or three best practices typically emerge as the "tall poles in the tent," deserving significant further attention. Quite often, action plans are agreed to for pursuing these best practices. Actions may involve adoption or development of approaches to supporting best practices, or they may simply involve more discussion by the team.

At this point, a critical juncture emerges. Once the team leaves the meeting, action plans may slip in priority, especially if their impact is primarily long term. These plans become "nice to haves "rather than mission critical. Of course, this is not that surprising. As emphasized throughout this book, day-to-day business life has a tendency to intervene and demand attention.

Furthermore, making progress in implementing best practices may be far from straightforward, involving needs to focus and change, as well as invest significant time. One challenge leads to another, and abilities to resolve one depends on successfully addressing another. That's why these essential challenges of strategic management keep managers awake at night!

CONCLUSIONS

In many years of working closely with top managers, I have repeatedly been asked, "Should I make a major commitment to X?" X has ranged from TQM to BPR to LT to QFD to ABC to OBM to CI to KM to ERP to BS, with metrics ranging from ROI to NPV to NOV (see the Index for definitions of these acronyms).

My answer has always been, "What problem are you trying to solve?" The alphabet soup of management methods and tools only represents alternative means to addressing significant business issues. There is no right or wrong, good or bad, when considering these methods and tools. There are only business problems to be solved.

My question, "What problem are you trying to solve?" usually results in a variety of answers. Reflecting on the thousands of managers to whom I have addressed this question, in one form or another, provided the basis for the challenges discussed in this book. The essential challenges discussed here transcend any particular practices, methods, and tools.

These challenges were clearly manifest in my studies of industries over the past two centuries (Rouse, 1996) and in my studies of how a wide range of contemporary organizations become trapped by persistent false beliefs (Rouse, 1998b). These challenges are pervasive and fundamental, crossing markets, technologies, and time. All managers must—or at least should—address these challenges.

I now respond differently to managers' question, "Should I make a major commitment to X?" I now emphasize the essential challenges discussed in this book. Make whatever commitments you can afford to addressing the essential challenges. To the extent that the alternative you are entertaining does not help you to deal with one of the essential challenges, my intuition is that it is not a good investment. If you just focus on dealing well with these challenges, everything else can be delegated, outsourced, or forgotten.

REFERENCES

Rouse, W. B. (1996) *Start Where You Are: Matching Your Strategy to Your Marketplace*. San Francisco, CA: Jossey-Bass.

Rouse, W. B. (1998a). Computer support of collaborative planning. *Journal of the American Society for Information Science* 49(9): 832–839.

Rouse, W. B. (1998b). *Don't Jump to Solutions: Thirteen Delusions That Undermine Strategic Thinking*. San Francisco, CA: Jossey-Bass.

Sage, A. P., and Rouse, W. B. (Eds.). (1999). *Handbook of Systems Engineering and Management*. New York: Wiley.

Key Questions

GROWTH

- What are your growth goals, what will achieving these goals enable, and what consequences will result if you fail to achieve these goals?
- What are your current and emerging relationships with your markets, and what key indicators would have to change to improve your situation?
- Where can you create the market space you need to grow, and how capable are you of making this happen?
- What is your overall growth strategy, what plans have been formulated, who is responsible for these plans, and how will you measure progress?
- What methods and tools are you using to support your growth strategy?

VALUE

- Who are the stakeholders in the value provided by your enterprise?
- What is the value provided to these stakeholders by your products and services?
- How has this value changed in recent years and likely to change in the future?
- How well does your organization transform inventions into innovations?
- What are success and failure stories and what factors impacted these results?
- Which of the common barriers to innovation are prevalent in your enterprise?
- What is your value/innovation strategy and how is it supported?

FOCUS

- Do you have a well articulated and well-understood process for making major decisions, especially those involving unfamiliar and infrequent elements?
- Does this process ensure consideration of several alternatives, ranging from status quo to incremental change to radical change?
- Does this process ensure that the number of investments matches the resources available and needed for these investments to succeed?
- Does this process have multiple stages that result in regular termination of investments that are not progressing as needed?
- Has this process resulted in your enterprise being focused on a few key investments that are receiving the attention and resources necessary for success?
- To the extent that your answers to the above questions are "no," are you pursuing development of the processes necessary to answering "yes"?

CHANGE

- Which delusions may be affecting your organization's abilities to recognize needs for change and develop appropriate change strategies?
- What individual and organizational needs and beliefs are likely to underlie any persistent delusions, and how might these hindrances be overcome?
- What is your organizational baseline in terms of the reality of how information flows, how decisions are made, and how resources are allocated?
- Are you prepared to lead change by demonstrating sustained commitment at all levels of change processes?
- Do you have the methods and tools needed to understand and characterize needed changes and overcome obstacles to achieving these changes?

FUTURE

- What is your forecast for the future of your markets 5–10 years from now?

- What are your alternative scenarios for how you might compete in this future?
- How might these scenarios be improved using historical benchmarks?
- What current long-term investments do these scenarios imply?
- What metrics do you use for valuation of long-term investments?
- Does the size of your investment portfolio match the resources available?
- How do you formulate, evaluate, implement, and review your future strategies?

KNOWLEDGE

- What business issues drive your organization's information strategy?
- What does knowledge management mean within your organization?
- Does your organization know what it knows?
- How do you measure the value of knowledge in your organization?
- What is your knowledge strategy in terms of content, scope, and approaches?
- How do you support your knowledge strategy?

TIME

- What percent of your time is trapped by the urgent but unimportant?
- How is your time allocated between management and leadership?
- How is your time strategy linked to your strategic agenda?
- What methods and tools do you use to support your time strategy?
- How would you assess your management team's strategic thinking skills?
- How often does your team have significant strategic thinking opportunities?

SUBJECT INDEX